862.3 142849
Pér
Par

　　　　Parker.
　　　　Juan Pérez de Montalván.

Learning Resources Center
Nazareth College of Rochester, N. Y.

TWAYNE'S WORLD AUTHORS SERIES
A Survey of the World's Literature

Sylvia E. Bowman, Indiana University
GENERAL EDITOR

SPAIN

Gerald Wade, Vanderbilt University
EDITOR

Juan Pérez de Montalván

TWAS 352

Juan Pérez de Montalván

Juan Pérez de Montalván

By JACK HORACE PARKER
University of Toronto

TWAYNE PUBLISHERS

A DIVISION OF G. K. HALL & CO., BOSTON

Copyright © 1975 G. K. Hall & Co.
All Rights Reserved

142849

Library of Congress Cataloging in Publication Data
Parker, Jack Horace.
Juan Pérez de Montalván.

Twayne's world authors series ; TWAS 352 ; Spain)
Bibliography: p. 155-58.
Includes index.
1. Pérez de Montalván, Juan, 1602-1638.
PQ6420.P3Z833   862'.3   74-23740
ISBN 0-8057-2625-X

MANUFACTURED IN THE UNITED STATES OF AMERICA

To
Marjorie, Geoffrey and Ceciley

Contents

About the Author
Preface
Chronology
1. Life of Montalván   15
2. The Plays of *Para todos* (For Everybody)   26
3. The Plays of the *Primero tomo* (Volume One)   39
4. The Plays of the *Segundo tomo* (Volume Two)   52
5. Other Plays and a Contemporary Assessment   63
6. Problems of Authorship, including the *Orfeo en lengua castellana* (Orpheus in the Castilian Language) 69
7. Prose Writings   82
8. *Para todos* (For Everybody)   106
9. The First Biography of Lope de Vega: *Fama póstuma* (Posthumous Fame) 119
10. Miscellaneous Poetry   125
11. Conclusion   130
    Notes and References   135
    Selected Bibliography   155
    Index   161

About the Author

Jack Horace Parker, a Canadian by birth, is Professor of Spanish and Portuguese at the University of Toronto, where he received his B.A., M.A. and Ph.D. From 1966-69, he was Chairman of his Department and from 1969-73, Associate Dean (Humanities) in the University of Toronto's School of Graduate Studies. In 1973-74 Professor Parker enjoyed a Canada Council Leave Fellowship enabling him to complete his study of Juan Pérez de Montalván.

During World War II, while serving in Ottawa, Dr. Parker pioneered classes in Spanish and in Portuguese at Carleton University and, after the war, was a visiting professor at the Universidad de San Carlos, Guatemala. Professor Parker has also taught at Columbia University, Indiana University, the University of Illinois, the State University of New York at Buffalo, and the University of British Columbia.

Professor Parker has served as Chairman of several groups of the Modern Language Association of America and of the American Association of Teachers of Spanish and Portuguese and as Vice-President of the Instituto de Literatura Iberoamericana. In 1968-70 he was President of the Canadian Association of Hispanists, and in 1975 will be the first Canadian President of the American Association of Teachers of Spanish and Portuguese.

A member of the Editorial Board of the *Canadian Modern Language Review*, *Hispanófila* and the *Kentucky Romance Quarterly*, Professor Parker is also the author of *Breve historia del teatro español* (Mexico, 1957) and the co-author of *Lope de Vega Studies 1937-62* and *Calderón de la Barca Studies 1951-69* (University of Toronto Press; 1964 and 1971). He prepared the Twayne monograph on *Gil Vicente* (1967), having contributed the article on that Portuguese dramatist in the *Encyclopedia Americana*. Parker has published widely in critical periodicals on Spanish and Portuguese literatures, and is continuing his research in his special interest, the Spanish *Comedia* of the Golden Age.

In 1966, Professor Parker's native land conferred on him its highest academic honor, a Fellowship in the Royal Society of Canada (F.R.S.C.).

Preface

Juan Pérez de Montalván,[1] although of second order among the vast number of writers of Spain's Golden Age, is in many ways a fascinating exponent of several *genres*. His life was a short one, but a feverish one, and during the first third of the seventeenth century he was in the center of the literary whirl in Spain's capital city. That epoch, as Victor Dixon puts it in his discussion of *For Everybody*, was "unquiet but always colourful," and in that epoch, under Philip III and Philip IV, Montalván himself was "an erratic but always exhuberant author."[2] He was a close friend and protégé of the great Lope de Vega, and was his imitator in many ways. However, as Maria Grazia Profeti states in her monograph on Montalván, at times "Calderón is much closer than Lope"[3] in Montalván's literary endeavors. Montalván was at his best in drama, and in addition to being very popular and successful among his contemporaries, he produced several plays which have stood the test of time. In addition, he tried his hand at other branches of literature. In lyric poetry and in novelistic prose, he is not to be scorned; although the former is a very small output and the latter followed the more popular tastes of the day. In a philosophical-theological-"scientific" compilation Montalván showed that he possessed an encyclopedic mass of knowledge, born of his reading and his frequenting of the academies, or cultural circles, so prominent in his native city. His biography of his master Lope de Vega is no example of accuracy, but it is a sincere attempt to put in words a deep-felt appreciation. The *Orpheus in the Castilian Language*, if it was not ghost-authored by Lope de Vega himself, was only an exercise in erudite learning and a step in the literary polemics of the day, as was his later short prose satire, *The Trumpet*. The pages in prose dedicated to the life and purgatory of Ireland's St. Patrick reveal that the Spaniard of the seventeenth century had a deep, though vague, interest in that trouble-torn land.

A British scholar (Victor Dixon) and an Italian scholar (Maria

Grazia Profeti) are in modern times carrying the torch of Montalván scholarship, and their work continues to show that Montalván merits the twentieth century's attention. It is a truth in need of correction that Dixon could write in his review of the Profeti monograph that Montalván, "though immensely popular in his own century, is today almost forgotten, except as the target of Quevedo's *Perinola* and as the first biographer of Lope."[4] Many details concerning him and his works are still in doubt, and additional assessments need to be made of the literary production of "the imaginative and original craftsmanship of an unjustly neglected author," as the late Edward Glaser characterized Montalván, very rightly, some years ago.[5] Juan Pérez de Montalván's worth in world letters must be put forth even more strongly, and this small volume attempts to assist in that fruitful task. Joaquín de Entrambasaguas' statement of 1947 that Montalván "is very much in need of a monograph in which there will be definitely established the value and extent of his authentic work"[6] has been largely overcome by the Dixon-Profeti research and publication, but a great deal still must be done to determine what Montalván really wrote and when. Furthermore, his plays, except for a very few, are generally unavailable, and they must achieve modern editing.

I wish here to express my gratitude to the Canada Council for grants awarded me to visit libraries in Europe and for a generous Leave Fellowship, 1973-1974, to enable me to complete the preparation of this monograph. My gratitude also goes to the Humanities and Social Sciences Committee of the Research Board of the University of Toronto for grants in aid of research in libraries in North America and for funds for a final typing of the MS for the publisher. I am grateful to Dr. Colbert Nepaulsingh, who in years past advanced immeasurably my collecting of Montalván materials; and a very special word of thanks is due to Mr. Juan-Guillermo Renart, M.A., my research assistant during several academic sessions, whose always cheerful and efficient support encouraged me greatly to bring many years' meditation to fruition. To Mrs. T. B. Barclay, M.A., I express appreciation for carefully typing the manuscript for the press. Finally, and above all, to Dr. Gerald E. Wade, editor of this series, I offer many, many thanks for his unfailing help and suggestions in the preparation of this and my previous book on *Gil Vicente* (1967) for Twayne's World Authors Series.

JACK HORACE PARKER

University of Toronto

Chronology

1601/ Juan Pérez (de Montalván) born in Madrid, exact date un-
1602? certain. Friendship begun with Lope de Vega and other men
     of letters in his father's bookshop in Madrid.
1617 The Licentiate in Philosophy and the Humanities granted to
     the young Juan by the Universidad de Alcalá de Henares.
1618 About this time, during student days, perhaps encouraged by
     Lope de Vega, he began to write plays; probably *Morir y
     disimular* (To Die and to Conceal), *Cumplir con su
     obligación* (To Do One's Duty) and *La ganancia por la mano*
     (Success in One's Plans).
1620 Participated in a poetic contest to celebrate the beatification
     of San Isidro, Madrid's patron saint, and was praised by Lope
     de Vega, the Master of Ceremonies.
1622 Participated in poetic contests in honor of the Canonization
     of San Isidro, San Francisco Xavier and San Ignacio de
     Loyola. Prizes won and praise received.
1624 Publication of the *Sucesos y prodigios de amor* (The Happen-
     ings and Prodigies of Love), eight exemplary novels.
1624 Publication of the *Orfeo en lengua castellana* (Orpheus in the
     Castilian Language), a poem which may have been ghost-
     authored by Lope de Vega.
1625 By this time, ordained a priest. Served as chaplain in the
     parish of San Juan, town of Ocaña.
1625 In the month of May, admitted with his close friend,
     Francisco de Quintana, into the Congregación de San Pedro
     de Sacerdotes Naturales de Madrid.
1625/ The Doctorate in Theology awarded by the Universidad de
1626? Alcalá de Henares.
1627 Publication of the *Vida y purgatorio de San Patricio* (Life
     and Purgatory of St. Patrick), a prose work.

1629	Participated in a poetic contest in memory of San Pedro Nolasco, founder of the Order of Our Lady of Mercy. Prizes won.
1632	Publication of the miscellany, *Para todos* (For Everybody).
1632	In December, elected a *discreto* in the Venerable Third Order of St. Francis, for 1633.
1633	By this time, a Notary of the Inquisition.
1635	Publication of the *Primero tomo* (First Volume) of twelve plays, prepared by the author.
1636	Publication of the *Fama póstuma* (Posthumous Fame), in memory of Lope de Vega.
1636-1638	Severe mental ill health. In the last months, in an *asilo* in Madrid.
1638	Died June 25.
1638	Within a month of his death, publication of the *Segundo tomo* (Second Volume) of twelve plays, prepared by the author's father.
1639	Publication of the *Lágrimas panegíricas* (Panegyric Tears) in memory of Montalván.

CHAPTER 1

Life of Montalván

I *The Biographers*

GEORGE William Bacon, who has given us the most comprehensive, albeit now out-dated and old-fashioned, account of Juan Pérez de Montalván and his dramatic works,[1] brings to our attention in his Preface (p. 2) that there are lacking many "details concerning our author, especially the exact date of his birth." Thanks to the magnificent research of Victor F. Dixon in the last fifteen years, many solutions have been found to Montalván problems,[2] and thanks also to the encouraging work of an Italian investigator, Maria Grazia Profeti, Montalván scholarship is at the present time being greatly furthered.[3]

II *Parentage*

Montalván was presumably born in Madrid, and the year 1602 has been generally accepted as his date of birth. However, as Dr. Dixon has pointed out, "more probably he was born in 1601."[4] No baptismal certificate has been found for Juan Pérez de Montalván, although certain documentation is available for the family.[5] Juan's parents were Alonso Pérez and Felipa de la Cruz, who were married in 1592 in Madrid, although they had apparently come some time previously from nearby Alcalá de Henares, where Juan was later to pursue university studies. The father, who had been a bookseller in Alcalá, had established his business in the larger center (Calle de Santiago, Madrid) while continuing certain interests in other places, including Valladolid, where he had contacts with Cervantes. In fact, from certain enmity arising between the two, Francisco Maldonado de Guevara has credited Alonso Pérez with the authorship of the false *Quixote*.[6] From the Alonso Pérez - Felipa de la Cruz union, at least five children were born: Cristóbal, Isabel, Petronila and Angela, as well as Juan. The family seems to have been extremely devout in an era of devout Catholicism, with the Church being a constant guide and end in its activities.

[15]

There has been a great deal of reference to the father's being of Jewish extraction and a descendent of a family converted to Christianity. Juan makes an oblique statement regarding this possibility when in *Para todos* (For Everybody), 1632, he speaks of "the art of the bookseller, which had its beginning with the Hebrews," and Quevedo's violent attack on our author in *Perinola* (Teetotum),[7] following *Para todos*, hints rather clearly at this Jewish blood at several points in the work. For example, when he refers to Montalván's literary quarreling with Jerónimo de Villaizán, Quevedo declares that it is better to sell manna in town than to gather it in the desert; the meaning being that Villaizán's father was an apothecary and Montalván's ancestry included the Israelites, who lived on the God-provided manna in their forty years of wandering (Exodus, XVI). Edward Glaser, whose untimely death cut short his fruitful studies of Hispanic-Jewish questions, accepted this idea of "Montalván's Jewish ascendancy," and pointed to some difficulties Montalván had with the Inquisition.[8] However, on another occasion, Glaser stressed the fact that Montalván and his family were thoroughly Catholic, as was notably true throughout Montalván's life.[9]

III Studies

Young Juan's schooling was first of all in Madrid, and his university education was at the then-famous University of Alcalá de Henares. Philosophy and the Humanities gave him the licentiate in 1617, and some years later, with a specialty in Theology, he was awarded the doctorate, in 1625 or 1626.[10] His fellow student and closest friend at Alcalá (they lived together) in the early 1620's was Francisco de Quintana. On May 13, 1625, they were both admitted into the Congregación de San Pedro de Sacerdotes Naturales de Madrid.[11] Juan had been ordained a priest before this date; and for his studies he had been assisted financially by a mortgage on the Calle de Santiago property assumed by his parents in 1623.[12] Furthermore, Montalván had served as chaplain in the parish of San Juan in the town of Ocaña, south of Madrid; and somewhere around this time he was further helped in a financial way by being granted a chaplaincy by Tomás Gutiérrez de Cisneros, a Peruvian merchant of Lima.[13] This businessman admired Montalván's writings from afar (reference is made to that by Montalván in the dedicatory preface of the Seventh Day of *For Everybody*), and was apparently also repaying a debt owed the father. Continuing his theological career, Montalván was elected in December, 1632, a *discreto* in the Venerable Third Order of St. Francis for 1633, and as early as this latter year he became a Notary of the Inquisition.

IV *Early Literary Activity*

Meanwhile, Montalván's literary activity, which had begun early for our precocious author, was impressive. He is supposed to have written a play (perhaps with Lope de Vega's assistance) at the age of seventeen: *Morir y disimular* (To Die and to Conceal); and it is possible that this, and his "second" play, *Cumplir con su obligación* (To Do One's Duty) — he calls it his second in his First Volume of plays, 1635 — as well as *La ganancia por la mano* (Success in One's Plans), belong to early student days. In the Spring of 1620, Montalván took part in a poetic contest which was held in Madrid to celebrate the beatification of San Isidro, Madrid's patron saint.[14] The poetic contest took place in the Church of San Andres, and Montalván entered poems in the second, fifth and seventh of the nine sections. He won the praise of the Master of Ceremonies, Lope de Vega, but it is not clear whether he won a prize for his poetry. His entries were for a sonnet, *glosas* and ballad meter (reproduced by Bacon, "Life," pp. 456-60). The participants were given the first and last lines of the sonnet, and the subject to be treated was the angels' ploughing for San Isidro while he was engaged in prayer and contemplation. Montalván's two *glosas* also deal with the ploughman saint, as does the ballad (limited to forty lines). Much praise is poured forth for the saint, and it is noted, in a very complimentary way, that Spain's monarch was also born in the same city.

The year 1622 brought, under Pope Gregory XV, the canonization of Santa Teresa, San Felipe Neri, San Isidro, San Francisco Xavier and San Ignacio de Loyola. Lope de Vega once again presided over the Madrid festivities to celebrate the important event for Spanish Catholicism. On June 25 a poetic contest was held by the Jesuit Order to honor St. Francis and St. Ignatius, and Montalván took part in the fifth, seventh and twelfth of the twelve sections: for tercets, *glosas* and *quintillas*. It is noted in records of the event that in the seventh contest there were over eighty participants, and Montalván did well to receive second prize, a gold clasp. In the twelfth contest there were only four rivals, including the young Calderón de la Barca, and here Montalván was rewarded with first prize, a silver pitcher.[15] Montalván's tercets deal with the prescribed subject: "the illustrious vision" of St. Ignatius; the *glosa* is on the glories of the two saints; and the *quintillas* are on another prescribed subject: "the victory which the glorious St. Francis Xavier had over death" (given by Bacon, "Life," pp. 464-69). As to the *glosas* (or seventh section), Bacon writes (p. 8): "and indeed the excellence of his [Montalván's] contribution justifies the verdict of the judges."

Three days later, the City of Madrid honored San Isidro again, this time by a poetic contest for his canonization. Montalván took part in the third, eighth and tenth sections, for octaves, *canciones* and *glosas*, receiving third prize, an earthenware drinking vessel, for his octaves. These dealt with San Isidro, his wife Santa María de la Cabeza and their miraculous crossing of the river Jarama on her cloak. The *canción* gave thanks to Pope Gregory on behalf of Madrid for canonizing Isidro, and the *glosa* celebrated Madrid's glory for having such an illustrious and saintly son (poetry reproduced by Bacon, "Life," pp. 464-69).[16]

The end of the 1620's (May, 1629) brought about another important *justa poética* in Madrid, to honor the memory of San Pedro Nolasco, the founder of the Order of Our Lady of Mercy. Montalván took part in the contests for a sonnet and *décimas* (second and fifth sections of ten), and won first prize, a mirror, for his *décimas*. The sonnet (given by Bacon, "Life," p. 470, and reprinted by José Simón Díaz[17]) meditates upon "that mysterious miracle which befell our glorious Father [San Pedro Nolasco], as a child, when he took into the palms of his hands a swarm of bees." The prize-winning *décimas*, unfortunately, have not been included in the published account of the *fiestas solemnes*.[18]

V Literary Polemics

Along with these poems for poetic contests, Montalván continued to write other occasional verse, some fifty plays, prose such as the short novels and the *Purgatory of St. Patrick*, the miscellaneous *For Everybody*, and a good many dedications and *aprobaciones* (in his duties as Notary of the Holy Office).[19] No doubt he stuck very close to Madrid and its environs, but his dedication to *Los templarios* (The Templars) in the First Volume of his plays (1635) indicates that he had been in Seville at some time previously, where his father had business interests. From 1632 on (including *For Everybody*, where he used it at least twice) he assumed the name "Montano" quite frequently as a pseudonym,[20] and he seemed to have been very busy indeed, throughout his short life, in literary pursuits and in his duties as a priest. That he got into the literary disputes of the day will be

Life of Montalván

very apparent in a later discussion of his relations with Jáuregui, Villaizán, Quevedo and others, and soon this quarreling became very bitter indeed. Jealousies and rivalries for Court favor seem to have been at the root of many a difference; and Bacon ("Life," pp. 24-51) has given us a detailed account of Montalván's "Relations with Quevedo," including an anecdote which, while it is probably not true, is illustrative of Court problems: "One day Quevedo and Montalván were together at Court while the king and courtiers were criticising a picture by Velázquez which hung there. It represented St. Jerome scourged by angels for reading profane books. At the king's suggestion, Montalván improvised these verses [translation mine]: 'The angels were vying with each other/In scourging the saint for reading Cicero...' Whereupon Quevedo, interrupting him, finished the stanza thus. 'By Heaven! What would have ever happened/if he had been reading Montalván!'"

Bacon (p. 51) finds some redeeming features in these literary battles. Speaking particularly of the bitter Quevedo-Montalván controversy following the publication of *For Everybody* in 1632, he writes: "For, along with other feuds, it not only entertained the public, but created a great demand for the work about which it waged. The six editions of the *Para todos* which appeared in two years did more to console Montalván for the abuse he suffered than all the felicitations and eulogies of his sympathizers."

VI *Literary Friends*

The more positive aspects of Montalván's literary experiences are many. It is to be noted that in the above-mentioned poetic contests he was in close contact with Lope de Vega, of course, and with many of his leading literary contemporaries such as Pedro Calderón de la Barca, Guillén de Castro, Juan de Jáuregui, Luis Belmonte, Sebastián Francisco de Medrano, etc. The last named was a very close friend, and no doubt, under his presidency, Montalván frequented the Academia de Madrid to read, listen to and discuss poetry and other aspects of culture.[21] These influences upon our author must have been fruitful; and indeed it is to be remembered that they started almost from the cradle in the beneficent milieu of his father's bookstore, where it is believed that the great Lope de Vega himself organized literary *tertulias*. Rafael Sánchez Mariño has studied the Lope de Vega-Alonso Pérez connection in an unpublished doctoral dissertation,[22] and Bacon ("Life," p. 5, note 5) and others give information about the many books which Alonso

Pérez published for the *Fénix de los Ingenios*. Furthermore, for many years Alonso was the official bookseller to the king (from 1604 on), and he must have held an important and dominant position in Madrid. So close were he and Lope de Vega that the latter mentioned him specifically in his will of February 4, 1627 ("Alonso Pérez to whom I owe so much and whom I esteem so much"), in addition to naming him an executor.[23]

We can imagine that Lope de Vega was at the bookstore very, very often, and that he took an interest in the book production, seeing the growing Juan from time to time and encouraging him in his work, to such an extent that Montalván later gave full credit to Lope de Vega for any of his success, writing in the prologue to the exemplary novels of 1624 that "the little which I have achieved in my youthful years I owe to his training." If Montalván thus explains that he owed everything in his early literary career to Lope de Vega's tutelage, Lope de Vega in his preface to his play *La Francesilla* (The Little French Girl), published in *Parte XIII*, Madrid, 1620, and dedicated to the young "licenciado" who was continuing his studies at the University of Alcalá de Henares, states that he became interested in young Juan because of obligations to his father, and owing to an occasion which demonstrated very clearly Juan's growing talents. These were shown emphatically one day when he defended himself very well before some learned men in the Madrid Real Monasterio de las Descalzas. In that same year 1620 Lope de Vega suffered the bitter loss through death of a beloved protégé, Baltasar Elisio de Medinilla, and some critics believe that Juan was taken under Lope de Vega's wing to fill an aching gap.[24]

"This intimacy" wrote Bacon, "Life," p. 5, "was destined to mean not a little for the young Juan, for during his visits to the book-shop Lope must have seen much of him, and soon begun to regard him with paternal affection.[25] As time passed, the timidity of the child, who had shrunk back in awe and wonder before the 'phoenix of Geniuses,' became transferred into love; and it gratified Lope to know that he was considered his inseparable friend and mentor. More mature years brought with them signs of great literary ability in Juan, whereupon Lope, confident of his success, urged him to try his hand at the drama . . ."

This fruitful relationship continued throughout the years, and one can trace it from laudatory poem to poem or preface to preface, up until Lope de Vega's death in 1635 and Montalván's *Fama póstuma* (Posthumous Fame) of 1636, in memory of his deceased mentor.[26]

Life of Montalván

The mutual compliments are usually exaggerated beyond the bounds of reason and truth, and they must be taken with care and caution as to their contents, for the literary mind is sometimes careless and forgetful about detail.[27] However, these utterances on both sides are the reflection of a helpful relationship, which is one of the most celebrated in Spanish literary history. "Forty years his senior" wrote Bacon, "Life," p. 20, in summing up, "Lope had from the first regarded our author with the deepest paternal affection. During his early efforts he had bent over him, breathing ideals into his ear, and guiding his tremulous hand. It was to this aid and encouragement that the young playwright owed much of his subsequent fame. And yet the self-satisfaction occasioned by the attainment of this fame was far overshadowed by his delight at his master's expression of admiration. What greater pleasure would there be for the protégé than to read such an eulogy as this:

> Dr. Montalván, from whose being
> there pours forth a sea of knowledge throughout the World;
> now portraying the foibles of Love
> in learned prose and in sonorous verse! . . ."[28]

There seems to have been one occasion only — but an important one — when Lope de Vega let his protégé down. From among the names of the polemists on both sides of the bitter *For Everybody* (Montalván) - *Teetotum* (Quevedo) controversy of 1632 and following, notably absent is the name of Lope de Vega. Bacon declares for the year 1631 ("Life," p. 37, note 1), that "the two [Lope de Vega and Quevedo] were not on friendly terms by reason of Quevedo's hostility toward Montalván," but the history of the period seems to attest to a continuing and constant very close friendship, as mentioned by Antonio Papell in his study of Quevedo's life and works.[29] Quevedo was honored by Lope de Vega on many occasions; in the *Jerusalén conquistada* (Jerusalem Regained) of 1609, and in *El Laurel de Apolo* (The Laurel of Apollo) of 1630, for example, and Quevedo's "aprobación" of Lope's *Rimas de Tomé Burguillos* (Rhymes of Tomé Burguillos) of 1634 could not have been more whole-hearted. There is no reason to believe that this mutual admiration was anything but sincere, although their mutual dislike of Luis de Góngora seems to have had a great deal to do with it. It is just one more enigma of the day that Lope de Vega should have been such an enemy of Góngora's *culteranismo*, because it was obscure in form,[30] and not have been the enemy of Quevedo's other "obscure" aspect of the baroque: *conceptismo* (obscurity in content). It is likewise a big question mark why Quevedo should not have respected, for the sake of his friendship with Lope de Vega, Lope's deep and enduring friendship with and protection of Juan Pérez de Montalván. But there seems to have been little rhyme and reason in those literary alliances of the time; Montalván's jealousy of Jerónimo de Villaizán and Lope's praise of him, or Quevedo's attack on Juan de Vidarte, who was lauded by Lope de Vega, being only two more mix-ups of the period. The final big question mark is why Lope de Vega, in spite of his friendship with Quevedo, did not vociferously enter the fray to protect his protégé; he would have been able to do so effectively. Who knows whether he did not attempt it, from behind the scenes? There were many unsigned and pseudonymous contributions to the controversy of the early 1630's, and who knows, for example, whether Lope de Vega may not have been behind *La trompa* (The Trumpet), to be discussed later, which was presumably Montalván's reply to Quevedo's scathing criticism in *Teetotum*.

VII *The Final Years*

Lope de Vega died in 1635, and Juan Pérez de Montalván moved forward to prepare for him a fitting *In memoriam*, the *Posthumous Fame*. Unfortunately, the end was not far off for Montalván himself. Around this time, though he was only in his mid-thirties, his health had been declining. A good deal of literary production had already been prepared, performed or published, and La Barrera[31] and others, following the explanation to be found in the *Lágrimas panegíricas* (Panegyric Tears), brought forth for Montalván himself in 1639, attribute this failing health to excessive study and overwhelming literary tasks and the sorrow experienced upon the death of Lope de Vega in 1635. However, there have been other explanations put forth for these unhappy last years of about 1635-38. The most "scientific" would lead us to believe that Juan shared in the general ill health which seems to have been the rule rather than the exception in his immediate family. The father continued a long and vigorous career in the book business, but both the elder brother Cristóbal and the elder sister Isabel apparently died very young, in the early years of the 1600's. To the mother, Felipa de la Cruz, blindness is attributed in her later years, and another sister Angela, who along with Petronila became a nun, is said to have suffered mental disorders in the form of hallucinations in her convent.[32]

Life of Montalván

Montalván's last six months seem to have been a period of out-and-out insanity, in an *asilo* in Madrid, and he had had several "attacks" over a period of several years. The violence of the Quevedo-Montalván polemic following the *For Everybody* of 1632 must have weighed heavily on a possibly weakened mind,[33] and at least half a year before Lope de Vega died Montalván had had a prolonged "fainting spell" (mentioned by him in the prologue to the *Posthumous Fame*), and some time after that, other "collapses" had come upon him. These attacks, according to Francisco de Quintana, writing in the *Panegyric Tears*, "reduced him, even in speech, to the state of a child." With reason completely gone, Juan Pérez de Montalván died on June 25, 1638. He was buried in the chapel of the Madrid Church of San Miguel de los Otoes, which is no longer standing. In his last years, Montalván was, naturally, only occasionally in a state of health sufficient to supervise his affairs, and he was unable, as Victor Dixon has shown in discussing the Second Volume of the plays, to put his house in order and leave us a certain account of his literary production. In addition to the published works which are ascribed to him, Montalván in the prologue to Lope's *Posthumous Fame* had promised a Second Part of *For Everybody*. Under his name in the index of writers of Madrid in *For Everybody*, Montalván announced *La prodigiosa vida de Malhagas el embustero* (The Prodigious Life of Malhagas the Trickster); and Quintana, in the prologue to the Second Volume of plays, 1638, said that Montalván had begun an *Arte de bien morir* (Art of a Good Death). None of these works has come to light.

Just as Juan Pérez de Montalván had rallied his friends to produce an *In memoriam* for Lope de Vega, the *Posthumous Fame*, so too Montalván's circle brought forth a collection of eulogies, the *Panegyric Tears* of 1639.[34] The tribute to Lope de Vega had contained his first biography (by Montalván himself; see later discussion), and the panegyrics of some one hundred and fifty-three different authors. Strange is the absence, on that occasion, of many dramatists, poets and prose writers of note, many of whom were friends of Lope's; but perhaps not so strange, for Montalván was not universally loved. Luis Astrana Marín explains the situation thus: "And with him [Quevedo] abstained, no doubt on account of differences with Montalván, the writers of greatest reputation then and afterwards such as Pedro Calderón de la Barca, Fray Gabriel Téllez (Tirso de Molina), Juan Ruiz de Alarcón, Antonio de Mendoza, Alonso de Castillo Solórzano, Vicente Mariner, etc., etc. Only three notables contributed to the *Fama*: Luis Vélez de

Guevara, Francisco de Rojas and Solís [Antonio de Solís y Rivadeneyra]."[35]

VIII The In memoriam to Montalván

The *In memoriam* for Juan Pérez de Montalván brought together the eulogies of some one hundred seventy-five contributors, stressed by the editor, Pedro Grande de Tena, to be "intimate friends" of the deceased. Many of those paying tribute were clerics and not men of letters; but several well-known names do appear: Calderón de la Barca, Tirso de Molina, Vélez de Guevara, Antonio de Solís, Antonio Coello, Castillo Solórzano, Matos Fragoso, Polo de Medina, María de Zayas Sotomayor, etc. Some who were notably absent in Lope de Vega's case must by now have forgiven and forgotten any differences to lend their names on this occasion. The *Panegyric Tears* were international in that there were three contributions by Portuguese writers and a poem in Italian by Francisco de Benavides Manrique. The budding dramatist Agustín Moreto (born 1618) provided some verse, and of this Ruth Lee Kennedy says: "This poem, the earliest product of Moreto's pen which cannot be questioned, is a sonnet printed in the *Lágrimas panegíricas* . . ."[36]

In this miscellaneous collection of "panegyric tears" shed for the deceased Juan Pérez de Montalván, not all the old quarrels of the bitter enemies were forgotten, or omitted. Fray Diego Niseno's funeral eulogy, of the *Panegyric Tears*, does not mention the archenemy Francisco de Quevedo by name, but it was clear against whom the orator was inveighing. "That such a feud was continued even over the lifeless body of Montalván (Bacon, "Life," p. 50) at a time when clemency should have softened anger, shows only too well how deeply rooted was the hatred it had engendered. And this hatred was not buried with our author, for many passages in the *Lágrimas panegíricas* prove it to be as much an invective against Quevedo as an eulogy of the deceased."

Father Niseno makes much, as is to be expected, of Montalván's virtues. Flattering comparisons are put forward concerning him and the great writers of the past. A point uttered very emphatically by Niseno is that envy was always on the enemies' side and that the very ones whom Montalván eulogized and rescued from oblivion were those who attacked him. Nevertheless, declares Niseno, Montalván went on speaking kindly of them; and one wonders immediately how sincere those words in return always were. Juan's motives in writing did not always seem to be the best — perhaps he tried too hard to

Life of Montalván

win friends and influence people; and was that a sign of an inferiority complex? It is possible that he never forgot his supposedly Jewish ancestry, in a country of intense Catholicism, and it is possible also that the "lowness" of his father's occupation, a tradesman, weighed upon his mind as he traveled in Court circles. Perhaps he did attempt to put on airs, and was pounced upon for this desire to rise into prominence beyond his station in life and his abilities. In his rather licentious novels, it is possible that Montalván was revealing a consciously or subconsciously repressed sexuality, never fulfilled in his strict religious and puritanical upbringing. His deteriorating health over a period of some years probably made him less than amiable at times, and his enemies seemed to have retaliated in a very cruel manner. Be that as it may, Montalván was very fortunate in having the almost constant defense of the greatest of the great, Lope de Vega. But in our judgment of Montalván, the man and the writer, we must look at him for himself alone. It was in drama that he made his most significant contribution. Therefore, let us begin with a study of his plays.

CHAPTER 2

The Plays of Para todos (For Everybody)

I *How Many Plays Did Montalván Write?*

IN *Para todos* (For Everybody), the miscellany of 1632, Montalván declared (in the index of writers of Madrid) that he had written thirty-six *comedias* and twelve *autos sacramentales* (sacramental plays). From the date of writing this entry about himself, let us say in 1631, until severe illness overtook him about 1635, perhaps he wrote another ten plays? (His average seems to have been about two and one-half plays per year.) Published in *For Everybody* are four three-act *comedias* and two *autos sacramentales*.[1] In the First Volume of Montalván's plays, of 1635, there are twelve *comedias*, no doubt authentic. Victor Dixon's careful study of the Second Volume of 1638 (see Dixon, "*Segundo tomo*") adds nine only (out of twelve) *comedias* as definitely authentic. That adds up to a total of twenty-five *comedias*, and two *autos sacramentales*, and to a great extent it is only a guess as to which ones of the many attributed to Montalván in other collections and in separate publication *(comedias sueltas)* are really his. Victor Dixon's careful research has made a decision, at least tentatively, in many cases,[2] and Maria Grazia Profeti has added *El caballero del Febo* (The Knight of Phoebus) to the *autos;* but uncertainties of the Montalván canon in drama remain legion. In addition, Montalván collaborated with his contemporaries for several titles, and it is not clear whether Montalván, whose factual accuracy was never high, was thinking of these in the *For Everybody* calculation.

II *Chronology and Classification*

The words used by Walter Poesse in discussing the drama of Juan Ruiz de Alarcón are very à propos for Juan Pérez de Montalván: "It is not possible, with our meager knowledge, to establish with any degree of certainty the dates of the composition of Alarcón's plays, nor the order in which they were written."[3] Over twenty years ago, I

The Plays of Para todos (For Everybody)

made an attempt to arrive at a chronology for Montalván, using the methods employed successfully for other dramatists by M. A. Buchanan, Morely and Bruerton and others — that is, a study of trends in versification — but that study must be thoroughly revised in view of information which has been brought forth since 1952 concerning what Montalván wrote or did not write.[4] Traditionally it has always been stated, perhaps correctly, that Montalván's first play was *Morir y disimular* (To Die and to Conceal), written about 1619. Montalván's dedication of *Cumplir con su obligación* (To Do One's Duty), of the first volume, declares that it was the second play which he wrote in his early years. Victor Dixon has expressed a considered opinion that *La ganancia por la mano* (Success in One's Plans) is an early play of Montalván's student days ("*Segundo tomo*," p. 96, note 22). Odd bits of information are available for the odd play as will be noted in discussing individual plays, but that is as far as it can go at the present time. As mentioned above, Montalván collected four *comedias* and two sacramental plays for *For Everybody*, 1632; he collected twelve more *comedias* for his First Volume, 1635. But in drama, it seems, that was the extent of his personal collecting. The Second Volume of *comedias*, 1638, was long believed to be the dramatist's own compilation, but it is not. Since, as Poesse wrote for Ruiz de Alarcón, "any chronology is conjecture" (pp. 36-37), it seems best to discuss the Montalván plays in the order they appeared in the printed "Montalván" collections, of 1632, 1635 and 1638, with a consideration of attributed plays to follow.

Any attempt at classification brings many problems also. Bacon ("Life") attempted a division into "Comedias heroicas" (Heroic Plays), "Comedias de capa y espada" (Cloak and Sword, Adventure Plays), "Comedias de santos" (Plays on the Lives of the Saints) and "Comedias devotas" (Plays of Devotion), the last including the *autos sacramentales*. Godínez de Batlle ("Labor literaria") copied this classification from Bacon. Maria Grazia Profeti *(Montalbán)* has followed a similar path, with sections in her book on "la commedia eroica" (Heroic Comedy), "la commedia d'intreccio e onore" (Plays of Intrigue and of Honor), "la commedia storica" (Historic Drama), "la commedia 'de santos'" (Lives of the Saints) and "l'auto" (Sacramental Plays). "It is not easy," wrote Walter Poesse of Alarcón, p. 37, "to compartmentalize *comedias* . . . since the elements that predominate in one type are to be found in various degrees in the others as well." Montalván was "essentially exuberant and ill-disciplined" (to use the words of Victor Dixon in his review of

Profeti's *Montalbán*, p. 187), and Lope de Vega's keyword "variety" was his also. Classifications are worth putting forward, but in this study it seems more fruitful to take the *comedias* and *autos* one by one as they appeared in the various volumes and attempt an individual analysis. Hence, let us look first at the plays published in *For Everybody*.

III El segundo Séneca de España *(The Second Seneca of Spain)*[5]

The first play in *For Everybody* aims at paying high tribute to the memory of the glorious Philip II, looked upon by Montalván as a perfect prince and a man of Senecan virtue. (It is to be noted that Cloridano in the novel *The Enchanted Palace*, part of the entertainment of the Fourth Day of *For Everybody*, gives a discourse on "The Perfect Prince.") As in the case of all the plays chosen for inclusion in this collection of miscellaneous materials, Montalván is drawing upon some of his best and best-known plays from among those already staged successfully. Indeed, this *comedia*, which forms part of the entertainment of the Introduction to the whole week of *For Everybody*, is Montalván's "best drama," in the eyes of Federico Carlos Sainz de Robles.[6] Montalván wrote three plays on the famous King Philip and his contemporaries at court, the other two being *El señor don Juan de Austria* (published in the first volume of plays) and the second part of *The Second Seneca* (published in the second volume).[7] Dixon has called the first *Seneca* of Montalván's "the most interesting of his three plays about Philip II," and has agreed to a mid-twenties or late-twenties date: "there is some confirmation for a conjecture by J. H. Parker that it was written between 1625 and 1628" (Dixon, "*Para todos*," p. 40).

G. W. Bacon discussed what he believed to be the main source of the play, Luis Cabrera de Córdoba's *Filipe Segundo Rey de España* (Madrid: Luis Sánchez, 1619).[8] Cabrera de Córdoba was certainly consulted by the dramatist, but Victor Dixon points out that the play's chief historical source — mentioned by Montalván himself in *For Everybody* — was a book printed for Montalván's father by the Viuda de Alonso Martín in 1625, Lorenzo Vander Hammen's *Don Filipe el prudente, Segundo de este nombre*. The play may have been performed in Valencia in 1628; hence the probability of a 1625-28 date of composition.

The plot of Montalván's *Second Seneca* (Part I) is as follows: Against the background of the Duke of Alba's being sent to the Low Countries to eliminate rebellion and Don Juan de Austria's being

The Plays of Para todos (For Everybody)

sent south to quell the Moors, Felipe II prudently tries to solve domestic problems arising from his jealous and inept son Prince Carlos. After many ups and downs and many painful controversies, the play comes to an end with Don Juan de Austria about to lead the Pope's forces in the Eastern Mediterranean against the Turks and with King Philip about to be married to his niece, Ana of Austria, daughter of the Emperor Maximilian.

At the beginning of the play Felipe II takes refuge from a storm incognito in the humble home of a peasant mayor, Juan Rana, and Noël Salomon has remarked on the humor arising in this play from the "alcalde-comique," and the dignity revealed by this character of lower rank.[9] Indeed, thinking of "alcaldes" (mayors) in the *Comedia*, one is reminded of such admirable persons as Calderón's peasant mayor, Pedro Crespo, of *El alcalde de Zalamea* (The Mayor of Zalamea), and even of Philip II himself, who acts in a dignified and considerate way throughout the play. It is clear that character delineation, and above all character delineation of the king, is the main feature of Montalván's *Second Seneca*. Consummate skill is shown by Montalván in presenting the monarch to his audience. Philip is a man of perfect nobility, in both word and deed. No doubt the Spanish audience of the day was greatly attracted by this presentation, in dramatic form, with all the accompanying pomp and ceremony, in harmonious, sonorous verse.

IV   No hay vida como la honra *(There Is No Life Like Honor)*[10]

This play is likewise celebrated as being one of Montalván's best, and the author states that he chose it for inclusion in *For Everybody* (Day One) since it was one of his plays which had received greatest applause from the theater public. The number of times it was printed in the nineteenth century attests to its worth.

Don Fernando arrives in Valencia from Zaragoza to marry his cousin Leonor. Through a very common *Comedia* convention, a quarrel with a stranger, he finds himself in jail. By common *Comedia* coincidence, he meets Carlos, who is in prison also because he quarreled over his beloved (Leonor) with the Count Astolfo. Fortunately the two men are freed, and are again able to pursue their amorous interests, jealous of each other's intentions. One day when Carlos is calling on Leonor, he is forced to hide (another *Comedia* convention) while her father declares to his daughter that she now must marry the wealthy Astolfo. One night later on, Leonor admits into her chamber by mistake the persistent and obnoxious Astolfo.

Carlos, following along behind, challenges his rival to a duel and kills him. Carlos then flees to the mountains, since a high price has been put on his head. Leonor's father, meanwhile, dies and leaves her penniless. The noble-hearted Carlos gives himself up to the Viceroy so that the reward will go to Leonor. Fortunately all the characters converge on the Viceroy's home at the proper moment, and all ends well: it is recognized that the dead Astolfo was an evil man, Carlos is pardoned and given double the reward as retribution, Leonor marries Carlos, and Fernando marries Leonor's cousin, Estela.

As can be seen from these details of plot, *There Is No Life Like Honor* is a lively play, of a novelistic kind, in the best of the Lope de Vega *Comedia* tradition. The play has all the elements so dear to the entertainment-seeking audience of the day: adventure, intrigue, fast action, honor problems, good verse, colorful costuming, and a happy ending. It is a play of "intrigue and honor" (Profeti, *Montalbán*, pp. 74-76), and although Bacon ("Life," p. 471) classifies it as a "comedia heroica," it bears resemblance to the cloak and sword plays, except that some characters are of higher rank than is usual in that type. Attention is paid to characterization: the *gracioso* (comic servant), Tristán, as is usual in Montalván, is well drawn,[11] and Leonor, performed by the well-known contemporary actress Antonia Manuela (mentioned by Montalván himself in *For Everybody*),[12] shines above the conventional *galanes*, Don Carlos and Don Fernando. Romualdo Álvarez Espino cites this play as an example of one containing very effective and entertaining comic scenes,[13] and many years ago I suggested that a *jeu de scène* in Act I may have inspired a comic scene in Molière.[14]

It is not surprising that *There Is No Life Like Honor* can be credited with simultaneous performances in both public theaters of Madrid over a period of some days (an "unprecedented distinction" — Dixon, "*Para todos*," p. 40), with amateur performances and with presentation in Lima, Peru, by 1630.[15] In Mexico also, the play seems to have "enjoyed" notice and censure in the seventeenth century.[16] As to date of composition, a probable *terminus ad quem* is 1628, for Roque de Figueroa had produced the play at Court before March 28 of that year.[17]

V De un castigo dos venganzas
(For a Punishment a Double Vengeance)

This play (entertainment of Day Three) begins with a conventional *Comedia* adventure: one night Don Pedro surprises an un-

The Plays of Para todos (For Everybody)

known man at his sister Leonor's grating and is unfortunately killed by him. Leonor had mistakenly thought this Don Juan de Silva, immediately imprisoned for his crime, to be her lover Don Lope. Don Juan is released only on condition that he marry Leonor at once to restore her honor, a solution much to the dislike of all parties, including a neighbor girl, Violante, madly in love with Don Juan.

In Act II, Violante has turned to Don Lope, and the Juan-Leonor union of six months is marred by Juan's suspicions that his wife had and continues to have a lover, Don Lope. Violante, by this time dishonored by Lope, is violently jealous of Leonor, who is planning a rendezvous with Lope. Violante finds Leonor and Lope *in flagrante delicto*, and kills both of them with a dagger. Juan, arriving at that moment, at the end of Act III, takes the blame for the double murder, and is pardoned (to later marry Violante) as the defender of his family honor.

Associated with this play is a great deal of controversy with the contemporary dramatist Jerónimo de Villaizán, and the desire for Court favor (as outlined by Dixon, "*Para todos*," pp. 44-49). The setting of the play is in Portugal, with a reference to an expedition to Brazil against the Dutch. Bacon ("Life," p. 390) dated the play as 1625-26 with this historical allusion before him, but Dixon ("*Para todos*," p. 46) is of the opinion that "we need not take this apparent 'periodismo' too literally; Montalván was writing a *drama de honor* — an unconventional one in that the guilty wife and lover are murdered not by the husband but by the lover's discarded mistress — rather than a 'documentary' like Lope's *El Brasil restituido* (1625). He could have chosen the departure of the expedition as the background of his play years after the event." From a performance of the play, 1630, by the Company of Manuel Vallejo, Dixon suggests "about 1630" as the play's date.

Considering *For a Punishment a Double Vengeance* to be "one of Montalván's best productions" — and Montalván himself in *For Everybody* speaks of the play's having been "very much applauded" and having enjoyed a continuous performance in Madrid of twenty-one days — Bacon ("Life," pp. 390-91) is shocked by the "repulsive horrors" of the plot but filled with admiration by the play's logical development, the "pure, energetic language," the "almost total absence of *culteranismo* and the usual obtrusive *gracioso*." "The blind and fatal devotion of Leonor and Lope is skilfully drawn, and the awful closing scene forms a fitting and effective climax to the prophetic gloom which lies over the entire piece." *For a Punishment a Double Vengeance* is another of the Montalván plays which has caught the special attention of Dr. Profeti, and she analyses it with perception *(Montalbán,* pp. 78-79, passim).

VI La más constante mujer *(The Most Devoted Fiancée)*[18]

The Most Devoted Fiancée, as Bacon puts the title, was written, Montalván tells us himself,[19] "to vindicate his reputation at a time when it was menaced by the machinations of jealous rivals" (see Dixon, *"Para todos,"* p. 51). The play was apparently composed "in April and May of 1631" (Dixon, p. 52), in a period of "four weeks" (Montalván), "rehearsed in one week" and "performed for many days" before adjournment for Corpus Christi (June 19, 1631). After that Montalván interrupted his play writing, rather bitter and disillusioned despite the play's success, to compile his miscellany, *For Everybody* (1632).

The plot of *The Most Devoted Fiancée* (entertainment of Day Seven) hinges around the rivalry of two Italian families, the Esforcias and the Borromeos, and this rivalry is the source of despair for the two young lovers, Carlos and Isabel. The Duke of Milan wants Isabel, but this "más constante mujer" vows to remain true to Carlos until death. The Duke asks Carlos to aid him in pressing his suit, and the Duke's sister, Rosaura, in love with Carlos, asks Isabel to help her win him! Feeling that they have no alternative but to flee to France or England, they are about to depart on horseback, but are intercepted by the Duke's men. Isabel is seized and brought back; Carlos, at Isabel's insistence, escapes. Shortly afterwards, Carlos returns to the ducal palace in an attempt to free Isabel, but is captured and imprisoned. With sword in hand before the door of Carlos' cell, Isabel prevents a planned assassination of her beloved. Moved by her constancy, the Duke gives Isabel to Carlos, and Rosaura will marry her former suitor, the Duke of Ursino.

Bacon ("Life," pp. 345-46) and Profeti *(Montalbán,* pp. 52-53) attest to the success of *The Most Devoted Fiancée* in performance, publication and translation (into Italian and Dutch). Also, the play reached the New World, and performances were taking place in Peru at the beginning of the eighteenth century.[20] This is a "commedia eroica" (Profeti, p. 51) or perhaps a "palace play" ("comedia palaciega") rather than a "comedia de capa y espada," since the action takes place among the nobility and not among persons of lower rank. It is evident that the play has the characteristics very appealing to the audience of the day: a fast-moving plot, a great deal of action, the usual problems of love and honor, a dynamic

The Plays of Para todos (For Everybody)

heroine, and hero too, good lyric verse and the very desirable satisfactory ending.

VII   *The "Autos sacramentales" (Sacramental Plays)*

For Everybody incorporates two sacramental plays, *El Polifemo* (Polyphemus) and *Escanderbech* (Skander Beg), which form part of the entertainment of the Fifth Day of the week's activities. These two *autos* seem to have been written for Madrid's Corpus Christi celebrations of 1628 and 1629, respectively (see Dixon, "*Para todos*," pp. 41, 42).

Pedro Calderón de la Barca was "the most accomplished of all composers of the *auto sacramental*," writes Everett W. Hesse correctly in his Twayne monograph on that dramatist (p. 150). Hesse's words are very helpful in explaining what an *auto sacramental* was and what its function was: "This one-act religious piece, usually allegorical, which centered around the Eucharist, was performed either on carts in the street or in the plaza on the festival of Corpus Christi."[21] After the usual religious procession through the streets to the square, these little sermons in dramatic form were performed for the edification of the people, amid an atmosphere of joyful festivity. Drama, in the Corpus Christi celebrations, was no doubt looked forward to with great anticipation by the people, and no doubt the people benefited in a spiritual and esthetic way, in great measure.

VIII   El Polifemo *(Polyphemus)*[22]

The one-eyed Polyphemus, living with his cyclops on an island, relates (in harmonious verse) that God had cast him out of Heaven for the sin of pride. In vengeance, he has been spreading evil, whenever possible, throughout the history of Mankind. With the coming of Christ there was a confrontation (when he was sleeping Christ bored out one of his eyes with a stick); and Christ, the divine Ulysses, has begun his victorious mission in Jerusalem, wooing Galatea, the soul of Man. At the beginning of the play, Polyphemus asks for help, and several cyclops (one of them representing Judaism, for example) respond. Polyphemus decides to join battle in Jerusalem, and — as an illustration of startling stage effects in these *autos* — his island sinks into the sea amid a discharge of rockets. In Jerusalem, Polyphemus tries to court Galatea, while the cyclops play guitars and Alegría (Mirth) dances and sings to the music. After a long and bitter verbal and physical battle, Christ pays for the sins of Mankind through the shedding of his blood. The *auto* ends with the triumph of Christianity and the defeat of Polyphemus. And before the audience is a tableau of the cross, a chalice, the Host and the Christ Child, whose hand the redeemed Galatea clasps.

Francisco de Quevedo, in his *Teetotum*, attacking *For Everybody*, visited upon *Polyphemus* "a censure as harsh as well merited" (in the opinion of Bacon, "Life," p. 425). Among other things, Quevedo (being most upset by the identification of Christ with Ulysses) wrote that Montalván was a clumsy writer, a despicable scholar and a Christian of questionable orthodoxy. Bacon would agree wholeheartedly with Quevedo, declaring (p. 424) that "so offensive is the allegory of this extravagant and tedious production, that one cannot understand how the Church should have allowed its performance. The conception of the Savior boring out the eye of Polifemo with a stick, seems almost a burlesque upon Christianity." However, Edward Glaser some years ago took up the defense of the Montalván presentation, and with skill and deep understanding refuted Quevedo's and others' interpretations.[23]

Recalling that there was wide interest in the Polyphemus theme in Montalván's day, as exemplified by Luis de Góngora's *Fábula de Polifemo y Galatea* (1613) and Lope de Vega's *La Circe* (1624), Glaser points out that the accepted interpretations of Ulysses in Portugal and in Spain could have no misgivings in "pressing the allegorized Ulysses into the service of Christian piety." "To Patristic authors, steeped in nautical symbology, the exploits of the Greek seafarer logically suggest episodes from the history of the redemption" (p. 113). Denouncing Quevedo's ill-founded and malicious attack — he should have known better — Glaser concludes that "Traditional and then current hermeneutics fully sustain Montalván in accommodating the Odysseus myth to Christological explanation" (p. 115). "From the viewpoint of orthodoxy the basic ideas of the play are unassailable. Their dramatic presentation in the *Polifemo* manifests the imaginative and original craftsmanship of an unjustly neglected author" (p. 120). "The didactic aim of Montalván is not achieved at the expense of the poetic unity of the play. On the contrary, the theological disquisitions are closely woven into the fabric of the *Polifemo*, for they lead in logical sequence, to the eucharistic apotheosis that is of the essence in every *auto sacramental*" (p. 119).

Glaser's arguments in favor of Montalván's procedures seem very logical and very effective; but Victor Dixon is not very enthusiastic, to put it mildly, about Montalván's results: "Indebtedness to this source [Lope de Vega's *La Circe*, especially the second canto]

The Plays of Para todos (For Everybody) [35]

probably explains Montalbán's decision (an ill-conceived one in my opinion, Glaser notwithstanding) to interpret *a lo divino*, within a single play, both the blinding of Polyphemus by Ulysses and (as a *later* episode) his rivalry with Acis over Galatea. It would similarly explain the plot-structure of the *comedia Polifemo y Circe* [Polyphemus and Circe], written in 1630 by Mira de Amescua, Montalbán and Calderón, and very possibly planned not by Mira (*pace* A. E. Sloman, *The dramatic craftsmanship of Calderón* [Oxford, 1958], p. 132), but by Montalbán, who was able in his act to borrow lines not only from *El Polifemo* but also, as we shall see, from two other works of his own. Cf. *La Circe*, ed. C. V. Aubrun & M. Muñoz Cortés, (Paris, 1962), p. xl'' (Dixon, "*Para todos*," p. 41, note 23).[24] Dixon later mentions, pp. 42-43, a *canción* in Montalván's second act of *Polyphemus and Circe* which has versions in the Montalván play *A lo hecho no hay remedio* (What's Done Can't Be Undone) and the novel *Al cabo de los años mil* (At the End of One Thousand Years).

IX Escanderbech *(Skander Beg)*

"The *auto Escanderbech*," writes Dixon, "*Para todos*," p. 41, is "an ingenious recasting *a lo divino* of the first of Vélez de Guevara's two plays about Skander Beg, *El príncipe Escanderbey*." Dixon also gives some details about performance, and is led to believe, as was mentioned before, that Montalván wrote the sacramental play for the City of Madrid, Corpus Christi, 1629.

Before giving the text of the *auto* in *For Everybody*, Montalván provides a brief account in prose of the story of Jorge Castrioto (Escanderbech), in the manner of the prologues (or *proemios*) of the old plays of the sixteenth century, "so that those who did not know about it would be grateful for the propriety of the allegory." Then the play, in verse, is given. The plot in brief is as follows: Amid a background of battle, Cristerna María, with a cross for a sword and with the Holy Sacrament painted on her shield, comes on stage pursued by Escanderbech, in Turkish costume. He has been much taken by her beauty and charm, and she agrees to marry him provided he abandon the Sultan Amurates, his Lord. But he cannot make that decision, and they separate. Meanwhile, at home, Rosa, the Sultana, sings of Escanderbech, the noble Albanian, who has been raised to high position by the Sultan. On arrival, Escanderbech relates his many victories and tells of his meeting with the Christian Cristerna María. The Sultan orders Escanderbech to take that woman prisoner.

Since Cristerna María had offered him aid in all troubles, in his perplexity Escanderbech calls out to her and is surprised when she appears immediately. Escanderbech tells her that, among other things, on his homeward journey he saw the body of a young man, nailed to a cross and surrounded by a brilliant light. Cristerna María then enters into a long theological explanation of Christianity and exhorts Escanderbech to turn against the infidel and accept baptism. This Escanderbech does, setting fire to the Sultan's tent and winning a miraculous victory for Christendom through the aid of the supernatural. Amid the firing of rockets and the playing of music, on high on the "stage" appears Alberto, one of Escanderbech's supporters, on horseback with a drawn sword, and dead at his feet a seven-headed, fire-exhaling dragon.

It can be immediately seen that this is not the ending of the usual *auto sacramental*, which normally turns to adore the Blessed Sacrament, with the eucharistic apotheosis; but it is the proclamation of a victory for Christianity. In the play, Montalván, very desirous of instructing in things pious, pours forth explanations of Biblical matters and liturgy, including among other information a philological discussion of the word "God." Bacon ("Life," p. 421) finds that "Montalván's production possesses little interest, the style being poor and *culteranismo* too much in evidence." And Profeti too *(Montalbán*, p. 110) finds an emphasis on the intellectual in the play and, through a great desire to teach, a tendency to present a symbolical scenography in the Calderonian manner, "symptomatic of future development" (p. 112). In spite of any apparent shortcomings, *Skander Beg* no doubt fulfilled its purpose at Corpus Christi, 1629, to give example of Christian piety and to assure the populace of the continuing and eternal victory of the True Faith.

X Other "Autos sacramentales" Attributed to Montalván

In discussing the *autos* of *For Everybody*, it is well to remember that Montalván is credited with *Las santísimas formas de Alcalá* (The Most Sacred Host of Alcalá) — see Bacon, "Life," pp. 316 and 426 — and *El caballero del Febo* (The Knight of Phoebus). The first mentioned *auto* was printed in a collection entitled *Navidad y Corpus Christi*, Madrid, 1644; and the second, *The Knight of Phoebus*, existing in a holograph manuscript in the Biblioteca Palatina, Parma, Italy, was published by Maria Grazia Profeti in 1967.[25] As mentioned previously (in the Preface), the Parma MS bears a Montalván signature, as does a MS (partly autograph) of *The Most Sacred Host of Alcalá*, housed in the Biblioteca Nacional, Madrid.

In *The Most Sacred Host of Alcalá*, a bandit, Andrés Corbino, is

The Plays of Para todos (For Everybody) [37]

the possessor of a silver box containing a reliquary with the Host, and the dramatic action is mainly made up of the Devil's and the bandit captain's attempts to steal the Host, destroy it and do harm to Andrés. Continually the Host and Andrés are miraculously protected, and Andrés succeeds in transporting the Host to Alcalá for safe deposit with the Jesuits. There the various Faculties of the University of Alcalá de Henares (Philosophy, Medicine, Theology and Canon Law) all agree that only a miracle could have preserved the Host unimpaired through so many vicissitudes. The play ends with the defeat of the Devil and the victory of the guardian angel. At the latter's bidding the Jesuits place the Host on an altar for veneration.

"Although," writes Bacon, "Life," p. 426, "this piece bears the title *Auto famoso sacramental de las santísimas formas de Alcalá*, it is not a true *auto* but a *comedia devota*, since it does not possess the characteristic feature of the former — a *dramatis personae* consisting exclusively of allegorical characters. . . . The work offers but little interest, and the scene at Alcalá is tedious. The elaborate stage-setting of this scene, however, merits remark." A similar statement may be made about *Skander Beg*, and Bacon classifies this play also as a *comedia devota* (play of devotion) rather than an *auto*; but there could be some debate as to whether all characters of an *auto sacramental* have to be allegorical. In a wider interpretation of the *genre* there may be a mixture, and a mixture is found in *The Knight of Phoebus*.

The Knight of Phoebus combines characters of flesh and blood with allegorical ones; and we find together in the play the Knight of Phoebus, the Emperor Trebacio of France, Princess Lindaraxa, Amadís of Greece, an old man Fisberto, Montesinos, Prince Lucidoro a Moor, giants, Christ, Mankind, Divine Love, St. John the Baptist, Appetite, Understanding, Lucifer, Pride, the Devil, Guilt, and Will. From this list, we can see that Montalván has been reading books of chivalry (which he used in some plays attributed to him) and books of theology. Dr. Profeti in her study of the piece (p. 239) believes that the date of *The Knight of Phoebus* is just before 1631. Perhaps it was performed for the City of Madrid, in a Corpus Christi celebration, in, let us say, the Spring of 1630? Just guessing, it could have followed, in an annual presentation, Montalván's *Polyphemus* (1628) and *Skander Beg* (1629). Whenever it was presented, like the others it must have made a lasting impression upon the people, for it has a dynamic message concerning the nothingness of the vanities of the World and the eternal values of things of real substance.

Dr. Profeti has carefully compared the handwriting of the Parma

MS of *The Knight of Phoebus* with the partially autograph MS of the Biblioteca Nacional's *The Most Sacred Host of Alcalá*, and has reached the definite conclusion that the MS is an authentic holograph. The signature (a "b" in one, and a "v" in the other, respectively) causes concerns, but the discrepancy can be attributed to Montalván inconsistency. It is to be noted in this case, and it is most gratifying, that additional works of the unavailable Montalván are even today being made available to students of the *Comedia*.

Looking at all of the Montalván *autos*, one is inclined to agree with Sainz de Robles ("El ciclo dramático de Lope de Vega," p. 285) that "Montalván's *autos* are not very successful. A sin in them is coldness or confusion." They are symbolical, theological, allegorical and lyrical, but they overdo the didactic element and are possibly too "intellectual," as noted previously by Dr. Profeti. At times they compete in extravagances and bad taste with the worst of the day. Aside from their poetic qualities, dramatic stage devices and presentations and perhaps their theological discussions, these sacramental plays, generally considered, add little to Montalván's dramatic reputation.

CHAPTER 3

The Plays of the Primero tomo *(Volume One)*

I   *The Plays of* Volume One

THIS volume, which includes, as was customary, twelve three-act plays, was prepared by Montalván himself for the press (Madrid: Imprenta del Reino, for Alonso Pérez, 1635). At the beginning of the book is a "Long Prologue" in which Montalván complains of thefts of his plays and the publishing of plays of others under his name. Each *comedia* is preceded by a dedication to a contemporary individual, but curiously enough no play is dedicated to Lope de Vega.[1] The volume, in its first edition, is very rare (see Dixon, "*Segundo tomo*," p. 92, note 4). The plays were printed in the order followed below in the discussion.

II   A lo hecho no hay remedio, y príncipe de los montes *(What's Done Can't Be Undone, and the Mountain Prince)*

Aurora, Princess of Albania, banished from Court by her jealous stepmother, through her faithful friend and companion in exile, Clavela, meets a "wild man," Segismundo, in the forest. (Dressed in skins and unkempt, but filled with broad culture and noble aspirations, he is reminiscent of Calderón's Segismundo of *La vida es sueño* [Life Is a Dream]). Segismundo and Aurora fall in love, but unfortunately Clavela is in love with Segismundo also, and his desirability is enhanced when it is revealed that he is a prince of Greece.

Restored to the palace, after many vicissitudes in love through rivalry with Clavela, Aurora is told by her father that she is to marry Segismundo, king of Greece. Thinking that it is her beloved, she is overjoyed, but her joy turns to dismay when the man who appears is someone else. After much confusion the problem is cleared up: two princes of Greece were called Segismundo, but the Senate had decreed that our hero was the rightful ruler. However, his brother had usurped the throne and sent him into exile. Now all is set right.

The usurper flees for his life to the mountains, Princess Aurora is to marry her Segismundo, lawful king of Greece, and Clavela finds a husband in Ricardo, who had wanted her all the time.

For Bacon ("Life," p. 60, note 1) this is a *comedia heroica*, rather than a *comedia de capa y espada*, in that "the former bring on the stage personages in a higher rank of life, such as kings and princes; and generally have, or pretend to have, an historical foundation. They are often based on intrigue, like the *Comedias de Capa y Espada*."

As was mentioned before, an example of self-plagiarism is evident in this play (as well as in many others). The Montalván novel, *Al cabo de los años mil* (At the End of One Thousand Years), which was printed in *For Everybody* (1632), but no doubt written earlier, seems to contain the original version of a *canción*, "Within sight of Barcelona lies Montserrat," stanzas of which are found in Act I of the play under discussion, as well as in Act II of *Polyphemus and Circe*, in collaboration.[2] And one cannot help being struck by the fact that in a play such as *What's Done Can't Be Undone* we are in a novelesque or "novelistic" drama, very close to the plot, action and development as found in Montalván's short novels. Profeti *(Montalbán*, p. 20) notes this continuous repetition of action and theme, giving as an example our present play and the novel, *La hermosa Aurora* (Beautiful Aurora), in which both young princesses, of the same name, are sent from Court by the machinations of a jealous stepmother, and for whom all turns out well in the end after many trials and tribulations. "This close relationship between novel and *comedia*" (Profeti, p. 20, note 10) is supported by bibliography which is very convincing.[3] Whether it be a case of a play or of a novel, the purpose in Montalván's hands was entertainment and a moral lesson. The audience of both *genres* surely drew that from them, in varying degrees of intensity.

The date of *What's Done Can't Be Undone* is uncertain, though one is tempted to think of a relationship in time with Calderón's *Life Is a Dream* of the early 1630's (through the "wild man" Segismundo in both), but any relationship may be only coincidental.

    III   El hijo del serafín, San Pedro de Alcántara
(The Son of the Seraphim, St. Peter of Alcántara)

Characterized by Bacon ("Life," p. 472) as a *comedia de santos*, this play relates the exemplary life and miracles of the Franciscan Peter of Alcántara (1499-1562), who was beatified by Pope Gregory XV in 1622 (canonized in 1669).

The Plays of the Primero tomo (Volume One) [41]

Rejecting all temptations of the flesh, Pedro is able during his student days, and afterwards, to withstand the advances of a young woman Dorotea, who even availed herself of the assistance of the devil to try to make him fall. Later on in the play unbridled desire causes Dorotea to become insane, and Pedro's treatment (exorcism) in one of her spells is to slip the garb of a Franciscan over her head, exhorting her to become a nun, which course of action she follows on regaining sanity. The devil's later machinations against Pedro are of no avail, and the *comedia* ends with the devil's being forced to witness Pedro's ascent to Heaven on a throne, accompanied by the Child Jesus.

There were several plays in Montalván's time which dealt with the soul's being sold to the devil in an attempt to win some worldly advantage; and we have already noted in *The Most Sacred Host of Alcalá*, a short sacramental play, that the theme of the devil's being thwarted in his evil purposes, with the glorification of the Faith, was popular. The theological question of free will versus predestination also occurs in *The Son of the Seraphim*, and that was a theme hotly debated by the theologians of Montalván's day, with a frequent reflection in drama.

As was customary in the *Comedia*, history is often worked in as a background; and committing an anachronism, Montalván associates in a very good scene of Act II Pedro and the young King Sebastian of Portugal, who is planning a religious campaign in North Africa (1578). Pedro has divine foresight and knows that disaster will befall the Portuguese, but Pedro can only give the young fanatic his blessing and promise to pray for him daily. Act III reports that the Portuguese have been cut to pieces, and the devil tries, unsuccessfully, to prove the futility of Christian prayer. More historical and true are meetings between Pedro and Santa Teresa de Jesús (1515-82), who knew him well and recorded in her writings that "As for women, for many years he never looked at a single one"; indeed "he never lifted his eyes from the ground."

The play in question contains (as Profeti points out, pp. 35-36; see also pp. 105-106) poetic stylistic devices very close to those of the poem (attributed to Montalván), the *Orpheus in the Castilian Language* of 1624.[4] The beatification of Peter of Alcántara took place, as was mentioned above, in 1622. This may well have been an event which inspired Montalván to write his *comedia* on the life of the saint. The versification of the play has the appearance of the Montalván of the mid twenties, roughly. Perhaps my dating (Parker, "Chronology," p. 196) of around 1625 is still valid.

IV Cumplir con su obligación *(To Do One's Duty)*[5]

To Do One's Duty is a complicated account of several pairs' love problems at the Florentine Court. Don Juan, a mysterious Spaniard, seeks the hand of the duke's sister Camila, and his affection is reciprocated. One problem is that Camila is formally betrothed to the absent Marquis Arnesto, and Juan is being pursued by Celia, who is loved by the Duke of Florence. A further complication is that Juan has come to Italy to seek the seducer of his sister Estela. It turns out, after many trials and tribulations of love, that the seducer of Estela is Arnesto, who is now willing to marry her; the duke wins Celia; and Juan and Camila can pair off, as they desired.

"Written in pure, energetic language, this is an entertaining piece," wrote Bacon, "Life," p. 335, "in spite of the fact that it is rather unskillfully constructed. Jealousy plays quite an important rôle. . . . *Cumplir con su obligación*, as a whole, resembles one of the better plays of Lope de Vega." Álvarez Espino *(Ensayo histórico-crítico*, p. 145) singles out this play of Montalván's for examples of the epigrammatic style; and the editors of the 1827 volume praised the play's lyric poetry above all, pointing to some favorite lines: "Persuaded of this opinion we shall admire and copy with pleasure these beautiful selections, and we shall prefer them eternally to the coldness, languor and prosaic qualities (very verisimilar, it may be, but very insufferable) of other more modern writers" (p. 142).

Montalván's dedication of the play, in his *Primero tomo* — to repeat information given previously — declared that *To Do One's Duty* was his second play. This may well be so, which would date the play in the late "teens," both for Montalván and for the seventeenth century. The play, as is usual with Montalván, contains a very well developed comic servant *(gracioso)*, Mendoza;[6] and this character, as we know, well presented, was a constant in our dramatist. Perhaps he ran into many examples of this type in Madrid and in his university student days, and the resultant product in the plays is born of keen observation.

V Los templarios *(The Templars)*

The Templars relates the ups and downs, and the final suppression, of a religious-military order which was founded in Jerusalem in 1118 by French knights who had accompanied Godefroy de Bouillon on the first crusade at the end of the eleventh century. It also relates the love affair of Albante, leader of a band of outlaws, with Casandra, a captured pilgrim, and that of his associate, Germano, with

The Plays of the Primero tomo (Volume One) [43]

Flora, a peasant villager. The Templars rout the bandits, capturing some of them, and the young women decide to join the knights, dressed in male attire. Victories are won over the Moroccans and the Turks, and an expedition sets forth from Rhodes to attempt to wrest Jerusalem from the hands of Saladin, who has just taken it (1187).

The Master of the Templars attempts to lay down very strict laws of conduct for the Order's members, but among some knights morals seem to be very lax, although the majority appears to be very high principled. Albante and Germano, escaping from prison after a period of three years of confinement, through spite and resentment go to the Pope and demand that the Templars be investigated. The Pope, who has already been scrutinizing "the perverted life" of the Templars, decrees that every Templar, without a single exception, is to be put to death. Flora and Casandra, recognized to be women, are spared.

Irrelevant scenes, a lack of any feeling of sympathy or horror for the awful ending, an over-abundance of "culteranismo," and a very large number of characters (nineteen) make *The Templars* one of Montalván's least successful plays. The main plot is more or less historical. What could be called a sub-plot, the love affairs of Albante, Germano, Casandra, and Flora, may have been put in for the *vulgo*, the common audience of the day. The love affairs do have some bearing on events, of course. Albante and Germano lose out, and this losing out (in love and through imprisonment) gives rise to their perfidy.

This play contains good examples of a dramatic device advocated by Lope de Vega in his *New Art of Writing Plays:* the woman dressed as a man, when Casandra and Flora, as noted previously, join the Templars and assume male disguise.[7]

VI   La doncella de labor *(The Waiting-Maid)*[8]

The Waiting-Maid is a better play, and its qualities support Montalván's statement in his dedication that it is "the most ingenious and best written play" of all he had composed. Outstanding is the heroine Isabel, who is filled with clever stratagems to further her love for Diego, who already has a beloved, Elvira. First she must make his acquaintance, and she does so by rushing into his house, begging protection against an angry (non-existent) husband. Isabel's suitor and Diego's friend, César, appears on the scene and causes her to take refuge in Diego's bedroom. This episode reaches Elvira's ears, and anger and jealousy take the place of peace and harmony.

To continue her campaign to separate Diego and Elvira, Isabel, disguised, enters Elvira's service as a waiting-maid. Making use of her own servant Inés, Isabel continues her game and increases more and more Elvira's suspicions of Diego. In fact, Isabel very subtly causes Diego to fall in love with her, thus achieving the purpose she had in mind from the beginning, to bring about her marriage to Diego. Elvira must be content with César; and of course there is a *gracioso* to pair off with Inés.

Bacon has very rightly classified *The Waiting-Maid* as a cloak and sword play *(comedia de capa y espada)*. Veiled women, disguises, hiding in bedrooms, jealousies, coincidences, . . . all these qualities give the audience a very attractive play, with fast action and brilliant dialogue. A "comedy of intrigue and honor" Profeti has called it, and *The Waiting-Maid* is also surely that. It compares well with Calderón's very popular and enduring series of *capa y espada* plays, which in some ways are the *genre* which is the "essence" of the *Comedia*. Everett Hesse *(Calderón*, pp. 55-56) has summed it up succinctly in the following words: "The criticism most often leveled at the Cloak-and-Sword plays is that they lack profundity of theme and that all their brilliance is only superficial. It must be admitted that, while there is depth in the notion that one cannot be kept from or forced into a marriage either acceptable or repugnant to one's desires, it is overshadowed in the play by the intrigue, comic situations, the highly lyrical and baroque style and the clever interweaving of the action, all of which provide 'good theater.' Furthermore, the audience enjoys 'being in' on the tricks and deceptions, and interest is maintained by its natural curiosity to ascertain the working out of the intrigue."

VII El mariscal de Virón *(The Marshal of Virón)*

The Mariscal de Virón, Don Carlos, is in love with Doña Blanca, and she with him. Unfortunately their king, Enrique (Henri IV of France), is in love with her too; but magnanimously the king withdraws his suit, plans the Carlos-Blanca marriage, and creates Carlos Duque de Virón and a Peer of France. Carlos, however, feels that he is not yet being sufficiently rewarded for his many services to the realm, and starts intriguing with France's enemy, Savoy. But repenting of his treachery, in battle he leads the faltering French to victory. The king, knowing many details of Carlos's perfidy (and that he was also negotiating a marriage with the Duke of Savoy's sister), offers Carlos a pardon if he will ask for it. But Carlos insists that he is innocent, and through arrogance, false pride and vanity, will not

The Plays of the Primero tomo (Volume One)

humble himself. The judges pass the death sentence on him, and he is beheaded publicly.

Quevedo, in his *Teetotum* denouncing *For Everybody* immediately after the volume's publication in 1632, pointed out that the source of the play was Juan Pablo Mártir Rizo's *Vida del duque de Virón* (which was first published in 1629).[9] Like *The Templars*, *The Marshal of Virón* ends unhappily, and is a tragedy in a sense. Montalván in both cases is following history, as interpreted by him, and he is not providing any surprises in the dénouement. In the historical account, the marshal perished on the scaffold, in public view, but in the play this sad event is related by Blanca to the king in moving terms, and in some detail. Profeti *(Montalbán, pp. 44-48)* points out that the play's theme is the magnanimity of a king versus the treachery of a vassal, adding that the description of feminine beauty in Blanca and her characterization are outstanding. Profeti also notes that the play is worth examining carefully on the side of baroque style in poetry.

The Marshal of Virón is credited with popularity on the stage and frequent publication in the seventeenth century, and Winifred Smith, fifty years ago, showed that the play's influence spread to Italy's *commedia dell'arte*.[10] *The Marshal of Virón* belongs to a *Comedia* grouping which one might designate as the rise-and-fall of a favorite, which is well exemplified by Montalván's Sejanus play discussed later in this chapter.

VIII La toquera vizcaína *(The Cap Seller of Biscay)*[11]

Doña Elena living in Valladolid has two suitors: Don Diego, whom she dislikes, and Don Juan, her favorite. A duel takes place between the two rivals, and Diego is killed. Juan flees to Madrid, where he takes refuge with Don Lisardo, originally from Zamora. Elena pretends to become a nun (she has her maid's sister enter a Valladolid convent under her name) and sets out for Madrid looking for Juan.

Elena lodges in the home of Magdalena, a Basque headdress seller, and decides to enter the business herself in order to obtain entrance into as many homes as possible in her search for her lover. Elena finds him in due time, but he is being pursued by another young woman, Flora, courted by Lisardo. After much jealousy, many complications, intrigues, deceptions and clarifications, Flora declares her true love for Lisardo, and Elena, revealing her identity, will marry Juan.

It is obvious that we are once more in a "commedia d'intreccio e onore," in the Profeti classification, or as Bacon puts it, a "comedia de capa y espada," like *The Waiting-Maid* and others. *The Cap Seller of Biscay* has all of the usual adventures, the sword play, the hidings and disguises, amid, as Profeti states correctly *(Montalbán,* p. 66) "the most subtle psychological variations." There is a certain depth to the presentation of Elena especially. She is most skilful in her machinations, some of them highly improbable it is true, but that is forgotten in "this brilliant, lively *comedia* [which] is one of Montalván's best" (Bacon, "Life," p. 412). The action is fast, the conversation is clever, and the verse is very lyrical. Accompanying that is, no doubt, costuming fitting to the occasion, colorful and attractive, as the characters flit around, heroine accompanied by maid, hero accompanied by man-servant. For the audience (similar to the readers of "escape" novels) there is a couple of hours diversion from the hum-drum realities of every day routine. This — to repeat — was the true *Comedia* for the people. Calderón, as mentioned several times, was outstanding in this *genre*. Montalván was occasionally not far behind him in giving the populace what it wanted; and *The Cap Seller of Biscay* is a good example of what he offered.

The date of composition of the play is uncertain. An attempt to use "internal evidence" would be to take Elena's words in spoof that she has been married "about nine or ten years," and that she was married in the year 1619, to get 1628-29 (?).

IX El fin más desgraciado y fortunas de Seyano,
o Amor, privanza y castigo
*(Sejanus' Fortunes and Most Unhappy End,
or Love, Favor and Punishment)*

The Emperor Tiberius has raised to high position and honor his confidant, Sejanus (who has great ambition for power), while his son Drusus, to whom much reward is due, is neglected in every way. Also, Sejanus' wife Laura is treated with ever-increasing contempt as honors are received by her husband. Getting Drusus away on a military campaign, Sejanus turns to court the former's wife, Livia. Drusus and others perish through Sejanus' trickery, and Laura, in anger and jealousy, determines to take revenge. Her impassioned plea to the emperor convinces the latter of Sejanus' treachery, and he is arrested. He is put to death by being hurled from a high rock and dashed to pieces. Livia meets a similar fate, and Laura's desire for vengeance is thus satisfied.

The Plays of the Primero tomo (Volume One) [47]

Montalván's dedication for this play names it as one of his first, and his source seems to have been a *Life* of Elio Seyano *(Vida de Elio Seyano)*, published in Barcelona in 1621. It is likely that Montalván read this book and wrote his play at the beginning of the 1620's. Once again it is an historical play, with history as interpreted by Montalván. Laura's rôle in the play (in the source, Sejanus' wife Apicata) seems to have been greatly enhanced; and her characterization is that of a strong woman, who could be played by a prominent actress. Bacon concedes that the play is "entertaining" (p. 338), but notes that the treatment of the subject is mediocre, with "the action dragging so much as to be tedious." Like *The Templars* and *The Marshal of Virón*, *Sejanus' Fortunes* is in one sense a tragedy, and Profeti (p. 84) sees in the work an "ambitious effort to compose a 'tragedy' in the classic style."

The presentation, in drama, of the rise and fall of a favorite ("privado") was common in the Golden Age; and Montalván and his contemporaries had before them a very real case in the person of Don Rodrigo Calderón, secretary of the king's chamber, who was beheaded in the main square of Madrid on October 21, 1621. "As the most striking spectacle in the political drama that had long enthralled the country, Don Rodrigo Calderón's public execution was an awesome event indeed," writes Raymond R. MacCurdy.[12] "And inevitably poets and populace were prompted to recall the rise and fall of a much greater favorite, Don Álvaro de Luna, who was executed almost two centuries earlier [June 2, 1453]." Antonio Mira de Amescua (probable author) was inspired to write *La próspera fortuna de don Álvaro de Luna* and *La adversa fortuna de don Álvaro de Luna*, "outstanding examples of the *comedias de privanza* or 'fallen-favorite plays,' a type of drama widely cultivated during the first three decades of the seventeenth century because the high risks of *privanza* were a pulsating reality of the times." Perhaps a reading of the account of a life of Sejanus (1621) and the actual fall of Don Rodrigo Calderón led Montalván's interest to the rise-and-fall theme, and inspired him to draw upon the past for several plays on the vanities of Fortune.

X Olimpa y Vireno *(Olimpa and Vireno)*

Olimpa, Countess of Holland, is betrothed to Carlos, Dauphin of France, but in love with Duke Vireno. The situation is complicated by the fact that Vireno is about to marry Princess Fenisa of Hungary, and the king of Thrace wants Olimpa for his son Eduardo. The

French knight Roland is at the Dutch Court to see that the pledge to the dauphin is upheld. In his travels, Vireno is captured by Eduardo, his old enemy; and Olimpa journeys to Thrace to attempt Vireno's release. Vireno, who is very fickle in love, is released into Olimpa's care; and as they return home via the Aegean Sea, Vireno abandons Olimpa, having won all her favors. She catches up with him in Thrace, to which he had returned to dally with a princess, Irene. Olimpa shoots Vireno, as he rejects her once more. Olimpa is then pardoned for taking the restoration of her honor into her own hands.

Montalván has used materials from Ariosto's *Orlando furioso*, Cantos IX-XI for this play; interpreting and modifying the Ariosto account to his liking. Profeti *(Montalbán*, pp. 80-84) points out that the dramatist has singled out as an important motif that of the lady abandoned on a desert island, "although far from being deserted, this island is peopled with maids and men-servants, becoming therefore more similar to a painting of Rubens than the melancholy, solitary portrayal of Ariosto" (p. 80). Bacon finds ("Life," p. 350) that, as happened also in *The Marshal of Virón*, the heroine "in utter defiance to all the canons of good taste, tells of her lover's death in a long discourse, devoid of real sentiment and wholly artificial in style." The *gracioso*, Vireno's servant Clarín, and the *graciosa*, Olimpa's maid Fenisa, are so much in evidence on so many occasions that they are obtrusive and are used overly much for comic relief in a very serious drama.

XI Lo que son juicios del cielo
(What the Judgments of Heaven Are)

Leonor, in love with Duke Roberto, has been forced to marry the Marquis Alejandro. Alejandro must absent himself in Rome, and he leaves Roberto's brother and his good friend, Lisardo, to keep watch over Leonor. To complicate matters, Leonor's sister-in-law, Angela, is very keen on Roberto. Alejandro returns from Rome secretly, and spies on his household. Disguised as Roberto, he forces the maid Inés to let him in. Leonor uses incriminating words, and Alejandro decides that Roberto must die. He forces Leonor to send Roberto a letter inviting him to visit her that night. When he comes, Alejandro kills him. The blame for the murder falls on Lisardo.

It was Alejandro's custom to have masses said for the repose of the soul of any one of his subjects who had met violent death, but he fails to have this done for Roberto. The ghost of the dead Roberto appears and reproaches Alejandro for his negligence. God has

The Plays of the Primero tomo (Volume One) [49]

allowed Roberto to proceed through Purgatory, and has allowed him to visit Earth. Alejandro, greatly awed, decides to make amends to the best of his ability.

The visit of a specter also takes place in Lope de Vega's *El marqués de las Navas* (autograph MS, April 22, 1624), and Montalván may be indebted to that play in writing *What the Judgments of Heaven Are*. Profeti *(Montalbán*, p. 70, note 14, and pp. 90-93) finds the punishment of adulterous love (or at least the intent) vigorous and put forward in no uncertain moral terms. However, the question of a forced marriage is at the root of the problem, and Montalván may have been very consciously portraying the unhappy results arising therefrom. Montalván was a moralist, we know, amid his desire to entertain, and this could be one of his most moralizing of plays. However, *What the Judgments of Heaven Are* does not stand out as one of the dramatist's better efforts.

XII   El señor don Juan de Austria *(Don Juan of Austria)*

The Papal Legate arrives in Madrid to be sumptuously received by King Felipe, accompanied by Ruy Gómez and Don Juan of Austria. Juan's beloved, Porcia, cannot see the reception on account of the crowd, and it is described to her (and to the audience) by Juan's servant Morata. That night, as usual, Porcia receives Juan and his nephew the Archduke Alberto, and they entertain themselves by composing and reciting poetry (four sonnets) in the manner of a literary "academy" of the day. King Philip, however, objects to nocturnal visiting (he waits up for Don Juan) and warns him against going out at night.

The king orders Juan to Flanders as governor, much to his sorrow and Porcia's. Honors fall upon Juan from the Pope, much to Felipe's jealousy. Traveling to the Low Countries, Juan, accompanied by his servant Morata, is followed by Porcia and her maid. Juan's mother, Margarita of Austria, comes on the scene, amid great retinue, and Juan, at her request, recounts at great length his many achievements over the years.

Don Juan of Austria is the second of the trilogy of plays on Felipe II (the third, the second part of *The Second Seneca of Spain*, was published in Volume Two of the Plays). The main source for Montalván was Lorenzo Vander Hammen's *Don Juan de Austria*, printed in Madrid, 1627, by Luis Sánchez for Alonso Pérez (Dixon, "*Para todos*," p. 42, note 27). *Don Juan of Austria* covers the period 1571 to 1576, from the date of the visit of Alejandrino, the Papal Legate, to the sending of Don Juan to Flanders. Some liberties have been taken with chronology as well as with the facts of history. Margarita of Austria was Juan's older half-sister, for example, not his mother, and historically she was in Italy from 1568 to 1581. Character study, as in *The Second Seneca of Spain,* both parts, is Montalván's forte and his outstanding achievement in this historical play.[13] Felipe is always the stoic monarch of Senecan virtue, although in *Don Juan of Austria* he is unfortunately tinged by extreme jealousy of his capable half-brother. The latter is a very life-like figure, "proud, discreet, chivalrous, reverent and devoted to the Church" (Bacon, "Life," pp. 378-79). In the opinion of Bacon, who finds a great deal of influence of Luis Cabrera de Córdoba's *Filipe Segundo Rey de España* (Madrid, 1619), the scene at the end of Act II, where the King is scratched by the chape of Juan's scabbard, is, in its latter part, "almost a verbal transcription" of that historical work.

XIII Los amantes de Teruel *(The Lovers of Teruel)*

In *The Lovers of Teruel* the sincere and pure love of Don Diego and Doña Isabel, of Teruel, is threatened by Diego's poverty and Isabel's other suitor, Don Fernando. Diego, in turn, is pursued by Isabel's cousin, Elena. The tricks and machinations of Fernando and Elena, for their ends, are numerous. However, Isabel's father, who favors the wealthy Fernando, grants Diego three years and three days to achieve honor and fortune.

Diego sets out with the Emperor Charles V for North Africa and achieves valiant deeds, including rescuing the king, but the period is almost over without his having become famous or wealthy. Meanwhile, at home, Elena has intercepted all correspondence between the two lovers, but they both remain true to each other in absence, and full of hope. The false news is spread by Elena that Diego has been killed. Finally fortune does come to Diego from the king, and he sets out for home immediately. But unfortunately, he arrives home just two hours after the time allotted, and Isabel has been forced to marry Fernando. Diego finds Isabel in the bridal chamber awaiting the groom, and wildly seeks a way to nullify what has happened. Fearful that Fernando may appear and kill Diego, Isabel tells Diego that she detests him. At this Diego falls lifeless to the floor, his heart broken. Isabel, clasping the hand of her dead beloved Diego, falls dead upon his body.

A great deal of effort has been put forth by investigators to ascertain whether these lovers of Teruel really existed. Many documents

— false or authentic — have been brought forward, and two mummies in glass-topped coffins were found, with the date 1217 as the year of their death (for details, see Bacon, "Life," pp. 322-30). Emilio Cotarelo y Mori feels that the mummies cannot be authentic, but are two bodies, perhaps husband and wife, which were exhumed after the legend began to be widespread. Cotarelo maintains that the story of *The Lovers of Teruel* is a Spanish version of Boccaccio's Florentine tale of Girolamo and Salvestra, *Decameron*, fourth day, eighth story.[14] For Cotarelo, the theory put forth by some that Boccaccio picked up an actual occurrence at Teruel (in a period when Spanish literary influences on Italian literature did not exist) is untenable. The fact seems to be that Spanish writers drew the story from Boccaccio in the middle of the sixteenth century, Montalván's later dramatic version being one of several. However, some modern critics still insist that the story is indigenous.[15]

Montalván's source seems to have been a play of the same title attributed to Tirso de Molina, and dated by Blanca de los Ríos as 1615.[16] The Montalván version is considered to be one of the best in the Golden Age, and its excellences are many. The theme is well handled dramatically, the characters (especially Diego and Isabel) are skilfully delineated, and the scenes of tragic love (what might have been) are moving. The language is often the language of pathos, and Montalván has poured forth the lovers' hopes and despair in very lyrical verse. Defects found by Bacon ("Life," p. 329) are an obtrusive *gracioso* and "an occasional tendency to lapse into verbosity." The setting in the time of Carlos V (although the story is supposed to belong to the thirteenth century) is found in several of Montalván's Spanish predecessors. That love could simultaneously cause the sudden death of two young persons is perhaps unrealistic, but the audience must accept the fact that their hearts were really broken. It is to be recalled that this tragic material was enthusiastically and successfully handled by the romantic Eugenio Hartzenbusch in his drama of the same title in the early nineteenth century. In choosing a final play for his first volume, Montalván did very well indeed to select the one he had written on the historic love affair of Spain's famous pair of lovers, who are associated in literary history with Romeo and Juliet and Abélard and Héloise.[17]

CHAPTER 4

The Plays of the Segundo tomo (Volume Two)

I *The Plays of* Volume Two

BY some critics it was believed that Juan Pérez de Montalván prepared his Second Volume of plays for the press himself, for within a month after Montalván's death on June 25, 1638, this book of twelve plays, apparently authentic, was offered for sale. However, Victor Dixon has shown conclusively that "Montalbán's 'Second Part' — like Tirso's — was not necessarily what it seemed."[1] "Till now it has been assumed that Montalbán himself prepared *Segundo tomo* for the press. But there is no evidence for such a supposition. He shows concern, certainly, for the proper publication of his plays, and was personally responsible for two previous collections. In 1632, he included four *comedias*, together with two *autos*, in his miscellany *Para todos*. By this means, he suggested in his preface, he intended to expose and confound those publishers who had already pirated various of his plays. In 1635 he published his *Primero tomo*, a collection of twelve more *comedias*. There again, in his *Prólogo largo*, he inveighed against the pirates, adding this time that many plays by other writers had been published as his" (pp. 91-92).

"Later remarks in this prologue," continues Dixon, p. 92, "confirm what the very title *Primero tomo* implied, that he hoped eventually to publish a further collection of plays. But there is no indication that he had such a collection in preparation. A Second Part of *Para todos* was what he expected to publish next, and after that he had rather uncertain plans."

Indeed, it should be remembered that Montalván was in no state, mentally or physically, in the couple of years preceding 1638, to compile a volume for publication. The preliminaries to the *Segundo tomo* indicate that it was his father, Alonso Pérez, who prepared the volume and had it brought forth at his expense.[2] Whether the choice of plays as to authorship was intentional or unintentional is not

[52]

The Plays of the Segundo tomo (Volume Two) [53]

known; but Victor Dixon has shown that the collection was prepared for the press some nine months before Montalván's death, and that at least three plays therein are probably not Montalván's.

II *Spurious Plays*

Amor, lealtad y amistad (Love, Loyalty and Friendship) had been printed as Sebastián Francisco de Medrano's in *Parte XXV de diferentes autores*, Zaragoza, 1632 and 1633, and as *Lealtad, amor y amistad* in a collection of poems and plays of Medrano's in Milan, 1631. The *Parte* text was used for Montalván's *Segundo tomo*. Dixon's evidence "surely confirms that *Amor, lealtad y amistad*, though included in *Segundo tomo*, was the work of Sebastián Francisco de Medrano" (Dixon, p. 103; and see pp. 98-103).

El divino portugués, San Antonio de Padua (The Divine Portuguese, St. Anthony of Padua) "is attributed in a manuscript apparently much earlier and more authoritative than the *Segundo tomo* text, to one Bernardino de Obregón" (Dixon, p. 103). The problem of authorship is made very difficult by the fact that "another quite different play about St. Anthony was also published as Montalbán's" (Dixon, p. 104), in the form of *sueltas*. "We must consider it most improbable, in fact," concluded Dixon after careful consideration, "that Montalbán wrote both. The 'Bernardino de Obregón' play — or the other — may have been attributed to him in error."

Edward Glaser studied the *Segundo tomo* play as "one of his [Montalván's] best *comedias de santos*" and as proof of the author's great interest in a Portuguese theme.[3] Noting that Bacon gave a résumé of a play with the same title (but of little similarity to the one Glaser was working with) and published in *suelta* copies, Glaser came to the decision that "it is very probable that the publishers, wishing to avail themselves of Pérez de Montalván's fame, caused to be circulated in his name and with the same title an inferior play" (p. 136, note 13). Glaser's purpose in his essay is "to examine carefully the manner in which Pérez de Montalván brings the figure of Antonio to the stage" (p. 137); and Glaser has found in Montalván's presentation of the saint's life "a solid dramatic creation" (p. 140), with comic relief provided from time to time by the lay-*gracioso* amid a very serious treatment of the saint's miracles and achievements in his activity on earth. Although, finds Glaser, Montalván took considerable liberties in using his sources, yet he was guided very greatly by the popular image of Antonio.

clusion (p. 176) is that "the Spanish author gives [to Antonio] a profundity and complexity absent in his *Vitae.*" "*El divino portugués, San Antonio de Padua* results from a happy association of theater and hagiography . . . the central theme which unifies this work is the development of the personality of Antonio from the early days of the studious Augustine [he was first a monk of the Augustine Order] in the solitary cell of Santa Cruz until his consecration as a daring and active Franciscan. As to what refers to the life of the Saint, to his evangelizing efforts or to his miracles, every detail is treated in such a way as to illumine with greater efficacy the figure of the hero. The wealth of doctrinal material and the tone of its expression show that the Spaniard has captured all Antonio's importance as a theologian, a facet forgotten in the popular treatises" (Glaser, pp. 176-77).

The other *Divine Portuguese*, the different *suelta* version studied by Bacon, "is worse than mediocre" (Bacon, "Life," p. 414), and Glaser has noted its inferiority. Bernardino de Obregón (author of the version in the *Segundo tomo* and the one studied so carefully by Glaser) "may of course have been a pseudonym for Montalbán or anyone else" (Dixon, p. 103, note 45). Let us hope that time will show that Montalván really wrote the play published in the Second Volume, and that Glaser's enthusiastic words can be definitely applied to a Montalván creation.

El sufrimiento premiado (Suffering Rewarded) is another play of the Second Volume which Victor Dixon has shown almost conclusively to be spurious, not written by Montalván, but a "lost" play by Lope de Vega. Dixon's careful reasoning is contained in his article ("*Segundo tomo*," pp. 105-09) and in his subsequent edition of the play.[4] Dixon's critical work is such a perfect example of the handling and resolving of a problem of authorship and chronology that I shall refer to it at some length in a later chapter on problems of authorship.

III Como amante y como honrada
(Like a Lover and Like an Honorable Woman)

The apparently authentic plays of the Second Volume begin, in the order of their appearance in the book, with *Like a Lover and Like an Honorable Woman*. In this *comedia*, Don Lope returns from Flanders to marry his cousin Leonor. Running into sword play — so many of the Cloak-and-Sword *comedias* of the seventeenth century begin with this convention — he helps an old friend, Don Juan — let

The Plays of the Segundo tomo (Volume Two)

us note the coincidental meeting — to put the aggressor to flight. Don Juan is hoping to marry Leonor's sister, Ana, who cannot become engaged until the elder Leonor is married. Mistrust and jealousy arise, Lope postpones the wedding, and he challenges Juan to a duel. At the end of the usual three-act play, through the work of the *gracioso* Martín, the girls' uncle Don Pedro and the young women themselves arrive on the scene as the duel is about to commence. Much of the misunderstanding was due to Juan's having said that his intended had been in a convent for a whole year after the death of her parents some time previously, but that was true for Ana also. All doubts and problems being clarified and resolved, Lope will marry Leonor, and Juan, Ana, and the servants pair off too.

This "comedia de capa y espada" is "one of the very best of Montalván's efforts in this class," and the above-named *comedia* "is such a close second to his *La doncella de labor* that the reader cannot easily choose between them" (Bacon, "Life," p. 388). The play is set, as is common, in Madrid, the costuming is picturesque, the verse is very lyrical, there is plenty of action and suspense. The young gentlemen and young ladies, of comfortable physical circumstances, flit around through their psychological problems and sufferings, accompanied and aided by their servants, usually more clever and witty than the former, to finally have their affairs settled in the proper manner, with the conclusion that all is well that ends well.

IV Segunda Parte del segundo Séneca de España
(Second Part of the Second Seneca of Spain)

To impress upon his son, Fernando, that kings, as well as their subjects, are subject to death, Felipe II leads the young prince through the royal burial vaults. At the same time he points to the tombs of glorious predecessors and recounts their marvellous deeds. This awesome visit is interrupted by the bad news that the Invincible Armada (1588) has been wrecked by storm, and the king leaves immediately for the Escorial. For "local color," one might say during his trip he deals with various affairs of state. In a dream Philip sees his own funeral and feels that his death is not far off. In an affectionate meeting with his children, he gives advice to his successor, Prince Philip, and arranges the marriage of his daughter Isabel to his nephew Alberto, Archduke of Austria. Following that, the king takes Holy Sacrament and retires to his bedchamber. Shortly afterwards, it is reported to the audience that the king has died, conscious to the end, a very kingly death.

Part One of *The Second Seneca of Spain* (published in *For Everybody*, 1632) covered the years 1569 to 1570; *Don Juan of Austria* (published in Volume One of plays, 1635) covered the period 1571-1576; and this Second Part of *The Second Seneca* covers the period 1588-1598. Queen Ana of Austria, who historically died in 1580, appears briefly in Act I of this play; and Prince Fernando, who died in 1578, abruptly drops from sight about the middle of Act I, without any allusion being made to his death. Prince Philip, likewise, makes a very brief and abrupt appearance. Bacon's well-considered conclusion is that "the first part of *El segundo Séneca* is so far superior to the second, that one cannot but regret that the success attained by it induced our author to put forth a sequel" ("Life," p. 370). It is very evident that pageantry is a strong point in these historical plays. Royalty, in rich costumes, with much retinue, was a feast for the eyes of the audience, which must have been impressed by the great of the past. For this play, Montalván seems to have drawn once again to some extent on the previously-mentioned historian Luis Cabrera de Córdoba *(Filipe Segundo Rey de España*, Madrid, 1619). Certain details (the scene in the royal burial vaults at the beginning of Act I, for example) would suggest this. But the main source of information was, as for the First Part of *The Second Seneca*, the Lorenzo Vander Hammen book (already mentioned) of 1625.

V Don Florisel de Niquea. Para con todos hermanos y amantes para nosotros *(Don Florisel of Nicaea. Brother and Sister to the World and Lovers to Ourselves)*

Don Florisel and Clorinda are supposedly brother and sister, but the love between them is not that of relatives. A sealed paper left by her dying mother now reveals to Clorinda that she is not Florisel's sister. Unfortunately, Trebacio, Emperor of Constantinople, wants to marry her, and his supposed sister Briana wants Florisel. Abetted by Briana, Trebacio makes vigorous efforts to keep the lovers apart, to bring about his (and his sister's) desires. Imprisoned in separate cells, each is told that the other is dead. However, they escape and together seek refuge in an enchanted castle. There a ghost, that of Amadis of Greece, reveals the whole truth of their parentage. Clorinda is really Trebacio's sister, and Florisel is Briana's brother! Trebacio, in the face of irrefutable evidence, sees the error of his ways. Trebacio returns to his proper kingdom, Nicaea, and Florisel takes possession of Greece. The way is now open for the young lovers to marry and live happily ever after.

The Plays of the Segundo tomo (Volume Two) [57]

This play is a play of chivalry, and Montalván's source is the well-known romance *Don Florisel de Niquea*, of Feliciano de Silva, sixteenth-century writer of chivalric fiction. The story was available to Montalván through many printings. Magic gardens, enchanted fountains, magic shields and scarfs, terrible giants, magic potions, a specter which arises from a tomb . . . all this and much more is used by Montalván to lead his audience into an escape from reality (as he also did in some of his exemplary novels) in the tradition of one part of Spain's literary interests in the sixteenth and early seventeenth centuries. *Don Florisel of Nicaea* is verbose and not outstanding as a drama, but the abiding devotion of the young lovers, Florisel and Clorinda, through trial and tribulation, is a heart-warming experience for any audience or reader.

VI La deshonra honrosa (*Honorable Dishonor*)

Ordoño, prince of León, is courting the Duchess Flora, who loves Leonardo, of lesser rank. Ordoño's father, King Alonso, wants his son to marry the daughter of the king of Castile, for political reasons. Ordoño, to add to the complications, mistakenly believes that Flora's suitor is the Marqués Ludovico, Leonardo's closest friend. But Ludovico loves another, Laura. The prince, through letters, secret rendezvous and summons, tries to cause trouble among the young lovers, although he knows that ultimately he will have to accept his father's choice for him. He goes to such lengths that he spreads the rumor that Flora has lost her honor. Leonardo is so beside himself that he attempts to murder Flora who, fortunately, is saved in time. The arrival of the king on stage inspires the necessary explanations and clarifications. Leonardo will marry Flora, and Ludovico will have Laura, as the young persons desired.

It is possible that *Honorable Dishonor* is an early Montalván play, for a MS copy in the Biblioteca Nacional bears the date 1622, although the validity of that dating is far from certain. The play is rather weak as drama, and may well be one of the dramatist's youthful attempts to work in the genre.

VII El valiente nazareno, Sansón
(*The Valiant Nazarene, Sampson*)

The Philistine king's soldiers seize Sampson and, binding him, are transporting him on a cart. But the prisoner breaks his bonds and kills all of them, some one thousand, with the jaw bone of an ass. In a vision, an angel informs Sampson that he will be unharmed by any enemy provided that he avoids profane liquor and keeps his hair unshorn. Meanwhile, the king is trying to seduce Sampson's wife, Dalilah; and the king's sister, Diana, is mad about Sampson. Unfortunately, Dalilah, through misunderstanding and jealousy, and learning from Sampson the source of his strength, cuts off his hair while he is asleep. The helpless Sampson is seized and his eyes are put out. Sampson asks to be led to the two main columns supporting the roof of the pagan temple. As the play ends he is about to pull them down. His hair has now grown long and his strength has been regained.

The Valiant Nazarene is based on Judges, XV-XVI. Montalván alters the Biblical account on occasions when he feels he can achieve a greater dramatic and poetic effect. Dalilah's treachery, in the Biblical story due to corruptibility (she is paid a sum of money by the Philistines), is in the play explained by her jealousy, which on the surface seemed to be justified. The Spanish audience of the seventeenth century no doubt was attracted by Biblical stories in dramatized form, and so the appeal of the play can be explained. However, it does not impress a modern reader by any particular outstanding dramatic qualities. The poetry is very Gongoristic, and an involved use of stage machinery is to be noted.

   VIII Los hijos de la Fortuna, Teágenes y Clariquea
     (*The Children of Fortune, Teágenes and Clariquea*)

The beautiful Clariquea, rescued from the sea when she was a baby, fifteen years previously, is courted by many world rulers, including Teágenes, prince of Thessaly. Teágenes and Clariquea are deeply in love, but unfortunately Princess Sinforosa desires Teágenes. Wisely refraining from making a decision, for jealousies and dangers are many, Teágenes and Clariquea, properly chaperoned, flee by boat for Egypt. After a terrible storm they fall into the hands of pirates. Escaping that peril, they fall into the hands of another suitor, King Tiamis of Besanos. Escaping again, they set sail once more, and land on the island of Lotofagos, inhabited by cannibals. Running away again, they are trapped by another suitor, the King of Egypt; and later, are about to be sacrificed to the gods of King Hidaspes of Ethiopia. Clarification and explanation come in the nick of time. Teágenes is really the son of the King of Greece; Clariquea is King Hidaspes' daughter (born white to dark parents). All ends well, for Teágenes is to marry Clariquea and Princess Sinforosa will marry King Tiamis.

  Heliodorus' *Aethiopica* (or *The Loves of Theagenes and*

The Plays of the Segundo tomo (Volume Two) [59]

Charicleia) is the source of this fantastic play. There was a Spanish translation of the book published by Fernando de Mena in Alcalá de Henares, 1587, and in Madrid, 1615. Cervantes had made use of the story in his *Persiles y Sigismunda*, and years later Calderón de la Barca wrote a play on the subject with the same title as Montalván's. In the novel, this type ("wonderful" adventures, with constant change in setting, many peripetias and amazing coincidences and recognitions, and descriptions of far-off or legendary places, of the Heliodorus kind) has been called Byzantine; and Montalván wrote "Byzantine" novels, as the chapter on that *genre* will show.

The Children of Fortune, like Montalván's *Don Florisel of Nicaea, Palmerín de Oliva* (Palmerín of the Olive Tree), and other plays of the kind, is "escape drama"; "una fuga dalla realtà" (Profeti, *Montalbán*, p. 56), whether they be chivalrous, pastoral or Byzantine. Profeti finds that a Gongoristic, baroque style abounds in *The Children of Fortune*, and she is inclined to accept my dating of about 1634-35 (Parker, "Chronology," p. 210), being of the opinion that this play is definitely in a period of strong Calderón influence, "quite far from the *Comedia nueva* of Lope de Vega." "An intellectual and refined art" (p. 63) is herein found by Profeti, and "the motifs and techniques which are Calderón's could not be noted in a clearer manner." This may be a late play, under the Calderonian influence; and, at any rate, in this piece Montalván presents his audience with an enchanting fantasy, adorned with exotic tones, and with a true and pure love winning out over all obstacles put in its way.

IX Despreciar lo que se quiere *(To Scorn What Is Liked)*

Doña Leonor, the only daughter of her widowed father, has been betrothed to a Zaragozan, whom she does not know. One day she is rescued from the charge of a bull by a stranger, to whom she is greatly attracted. To maintain her modesty, she gives him her friend Ana's name and address. This "Don Juan de Guzmán," like Leonor, is betrothed to a young woman whom he has never seen. Both Leonor and Juan are being pressed to prepare for their marriages; and being very unhappy try to thwart the wedding plans in every way possible, not knowing that the two of them are planned for each other. Through the usual misunderstanding and misinformation, much confusion arises, and Juan and Ana's lover, Lisardo, are about to fight a duel in Ana's home. Fortunately, Don Rodrigo, Leonor's father, urged on by Leonor's servant Inés, goes to Ana's home just in time, straightens out the misunderstandings and brings about the desired pairing-off. The young lovers are overjoyed.

Once again this is a Cloak-and-Sword play, set in Madrid. "A wittily devised and cleverly executed piece, both in the drawing of character and sequence of events. It merits remark how cleverly Montalván defers the solution of the *enredo* till the immediate close of the third act, by preventing Juan and Rodrigo from meeting" (Bacon, "Life," p. 389). The words used by Everett Hesse (*Calderón de la Barca*, p. 48) about Calderón's plays of this kind could be equally applied to Montalván who, as we have seen on more than one occasion, is quite skilful in the Cloak-and-Sword play: "The audience is kept on edge by the rapidity of the action, the excitement of the chase and the various intrigues, duels, deceits, misunderstandings, cross-purposes, miraculous escapes and the moral issues involved. There is charm in the naturalness of the dialogue, the brilliant repartee and the lyric verses. The source of most plays of this type is in Latin comedy, in the inventiveness of the author, or in the works of immediate predecessors. The characters are usually the same and become almost stereotyped: two or three suitors, and their corresponding ladies, a father or squire and servants, the confidants of their masters."

Mabel M. Harlan, in her study of the sources of Moreto's *El desdén con el desdén* (Disdain Conquered by Disdain), suggests that Moreto may have made use of *To Scorn What Is Liked* to write his famous play.[5]

X La ganancia por la mano *(Success in One's Plans)*

Lisardo, having committed a murder in Alcalá, flees to Granada with his *gracioso*, Guzmán. On entering that city, he stops an incipient duel between Don Fulgencio and Don Feliciano over Doña Isabel. Later on Lisardo and Isabel become attracted to each other. To add to the "pairing," Feliciano has a sister, Nise, who is being courted by a Don Gerardo. Lisardo turns out to be Feliciano's cousin and he comes to reside in his home, becoming somewhat involved with Nise. Two years pass by, and the young people continue in their complications of love. Lisardo, in due time, is able to tell of his adventure in Alcalá, where he killed a rival over his beloved in that city. After many, many problems of mistaken identity, jealousies, coincidences, all the young people are brought together and a general pairing off takes place: Lisardo gets Isabel, Gerardo pairs off with Nise, as do the servants, Guzmán with Anarda (Isabel's maid), Estacio (Gerardo's man-servant) with Inés (Nise's maid).

The Plays of the Segundo tomo (Volume Two) [61]

Veiled ladies, evening meetings, letters being passed around and intercepted, threatened duels, jealousies, misunderstandings, rings given as pledges of love, and several pairs of lovers whose actions are parodied by their servants, make this play a typical but very complicated Cloak-and-Sword play. Delays in the action (such as the interpolation of Lisardo's story of adventure in Alcalá) cause *Success in One's Plans* to be one of the less attractive plays of its kind which Montalván wrote. We remember that Montalván spent some years as a student at the University of Alcalá de Henares; and Victor Dixon — to repeat — ("*Segundo tomo,*" p. 96, note 22) reminds us that Quintana, in his prologue to the Second Volume, "was saying, if we are to believe him, that one at least of the *Segundo tomo* plays was written then [in the early years] — perhaps *La ganancia por la mano*, in which the construction, versification, language and allusions to Alcalá suggest to me a 'student' play."

It is to be noted that in Act I of this play Anarda, in an attempt to lift Isabel out of her melancholy, suggests a reading of works by Lope de Vega, the *Arcadia*, a pastoral novel, or plays.

XI El valiente más dichoso, Don Pedro Guiral
(The Most Happy Braggart, Don Pedro Guiral)

Doña Angela is being forced by her father to marry Count Alejandro, but she loves her cousin, Don Pedro Guiral (who has gone to Rome to seek a papal dispensation allowing the cousins to marry). To complicate matters, Alejandro has dishonored one Lisarda, and she is trying to force him to marry her. Pedro returns from Rome, with his *gracioso* Beltrán, and visits Angela. This leads to a duel and Pedro kills the count. Pedro and Angela, properly chaperoned, escape to France and set sail for Algiers, but are shipwrecked. Pedro's attentions wander to another young lady, Serafina, but he turns back to Angela. Serafina, for revenge, will seek the aid of Moorish corsairs to seize Pedro. (Serafina is really Rosa, a Moorish Muslim.) Shipwrecked once more, Angela, with her maid Estefanía, and Pedro and Beltrán, are overtaken by the pirates, who carry off the men only. Dressed as Frenchmen, Angela and Estefanía succeed in reaching Algiers and find the men enslaved. With great constancy, Pedro defends Christianity and the King of Spain, while he condemns the Moorish faith. Rosa (or Serafina) is insisting that he become a Muslim, but through his refusal and violent assessment of Mohammedanism he is condemned to be burned at the stake. Angela is permitted to return to Spain, to report the martyr's end. Her decision is to enter a convent.

Loyalty to the King of Spain and steadfastness in the Catholic Faith are extolled by the dramatist in this play. The hero is well portrayed: he has human failings, but he ends up a Christian martyr. Some of the speeches by Pedro — after all, he is a happy braggart — are rather tedious, and his long account of his life to the King of Morocco, in Act III, is indeed too long. The plot, with its many cases of peripetia, is really fantastic. This Second Volume of plays does not end as attractively as Volume One, which Montalván prepared for the press himself.

CHAPTER 5

Other Plays and a Contemporary Assessment

I *Plays Attributed to Montalván in Other Collections or Published as "sueltas" (separate printings)*

IN addition to the plays published in the three volumes just discussed, there are a large number of other plays frequently attributed to Montalván, the main ones being:[1]

La centinel del honor (The Sentinel of Honor). Suelta.

Como padre y como rey (Like Father and Like King). Suelta. Available in *Comedias escogidas* of Montalván, II (Madrid: Ortega, 1831): 3-118; and in *Biblioteca de Autores Españoles*, XLV (Madrid: Rivadeneyra, 1858): 533-49.

Cómo se guarda el honor (How Honor Is Guarded). Suelta.

La desdicha venturosa (The Lucky Misfortune). Suelta.

Los desprecios en quien ama (The Disdain of One Who Loves). Suelta.

El divino portugués, San Antonio de Padua (The Divine Portuguese, St. Anthony of Padua). Suelta; and not the same play printed in the Second Volume. (See preceding discussion.)

Los dos jueces de Israel (The Two Judges of Israel). Suelta.

La gitana de Menfis, Santa María Egypciaca (The Gypsy of Memphis, St. Mary the Egyptian). Suelta. Dixon, "*La mayor confusión*," p. 24, note 16, records that this play, attributed to Montalván, was denounced and prohibited in Navarre towards the end of the eighteenth century. It continues to be mentioned by critics: for example, C. Russell Reynolds, "The Santa María Egipciaca Motif in Modern Brazilian Letters," *Romance Notes*, XIII (1971): 71-76: "The popular saint was the subject of at least one *comedia* during Spain's Golden Age. This was *La gitana de Menfis, Santa María Egypciaca*, by Juan Pérez de Montalbán" (p. 71).

Gravedad en Villaverde (Vanity in Villaverde). *Parte IX, Comedias nuevas escogidas* (Madrid, 1657).

Un gusto trae mil disgustos (One Pleasure Brings a Thousand Pains). *Parte XXIX, Doce comedias de Lope de Vega y otros autores*

[63]

(Huesca, 1634); and *Parte XXIX, Comedias de diferentes autores* (Valencia, 1636).

La monja alférez (The Nun Ensign). Suelta. From around the time of the edition and translation by James Fitzmaurice-Kelly (London: T. F. Unwin, 1908), there has been a good deal of interest in the story of the Nun Ensign. See, for example, J. H. Parker, "*La monja alférez* de Juan Pérez de Montalván: Comedia americana del siglo XVII," *Actas del Tercer Congreso Internacional de Hispanistas* (Mexico: El Colegio de México, 1970), pp. 665-71. Unfortunately for the Montalván canon, this play may be by Luis Belmonte Bermúdez (see Victor Dixon, Review of Profeti, *Montalbán*, p. 187). *The Nun Ensign* is one of the most famous cases of a woman dressed as a man, as discussed by Carmen Bravo-Villasante, *La mujer vestida de hombre*, p. 73, etc.

Morir y disimular (To Die and to Conceal). Suelta. The character Juanelo says, Act III, that this was the first play written by its author. Traditionally, in accounts about the dramatist, *To Die and to Conceal* was Montalván's first play, and written at the age of seventeen. It may or may not be Montalván's: " . . . *Morir y disimular* (if it was his, and his first play) . . . " (Dixon, "*Segundo tomo*," p. 96, note 22).

Palmerín de Oliva (Palmerín of the Olive Tree). *Parte XLIII, Comedias de diferentes autores* (Zaragoza, 1650). Montalván's *Palmerín* is "the definitive 'adiós' to the hero . . ." — Guido Mancini, *Dos estudios de literatura española* (Barcelona: Planeta, 1970), p. 100.

La puerta macarena, Parte I and *Parte II* (The Macarene Gate, Parts I and II). Sueltas. Many years ago, José R. Lomba y Pedraja categorized Part I as a good "historical" play in "El rey don Pedro en el teatro," *Homenaje a Menéndez y Pelayo*, II (Madrid: Suárez, 1899): 262. Recently, the two plays, based on the King Pedro cycle of ballads, have been discussed by D. W. Cruickshank, in his article on "Calderón's King Pedro: Just or Unjust?", *Gesammelte Aufsätze zur Kulturgeschichte Spaniens*, XXV (1970): 113-32. See p. 117 especially.

El reinar para morir (To Reign Only to Die). Suelta.

Remedio, industria y valor (Remedy, Industry and Valor). Suelta.

El rigor en la inocencia, o Privarse de privar (Cruelty in Innocence, or To Deprive Oneself of Favor). Suelta.

Santo Domingo en Soriano (St. Dominic in Soriano). Suelta.

Ser prudente y ser sufrido (To Be Prudent and to Be Devoted).

Suelta. Printed in *Comedias escogidas* of Montalván, I (Madrid: Ortega, 1827): 395-495; and in *Biblioteca de Autores Españoles*, XLV: 571-85. Victor Dixon has expressed the opinion that this play "was probably not by Montalbán" *("Para todos,"* p. 36, note 2). Charles David Ley *(El gracioso,* p. 174) finds that plays such as *Like Father and Like King* and *To Do One's Duty* contain "standard" Lope de Vega-type *graciosos;* but that in *To Be Prudent and to Be Devoted* there is "a first step towards the final transformation of the gracioso into the serious and bored 'confidant,' so typical of certain French writers of the period of Louis XIV." Unfortunately, if the play is not Montalván's, we cannot credit him with this development of the comic servant.

II "*Suppositious*" Dramas

We might add to the above listing quite a few other *comedias* associated at some time or other with Montalván's name (see Bacon, "Suppositious Dramas of Montalván," in his "Life," pp. 434-51). Examples, chosen at random, are:

La Gitanilla (The Little Gypsy Girl). Suelta. See J. H. Parker, "*La Gitanilla* de Montalván: Enigma literario del siglo XVII," *Actas del Primer Congreso Internacional de Hispanistas* (Oxford: Dolphin, 1964): 409-14. This is a version of *La Gitanilla de Madrid*, by Antonio de Solís y Rivadeneyra. There will be a later discussion of this play under "Problems of Authorship."

La lindona de Galicia (The Noble Lady of Galicia). Suelta. Also attributed to Lope de Vega and the subject of an article by G. T. Northup and S. G. Morley, "The Imprisonment of King García," *Modern Philology*, XVII (1919-20): 393-413. Mentioned in Morley-Bruerton, *Cronología*, p. 494: "It is not certain that the play is not Lope's. If his, the date could be 1631-35."[2]

La milagrosa elección de San Pío V (The Miraculous Election of Pius V). Suelta. Ruth Lee Kennedy, some years ago, expressed the opinion that "By elimination Montalbán seems the probable author" *(Modern Language Review*, XXXI [1936]: 408).

El valor perseguido y traición vengada (Valor Beset and Treason Avenged). Suelta. "Probably his" — Dixon, "*La mayor confusión*," p. 24, note 16. The play was discussed at some length by Irving A. Leonard, in a previously mentioned article, "Montalbán's *El valor perseguido* and the Mexican Inquisition," *Hispanic Review*, XI (1943): 47-56. "In 1682 the improprieties of a play entitled *El valor perseguido y traición vengada*, attributed to Juan Pérez de Montalbán, were regarded in such bad taste and as so irreverent that the Holy Office directed its banishment from the stage" (pp. 47-48). Leonard points out that Montalván was very popular in the Spanish Indies throughout much of the second half of the seventeenth century, "possibly enjoying acclaim only second to that of his master [Lope de Vega]" (p. 50). Noël Salomon (*Le Thème paysan*, p. 153) mentions this play ("attribuée à Montalbán") for its peasant character, Cardenio.

III Plays in Collaboration

Montalván wrote a few plays in collaboration with contemporary dramatists, and the following are to be noted in that category:

El monstruo de la Fortuna, la lavandera de Nápoles, Felipa Catanea (The Prodigy of Fortune, the Laundress of Naples, Felipa Catanea). *Parte XXIV, Comedias nuevas escogidas* (Madrid, 1666). Act I, by Calderón; Act II, by Montalván; Act III, by Francisco de Rojas Zorrilla (?). The play is available in *Biblioteca de Autores Españoles*, XIV: 449-70. The play was published as being by "Three dramatists" ("Tres ingenios"). Reasons have been put forth to support the above collaboration, but some doubts have been thrown upon the partnership. See Juan Bautista Avalle-Arce, "Una nueva pieza en títulos de comedias," *Nueva Revista de Filología Hispánica*, I (1947): 148-65, particularly p. 164, Anotaciones, xxv.

Polifemo y Circe (Polyphemus and Circe). *Parte II, Varios, antigua* (see La Barrera, *Catálogo bibliográfico*, p. 704). Act I, by Mira de Amescua; Act II, by Montalván; Act III, by Calderón. The play is available in *Biblioteca de Autores Españoles*, XIV: 413-28. It has been studied recently in Bernhard Paetz, *Kirke und Odysseus. Ueberlieferung und Deutung vom Homer bis Calderón* (Berlin: Walter de Gruyter, 1970), pp. 90-102.

El privilegio de las mujeres (The Privilege of Women). *Parte XXX, Comedias famosas de varios autores* (Zaragoza, 1636). Act I, by Calderón; Act II, by Montalván; Act III, by Antonio Coello. The play is available in *Biblioteca de Autores Españoles*, XIV: 397-412.

Los terceros de San Francisco; or *La tercera orden de San Francisco* (The Third Order of St. Francis). MS, Biblioteca Nacional, Madrid. Act I, by Lope de Vega; Act II, by Montalván; Act III, by both. The play is available in *Obras de Lope de Vega*, V (Madrid: Real Academia Española, 1895), pp. 425-63. In Lope de Vega's *Posthumous Fame*, Montalván recounts that he and Lope wrote this play in slightly over two days, and he goes into some detail about its composition.

IV A Contemporary Assessment: Pellicer's Analysis of Montalván's Dramatic System

In the *Panegyric Tears* (1639), one of the most promising (from its title) but most disappointing contributions is José Pellicer y Tovar's "Idea of the *Comedia* of Castille Deduced from the Plays of Dr. Juan Pérez de Montalván" ("Idea de la *Comedia* de Castilla deducida de las obras cómicas del Doctor Juan Pérez de Montalván"). The main disappointment, for any practical application, lies in the fact that the comments put forward are non-specific, in that the author has simply adapted an unpublished earlier treatise of his for the Montalván *In memoriam*.

As Alberto Porqueras Mayo and Federico Sánchez Escribano have put it, "On the occasion of Pérez de Montalbán's death in 1638, Pellicer was probably forced to collaborate, perhaps in great haste, in his *Fama póstuma*, which appeared in 1639, and he put his hand on his old treatise, unpublished, of 1635. What in 1635 was an essay of a general nature on the Spanish theater (without mentioning Pérez de Montalbán, nor any other dramatist except once Lope de Vega) was 'applied' now to the theater of Juan Pérez de Montalbán. Although reference to and the praise of Pérez de Montalbán (which, in reality, is the only new aspect in this second treatise of 1639) turn out to be very forced, they were theoretically 'possible' because Montalbán was a faithful disciple and follower of Lope de Vega, from whose art Pellicer de Tovar had taken inspiration in 1635 in composing his original treatise."[3]

The first-mentioned treatise, which for Porqueras Mayo and Sánchez Escribano is "one of the most important in the Golden Age" (p. 148), had been prepared for the Academia de Madrid and presumably read at a meeting of that body on an occasion similar to Lope de Vega's presentation of his *New Art of Writing Plays* (Arte nuevo de hacer comedias en este tiempo), some twenty-five years previously. Pellicer's title was "Idea of the *Comedia* of Castile. Precepts of the Theater of Spain and the Art of Modern Comic Style" ("Idea de la *Comedia* de Castilla. Preceptos del teatro de España y Arte del estilo moderno cómico"). When asked in a hurry by Fray Diego Niseno to participate in the *Panegyric Tears* for Montalván, Pellicer apparently picked up his previously delivered treatise. First of all, he removed the introduction and conclusion, the parts, as Maria Grazia Profeti says, which were "Most closely tied to the circumstances under which the essay originated."[4] Then Pellicer added praises of the deceased Montalván and some references to his practices in writing plays, "without paying attention to whether or not [his statements] corresponded in the slightest to the truth" (Profeti, p. 198). Picking up the points in the original, Pellicer stresses, for example, that the dramatist is much concerned with moral aspects (as Montalván the theologian surely was). Other previous statements are "applied" to Montalván's "system": the custom of breaking the unity of time, the adapting of verse form, with rhyme and reason, to the dramatic situation, the normal length of acts — in all a freer individual creativity aimed at a greater artistic validity. But growing tired of making changes in his original treatise, Pellicer leaves long passages intact, however abstaining once in a while from mere copying, "through fear," writes Profeti, p. 200, "that [his statements] will not agree with the practices followed by Montalbán." Even the conclusion of the *Idea Deduced* — further praise of the deceased — is not original to the occasion, but is the copying with the slightest modification of some passages from Pellicer's earlier words on Góngora! Miss Profeti has provided valuable insight into the Montalván treatise and Pellicer's unsatisfactory method of adaptation as she transcribes the text itself with critical comment and a listing of variants from the Academia de Madrid version of some three or four years previously.

As Porqueras Mayo and Sánchez Escribano (p. 138) have written, "from the point of view of dramatic ideology, the only sincere and genuine, systematic and organized document is the address of 1635."[5] The 1639 Montalván *Idea* is a literary curiosity but far from what its title promises. It is not a system deduced from an observation or analysis of Montalván's plays, but a previously established "system," poorly, hurriedly and superficially imposed. Very little of any value or truth for Montalván can be drawn from it.

CHAPTER 6

Problems of Authorship, Including the Orfeo en lengua castellana *(Orpheus in the Castilian Language)*

I *General Considerations*

PROBLEMS of authorship of plays even in a prepared volume of our dramatist's works have arisen, as has been discussed in the chapter on the *Segundo tomo*. Problems of attribution concerning the plays printed in other collections and separately (as *comedias sueltas*) are legion, and these plays can only be considered tentatively to be Montalván's until proven one way or the other.[1] Montalván himself complained of this chaos from time to time, as we know very well. He did so, for example, in the preface to *For Everybody*, where he gave as his fourth reason for ceasing to write plays for a while the fact that if it were said jokingly that a certain play was not Montalván's that error would be repeated and believed by others ("and while the truth is being ascertained," he wrote, "I go mad and my reputation suffers"). Quevedo, it is to be remembered, accused Montalván (in *Teetotum*) of having stolen a play of Villaizán. This charge Montalván vigorously rejected in his supposed reply to the satiric work *(La trompa* [The Trumpet]): "As for your saying that I add plays to my name, I say in plain Spanish that you lie!"[2]

Montalván gives a specific example of a play's being taken from him, as Lisardo of *For Everybody*, in the introductory words to *For a Punishment a Double Vengeance*, tells of seeing the play on the boards under someone else's name: " . . . so inventive is Envy, which adopts so many ways to take from the works of others." And of course the preface to *For Everybody* expands upon the problem: "I include here four plays of mine, only to proclaim that those which have been printed up until now without my permission, are false, lying, supposititious and adulterated . . . ," as does his "Long Prologue" to the First Volume of Plays: "because [in the way they are printed] they come forth full of errors, barbarisms, absurdities and lies even in the name of the author, attributing to me many which are not mine."

[69]

"Problems of authorship — and of date — continue to befog and bedevil the study of Golden Age drama," wrote Victor Dixon ("*Segundo tomo*," p. 91), "for all the scholarship which has been brought to bear upon them." And it is only necessary to look at the Morley-Bruerton *Cronología*, for Lope de Vega, to notice how many plays are uncertain or doubtful as to who wrote them and when. In addition to Montalván, many of his contemporaries spoke from preface to preface of damage to their reputation or financial position by having added to their credit wretched writings not theirs, or by having taken from them good works which would have brought them glory and fame, as well as monetary gain. Raymond R. MacCurdy, for example, has given us Rojas Zorrilla's words of complaint in his recent "life and works" of the dramatist: " . . . in Seville they print the plays of the least known authors under the name of those who have written most. If the play is good, they usurp the praise due its author; if it is bad, they detract from the reputation of the one who did not write it. . . . "[3]

Some concrete examples touching upon Montalván are worthwhile considering, especially in drama, and in poetry and prose also. Here will be discussed: (a) the problem of authorship of a play from Volume Two; (b) the problem of a play published separately (a *suelta*); (c) the problem of authorship of a poem attributed to Montalván; and (d) some questions which arise concerning a prose work — all of them bearing at some time or other the name of Juan Pérez de Montalván as author.

II A *Play of the* Segundo tomo: El sufrimiento premiado

We have already accepted Dixon's decision that three plays of the Second Volume (1638), *Love, Loyalty and Friendship; The Divine Portuguese St. Anthony of Padua;* and *Suffering Rewarded;* are apparently not by Montalván. Dixon has recovered for Lope de Vega this last title and, in addition to putting forth reasons in his article on the "*Segundo tomo*" (*Hispanic Review*, 1961), has repeated and strengthened these reasons in the previously mentioned edition of the play (London, 1967). In view of this careful documentation, it seems very worthwhile, in the bewildering chaos of seventeenth-century attributions, to follow closely Dixon's restoration of a significant early play to the Lope de Vega canon.

In the Prologue to his edition, Dixon speaks of his two-fold purpose (p. vii): "to rescue from oblivion, purify and clarify the text of a play both pleasant and original, and to examine the hypothesis — enunciated by me some years previously — that it is a 'lost work' of

Problems of Authorship

the Fénix de los Ingenios." In brief, some of the reasons for Lope de Vega's authorship put forth are: Lope de Vega mentioned a play of this title in his first *Peregrino* list of 1604; a manuscript with that title was in the hands of players in 1624; the plays of the Second Volume of Montalván's plays are not personally guaranteed by the dramatist (his last years, as we remember sadly, were plagued by illness); two fellow-plays in the volume, as mentioned before, are unlikely by Montalván; *Suffering Rewarded*'s system of versification is not Montalván's, but Lope de Vega's of the turn of the century (many *redondillas*, for example); and other characteristics of dramatic construction of the play are Lope de Vega's and not Montalván's. The last include character names and the attributes of characters:[4] a Carpio boasting of his coat of arms,[5] an old dame cynically exploiting her daughter's attractiveness, the braggart soldier, etc., and no *gracioso*.[6] In addition, says Dixon about *Suffering Rewarded* ("*Segundo tomo*," p. 108), language and allusions "could be shown to be typical of Lope."

"In view of the lack of studies on other aspects of Montalván's technique and style, it would have been a very wearying task to document my personal conviction that it cannot be his" (Dixon, Prologue to the edition, p. viii). On the positive side, Dixon's fruitful method in editing the play is to compare *Suffering Rewarded* with authentic *comedias* of Lope de Vega "to determine to what point we can say that it is a work characteristically his." Various details, as mentioned before, point to Lope de Vega's workmanship, and the question of characters is brought forth again, this time on Lope's side, for as Dixon says (Prologue, p. xix), "in questions of attribution, the very names of the characters of a play do not fail to have their importance, since each author had his own criterion of selection. Fortunately, there exists a study, that of Morley and Tyler, which permits us to determine easily if the thirteen which the author of *El sufrimiento premiado* chose were used by Lope for persons of similar kind or social rank."[7] "Well, as will be seen in the following table, all these names, except one, appear in authentic plays; and in the majority of cases are used for characters of the same general type. The fact does not prove, of course, that the play is Lope's; but it could contribute to refute its attribution to another writer of different predilections." And Dixon points out in a footnote on the same page that "Montalbán, for example, never used in authentic plays more than *two* of these names [in the long list of characters of *Suffering Rewarded*] Fabio and Celio."

Going on to considerations of "thought" and "culture,"

"language" and "versification," Dixon is able to find supporting evidence for his thesis that the play is Lope's, and his carefully weighed conclusion is that "As a consequence of this investigation, I believe that I can show, in the prologue and notes to this edition, that if on one side there is no proof whatsoever against, on the other side there are so many indications in favor of Lope's authorship that we ought to accept it as his. It will never be considered, unless documentary proof appears, as rigorously authentic, and it would be prudent to exclude it from any investigation about the Phoenix's technique, in view of the late date and evident incorrection of the texts which we possess. It is also possible that it is a recasting which Montalbán might have made of the work of his master; but as long as characteristics are not pointed out which will clearly deny the style of the latter, it seems more logical to suppose that it is, in its totality, the 'lost' play" (Prologue, p. viii). Victor Dixon's evidence and argument are overwhelmingly convincing, and critics will certainly agree with him: that we ought to accept *Suffering Rewarded* as not Montalván's but Lope de Vega's.

III A Comedia suelta: La Gitanilla

La Gitanilla, Cervantes' story of the little gypsy girl, in dramatic form, has been mentioned many times over the years as a play of Montalván's; but for many years its very existence or non-existence was continually debated.[8] In 1930, for instance, Eduardo Juliá Martínez, in editing Antonio de Solís' *Amor y obligación* (Love and Obligation) and referring to dramatized versions of Cervantes' exemplary novel of the same name, declared that he knew "no documentation" to prove the existence of a play by Montalván.[9] Juliá Martínez's opinion represents very well an interesting problem of authorship; befogged by a minimum of data and an overabundance of conjectures.

The old catalogues and listings of drama connected a play of the title with Montalván's name: Francisco Medel del Castillo's *Índice general* of 1735; Vicente García de la Huerta's *Catálogo alfabético* of 1785; Juan Isidro Fajardo's *Títulos de todas las comedias,* of 1787. The nineteenth century continued the attribution: the *Comedias escogidas* of Antonio de Solís, of 1828; Longfellow, in his preface to *The Spanish Student,* 1843; Adolf Friedrich von Schack in his *Geschichte der dramatischen Literatur und Kunst in Spanien,* of 1846; George Ticknor, in his *History of Spanish Literature,* of 1849; Ramón de Mesonero Romanos, in the *Semanario pintoresco español,* of 1852, and in the *Biblioteca de Autores Españoles*, volume XLVII, of 1858; but it is not clear which one, if any, of these writers had seen the play "by Montalván," or whether they were repeating hearsay. By 1860, La Barrera in his *Catálogo bibliográfico* was throwing a healthy doubt on the question and he wrote that "*La Gitanilla* [attributed to Montalván] is perhaps by Solís," and on a subsequent page asked: "Is it that of Solís?" However, twelve years later, Pedro Salvá's *Catálogo* (1872) of his library declared very vigorously that the play "is different from that of Solís, and not the same one, as La Barrera suspects." Louis de Viel-Castel, in France, in his *Essai sur le théâtre espagnol* (1882), speaks of Solís' having done a recasting of the Montalván dramatic version of Cervantes' exemplary novel; but Adolf Schaeffer, in his *Geschichte des spanischen Nationaldramas* (1890), stating that he had not seen *La Gitanilla* by Montalván, questions its authenticity and sheer existence. Hugo A. Rennert, in the early twentieth century, discussing chronology of Spanish drama (*Modern Language Review*, II, 1906-07), asks: "Montalbán? Solís?"; and some years later, George Hainsworth's conclusion (on Cervantes' exemplary novels in Italy, *Bulletin Hispanique*, XXXI, 1929) is that "In spite of the assertions of Salvá, who is not precise on editions, one tends now to believe with La Barrera that *La Gitanilla de Madrid*[10] attributed to Montalván is none other than the Solís play." However, the tradition has continued; for example, in Esther Crooks' *The Influence of Cervantes in France*, Baltimore, 1931; in Gregorio Palacín Iglesias' *Historia de la literatura española*, Mexico, 1949; in Charles Vincent Aubrun's *La Comédie espagnole (1600-1680)*, Paris, 1966; and in Juan Luis Alborg's *Historia de la literatura española*, Madrid, 1970, etc.[11]

That the problem of authorship was considered by widespread critics — in North America, France, Germany, Spain — and the fact that many sought the play in vain, make *The Little Gypsy Girl*'s story an intriguing one. Daniel E. Martell, writing a published thesis on Solís' drama (Philadelphia, 1902); George W. Bacon, studying Montalván's dramatic output (*Revue Hispanique*, 1907 and 1912); Wolfgang von Wurzbach, discussing Cervantes' Preciosa-story (Strasbourg, 1913); Ada Godínez de Batlle, writing on Montalván's life and works (Havana, 1920); J. A. van Praag, meditating on *La Comedia espagnole* (Amsterdam, 1922); Iris L. Whitman, investigating *Longfellow and Spain* (New York, 1927) — all these critics could not find a copy of the play, and in the *Revue Hispanique* of 1929, Eduard Fey (similar to George Hainsworth in the

Bulletin Hispanique of the same year) confessed that "The play has disappeared. . . . In Madrid and Santander my investigations were in vain."

Nevertheless, Milton A. Buchanan, reviewing Bacon's longer study (the "Life," in *Modern Language Review*, IX, 1914) had described a copy of the much sought-after play *(The Little Gypsy Girl,* by Montalván) in his private library, and later handed it over to a graduate student for investigation.[12] The Buchanan *suelta* copy was for a long time considered to be unique, but some years later Victor Dixon found a second copy in the Paris Bibliotèque Nationale and courteously informed me of the fact. Then Raymond Marcus did me the favor of describing the Paris *suelta* in detail; and with this assistance and from my own examination and observation, I concluded that without doubt the two copies (Toronto and Paris) are from the same printing (with neither place nor date). It may well have been a late seventeenth- or early eighteenth-century printing, and possibly from Seville, because of the very large type used for the word "Comedia" in the title: *La Gitanilla. Comedia famosa del doctor Juan Pérez de Montalván.*[13]

The *provenance* of these two *suelta* copies is impossible to trace. Professor Buchanan bought his copy (now in the University of Toronto Library) from some bookseller in London early in this century, and the Bibliothèque Nationale copy is reported by the Librarian to have come from the private library of the late Léo Rouanet in 1940. The interesting point about these two identical *sueltas (La Gitanilla,* Montalván) is that this version is very close indeed to the well-known *La Gitanilla de Madrid* (The Little Gypsy Girl of Madrid) by Antonio de Solís y Rivadeneyra (1610-1686), which was printed in Madrid in 1671 (in *Comedias nuevas escogidas de los mejores ingenios de España, Parte XXXVII).* The two plays are so close in lines that they can only be considered two versions of the same play; and their relationship is important in this discussion of authorship. Whether one looks at one version or the other (let us call them "M" for Montalván and "S" for Solís), the source is clearly Cervantes' exemplary novel, *La Gitanilla,* but a comparison of each with the novel has not been helpful in determining the relationship between "M" and "S." They both contain many similar details about the beautiful gypsy girl Preciosa and her adventures in love.

The first acts of "M" and "S" are almost identical. Neither the first lines nor the last lines are the same, but 60% of the lines of the poetry are identical and some additional 15% are very close. The

Problems of Authorship

differences and changes are to be found at the beginnings and endings of "scenes," if one considers entrances and exits of characters to indicate such. The characters, with a slight difference in servant-action, are the same, and the progress of the plot is identical in both "M" and "S." The second acts show greater variation: 45% of the lines are identical and 12% almost so. In the third acts the differences are notable: less than 10% of the lines are identical and under 5% partially so. The ending of the plot in both cases is the same: the forthcoming marriage of Don Juan, who took up the gypsy life to court the beautiful Preciosa, who is really of noble birth. It is to be noted that "M" contains only 679 lines in this final act, and "S" 970. Perhaps "M" in its third act is incomplete. In total, "M" contains 2703 lines, and "S" 2802.

There exists the possibility that "M" and "S" are descended from a lost original, "X"; but it is more likely that one is related to the other in a very close manner. It seems that one play is a re-writing of the other, and that conscious and intentional changes, more and more free as the recasting progressed, have been introduced. The changes, which exist above all in the beginning and final lines of the acts and "scenes," reject the possibility that it was a case of a good memory writing the play down after a performance, for memory would probably have retained the first and last lines, which in our two versions are usually quite different.[14] Nor can we accept, in view of the fact that "M" and "S" are really one and the same play, the opinion of Francisco A. Icaza that "Solís was able, without doing more than making slight modifications to the work built by Montalbán on Cervantes' *La Gitanilla*, to have it pass as his own."[15]

My belief is that both "M" and "S" belong to one dramatist, and that "M" is the first draft of the play which we know later, in an improved form, as Solís' *La Gitanilla de Madrid* (published 1671). (The vagaries of printing may very well, of course, have brought us corrupt texts, especially in the case of "M.") The versification of "M," if one can take these isolated cases as valid, is earlier than that of "S." Looking at the percentages of *redondillas, versos de romance* and Italianate lines, "M" is very close to the "style" of around 1630 (if such exists), and "S" is more in line with the Spanish dramatic manner of around 1650.[16] In dramatic structure, which is a most difficult matter, there are certain improvements which would indicate that "S" is a later re-writing of a first sketch. For example, "M" in a very few words mentions a meeting of the gypsy council (Act III); in "S" this council meeting takes place on stage, adding considerably to the impact of the play. Similarly, other gypsy customs (the distributing of "jobs" for the night, for instance), present in "S" but not in "M," bring with them an artistic value which the first version does not possess in these points. In addition, there seems to be an occasional correction of reading in "S" over "M," which urges the filiation of "M" before "S" in the process of creation (but we may very well in "M," as mentioned before, be dealing with a very corrupt text). Only very occasionally is it the other way around: "S" in line 2795 contains the name "Doña Ana," without explanation, whereas "M" makes it clear that that is Preciosa's real name. But in my opinion "S" over all is a much better play, with more conscious harmony of composition and a more developed and improved handling of dramatic art. For example, in "S," Don Juan and the *gracioso* Julio appear together felicitously and fruitfully in the first scene of each act to explain or to clarify what has occurred between acts, in sparkling dialogue; but in "M" their rôle in this regard is very limited. In general, all is more logical in the Solís version.

However, it is to be remembered that Fredson Bowers has remarked that "critical evidence is reversible," and, as to variants, frequently the case can be argued on both sides.[17] And there have been quite contrary pronouncements of very distinguished critics on these matters: for instance, Albert E. Sloman believed that *La vida es sueño* (Life Is a Dream), by Calderón, was inspired by *Yerros de naturaleza y aciertos de la fortuna* (Errors of Nature and Successes of Fortune), whereas others like George Tyler Northup and Rudolph Schevill considered the opposite to be the case;[18] and more recently Gerald E. Wade and Robert E. Mayberry, as well as María Rosa Lida de Malkiel, have found good evidence that *Tan largo me lo fiáis* (You Are Giving Me So Much Time) precedes *El Burlador de Sevilla* (The Trickster of Seville), while Emilio Cotarelo y Mori and Joaquín Casalduero had called the former a recasting of the latter.[19] Nevertheless, I continue to believe that Antonio de Solís was a recaster of himself in "M" to "S," and M. A. Buchanan, who owned both of the plays, was certain that that was the relationship of the two printed versions: "The *suelta* attributed to Montalván is certainly older. The two plays are often the same word for word, but there are many changes that indicate a recasting."[20] And away back in 1828 the unnamed critics of the *Comedias escogidas* of Solís spoke of the work of the "second" author: "He has only corrected some passages, made some suppressions, has added several scenes . . . he has improved it considerably."[21]

Problems of Authorship [77]

To repeat: as to the relationship of "M" and "S," I believe that to be the chronological order. As to the presence of Montalván's name on the *suelta* ("M"), we remember the confusion of names in the history of Spanish seventeenth-century drama, and Montalván's own words, already quoted, in his "Long Prologue" to the First Volume of plays: " . . . they come forth full of errors, barbarisms, absurdities and lies even in the name of the author, attributing to me many which are not mine. . . ." As to the date, and to the authorship too, of *La Gitanilla* ("M"), the first edition of *For Everybody* of 1632 (see later discussion) declares that "Don Antonio de Solís is writing a play which he calls *La Gitanilla*. . . ." The edition of 1635 changes the tense of the first verb, saying that "Don Antonio de Solís wrote *La Gitanilla*. . . ." Surely *La Gitanilla* ("M") is by Solís, and it seems probable that he wrote this first version of his play in 1632 or shortly afterwards.

IV *The Problem of Authorship of a Poem:*
Orpheus in the Castilian Language

There is associated with Montalván's name a very small amount of non-dramatic poetry, and there has not been in this *genre* the controversy regarding authorship and date which we find in the case of his plays; but the doubt about the "paternidad literaria" of one poem at least is a very intriguing one.[22] William L. Fichter wrote: "It is possible that we have not recognized all of Lope's anti-*culto* writings. . . . Cf., for example, the doubt that has sometimes been expressed about Montalván's authorship of the *Orfeo en lengua castellana* and the supposition that it was written by Lope."[23]

Whoever wrote this long (approximately 1800-line) epic poem in four cantos, the reason for its composition is clear: the literary battle between the learned poets led by Luis de Góngora and the plain-style poets captained by Lope de Vega. This battle had been going on apace for some years before the publication of the *Orpheus in the Castilian Language* in 1624, and Lope de Vega, with Montalván in his shadow, was deeply embroiled and concerned. From time to time, and quite frequently, Lope had been making comments, quite strong ones, in both prose and verse, not excluding the *Comedia* itself. Miguel Romera-Navarro has described the situation for Lope de Vega at the beginning of the 1620's: "The question of *culteranismo* seems now to preoccupy more than ever the mind of our poet: in the defense of the purity of poetic style he has seen himself so ill-treated by Góngora's friends that the question of principles has become a personal question, and his ironies and witticisms are filled with accents of anger."[24] Then this situation was exacerbated and brought almost to the breaking point by an unexpected blow to the plain-style cause: one of Lope de Vega's most competent supporters, Juan de Jáuregui, who had written vigorously against Góngora and his "obscure" style on several occasions, came forth with his *Orfeo* (Orpheus) in 1624. This poem was extremely "learned," as far as its classical allusions, constructions and vocabulary went, and its "baroque" style quickly roused the ire of Lope de Vega and his supporters. One of the latter in an anonymous comment had the hero Orpheus ask the heroine Euridice why she returned to Hell. To that her answer was: "Because the torment of Hell/Seemed more gentle to me/Than to hear you speak in your learned fashion."

It is not clear why the poet Jáuregui took this bold and traitorous step with his *Orpheus*, and Lope de Vega and those around him did not pause to investigate but immediately entered the fray with a violent attack. Supporting (and authoring?) a second *Orpheus*, this one in pure Spanish ("in the Castilian Language"), Lope de Vega in his preface to the poem did not mince words, as he denounced those "tinged" with Gongorism, who had been censuring others while walking in darkness themselves. It matters not here that this *Orpheus in the Castilian Language*, published under the name of Juan Pérez de Montalván, later in 1624, was itself semi-*culto* in the definitions of the day;[25] what matters in this consideration is that its authorship is a very "vexing question."[26] Away back in 1672, the *Biblioteca Hispana Nova* by Nicolás Antonio attributed the work to Lope de Vega, and through the years this nagging doubt has been in the critics' minds. A Biblioteca Nacional (Madrid) copy of the *Orpheus in the Castilian Language* (editio princeps, 1624, R/10394) bears a note in handwriting of the seventeenth century to the effect that "This *Orpheus* was written by Lope de Vega and he wrote it in four days," and Eustaquio Fernández de Navarrete, one hundred years ago, explained the authorship too simply when he wrote that "[Lope de Vega] presented [to Montalván] a work of his, the poem entitled *Orpheus in the Castilian Language*, so that the pupil might publish it under his name, which he did in 1624."[27]

Many others have been inclined to believe that this tradition of Lope de Vega authorship is the correct one; and recent writers such as Joaquín de Entrambasaguas[28] and Pablo Cabañas[29] are quite strong on the point. A great deal of weight is given to what has been

Problems of Authorship [79]

said about the authorship of the poem through the centuries, but Cabañas, for example, finds concrete positive internal evidence for Lope, such as extraneous references to mythology, common in some of Lope de Vega's works. Cabañas' conclusion, which I share myself, is that "We think that we have brought forth some literary proofs which seem to confirm the belief which has been sustained since Nicolás Antonio concerning the attribution to Lope de Vega of the *Orpheus in the Castilian Language* published under Montalbán's name. But documentary proof we do not have. Only this can clarify the mystery definitely" (p. 218). Also, "In the case of the *Orpheus in the Castilian Language* our scientific rigor, in spite of our personal conviction, prevents us from removing the question mark" (pp. 218-19). S. Griswold Morley has commented in a similar vein of uncertainty: "Proof will be forthcoming only by some accidental new discovery, and I shall not argue the question here. It is quite possible that Lope indulged his bent for foolery by fathering minor productions on others, as publishers often ascribed the work of rival dramatists to Lope."[30]

Victor Dixon ("*Segundo tomo*," p. 109) is clearly on the other side of the argument. "I have no faith," he wrote, "in the critical tradition that Montalbán shamelessly put his name to works in fact by Lope. (The 'evidence' for instance on which scholars assert that this happened in the case of *Orfeo en lengua castellana* is scandalously flimsy.)"[31] Yet it could have happened for the *Orpheus in the Castilian Language*, with Lope de Vega's indulging "his bent for foolery" as Morley put it; and I am inclined to believe that the evidence that Lope de Vega did this in this case is not without value. Gerardo Diego at one time went to the extreme of writing that Lope de Vega's *Orpheus in the Castilian Language*, "né under the name of Juan Pérez de Montalván," was a definite fact;[32] but we cannot go as far as that. Documentary proof is indeed lacking.

V   *The Question of a Work in Prose:* La Trompa *(The Trumpet)*

Just as for his poetry in general, so for Montalván's prose there has not been the discussion which has occurred regarding the authorship of plays. One interesting short treatise in prose, the afore-mentioned *La trompa* (The Trumpet), can have any doubt thrown upon its authorship only because of the confusion of contributions in the literary and personal battles of the 1620's and 1630's.[33] Montalván probably did write this little work immediately after Quevedo's attack *(The Teetotum)* on him following *For Everybody* of 1632. It is only possible that some friend of Montalván might have taken up his pen to defend him and to attack Quevedo, using Montalván's name attached to the title and within the work itself. For the preceding possibility of the *Orpheus in the Castilian Language*, in the Lope de Vega-Juan de Jáuregui quarrel, is still before us.

Del Piero, in his presentation of *The Trumpet*, reminds us (p. 40) that "No sooner had the copies of the debated book [*For Everybody*] come forth from the presses of Madrid, in May 1632, when a whole avalanche of satires, libels, attacks and counterattacks came to fall upon its young author, the innocent victim of the quarrels in which were involved Góngora, his master Lope, and his friends Luis Pacheco de Narváez and Fray Diego Niseno. The most celebrated of these satires (and at the same time the most merciless and the first, chronologically, among those which have come down to us) is the *Perinola* of Quevedo which, although it was not printed until the following century, attained immediately a great diffusion in manuscript, as can be seen by its numerous texts of the seventeenth century which have reached us." Del Piero feels that Quevedo's violent attack in *Perinola* (Teetotum), to be referred to again in a later chapter on *For Everybody*, was due to Quevedo's associating Montalván's name with those who brought about the Inquisitorial prohibition of many of Quevedo's works in 1631: "It is not clear that Montalbán had any direct part in this condemnation, but it is certain that Quevedo identifies him as one of the circle of his accusers, perhaps on account of his relations with the Holy Office, or (what is more probable) on account of his friendship with Niseno and Narváez, whom he praises in his book" (p. 41).[34]

It seems that Father Niseno jumped immediately into a defense of his friend in a "Reply" (now lost) to the *Teetotum*, and that many other "replies" followed, in favor of Montalván or vice versa. Some were anonymous, some were hidden behind pseudonyms, some bore real or fictitious names, as has been outlined by Agustín González de Amezúa in his study of "Las polémicas literarias sobre el *Para todos* del doctor Juan Pérez de Montalbán."[35] However, as Del Piero says, the critics had paid little attention to Montalván's own reply, *The Trumpet*, until Del Piero's article of 1961. The work was unpublished and known only in a unique manuscript in the British Museum, although Luis Astrana Marín had referred to its existence in his previously mentioned biography of Quevedo (*La vida turbulenta de Quevedo*, p. 437). That there apparently exists only one copy of the treatise, as a manuscript only, does not necessarily throw doubt upon authorship, for we remember that even the printed *The Little Gypsy Girl (comedia suelta)* seems to have only two copies in the world, and that the first edition of *For Everybody*, which surely must have consisted of hundreds of copies, is a great rarity today. "There are editions of the period," writes Del Piero (p. 43), "of which only a unique copy are known; and others, in short, which have been completely lost. And manuscript texts are usually still less resistant to the action of time."

The Trumpet has Montalván as its author, as has been mentioned, with the title, and Montalván's name several times within the text. Perhaps its style, which Astrana Marín (p. 437) characterized as "without wit" and "as heavy" as the style of Montalván's novels, is an argument in favor of Montalván authorship. However, to be fair to Montalván, whose prose is not always of the best, Del Piero reminds us that manuscripts of the seventeenth century became debased very frequently in transmission, and all of the leaden quality in the prose of *The Trumpet* need not be ascribed to its author, but partially at least to some careless and inept copyist.

The play *Suffering Rewarded* is certainly not by Montalván, nor is *The Little Gypsy Girl*. The *Orpheus in the Castilian Language* stands in the middle, his? or not his? *The Trumpet* is presumably Montalván's, and should continue to be accepted as his unless time proves otherwise. All of them are fascinating examples of questions which arise in the mind of the literary historian of the twentieth century with regard to many works of Spain's Golden Age.

CHAPTER 7

Prose Writings

I *Montalván's Prose Writings*

MONTALVÁN'S prose writings include *The Trumpet*, a satirical work already discussed, short novels in the style of Cervantes' exemplary novels, an account of *The Life and Purgatory of St. Patrick*, and prose portions of *For Everybody* (non-novelistic), as well as the usual dedications preceding a volume and his censorship and approval of volumes of others in his position as an officer of the Inquisition.

II *The Exemplary Novels*

In 1624, there was published in Madrid, by Juan González, the first edition of Montalván's *Los sucesos y prodigios de amor, en ocho novelas ejemplares* (The Happenings and Prodigies of Love, in Eight Exemplary Novels). The eight novels, running about 8500 words each, are: *La hermosa Aurora* (Beautiful Aurora); *La fuerza del desengaño* (The Force of Disillusionment); *El envidioso castigado* (The Envious Man Punished); *La mayor confusión* (The Greatest Confusion); *La villana de Pinto* (The Peasant Girl of Pinto); *La desgraciada amistad* (The Unfortunate Friendship); *Los primos amantes* (The Lover Cousins); and *La prodigiosa* (The Prodigious Story). In addition, four short novels were printed in *For Everybody* (1632), the titles of which are: *Introducción a la semana* (Introduction to the Week), containing the story of Don Francisco and Don Pedro, "exemplary and pleasurable"; *Al cabo de los años mil* (At the End of One Thousand Years); *El palacio encantado* (The Enchanted Palace); and *El piadoso bandolero* (The Compassionate Bandit).[1]

The influence of Cervantes' exemplary novels is immediately apparent in the title of Montalván's collection of 1624, and a reading of this collection and of the later-published novels (1632) shows that within the stories the influence of Cervantes and of other novelists of the day is considerable. The young Juan apparently did not wish to

[82]

rest his glory and fame on his activities as a poet and dramatist. He could see that great reputations had been made in the past by those who attempted prose; in fact, his master Lope de Vega, most successful in the poetic theater, continued to hope, throughout his life, for outstanding achievements as a novelist. It was a period when novels of all kinds, the Byzantine, the courtly, the chivalresque, the pastoral, the picaresque, etc., were continuing a waning popularity, and when inspiration was coming to budding novelists from both native and foreign writers, especially Italian, and Montalván, over the years, seems to have absorbed a great deal of the novelistic art.

Amezúa, in his introduction to his 1949 edition, points out that Montalván possessed one requisite to write good novels: imagination or creative fantasy; but that he lacked a second important one: a keen observation and study of the realities of life. "What reality," asks Amezúa (his edition, p. xii), "was it possible for that youth to perceive and capture, that youth who was not yet twenty-two years of age and who was just then opening his innocent eyes to the spectacle of the World?" "Where and how could he safeguard that equilibrium between reality and fantasy, wherein resides the perfection of the novel?" For as Fernando Gutiérrez wrote of Montalván in his edition of 1957 (p. 9), "Everything in his life was precocious and immature. He lived and died forcing time." Although there are odd glimmers of excellence on occasions in Montalván's novels, he did not have the time, nor the patience, apparently, for the observation and reflection so necessary for enduring success in novelistic writing. This lack of maturity Montalván could see for himself, for he wrote to the Reader in his prologue to *The Happenings and Prodigies of Love* (Amezúa edition, p. 13): "What I beg you to do, if you find any defects of style or substance, is to look upon them compassionately, excusing my youth." There was a potential there, it seems, for something worthwhile (Amezúa, p. xiii): "a lively and burning imagination; an affection for his characters; a success in the portrayal of these characters; good taste and a good sense of the novel, avoiding long and excessive moralizing, which he waives in favor of short moral declarations; and above all a constant dynamism, a great deal of action, which engendering moving and attractive episodes and events, with interest and pleasantness will carry out the novel's mission of giving solace and diversion to the reader." But time, and more probably talent, was not sufficient, and Montalván did not rise above mediocrity through all the novels he produced.

III La mayor confusión *(The Greatest Confusion)*

The Greatest Confusion, the fourth novel in the volume of 1624, has drawn the most attention from the modern critics. Caroline B. Bourland discussed its source in 1927,[2] and Victor Dixon, more recently, built upon the Bourland findings to throw more light on the problem of the sources and to discuss in depth Montalván's resolution of the plot.[3] Amezúa had given the story a good deal of thought, and he called it "one of the most repugnant and monstrous novels in the Castilian language."[4] And in his introduction to the 1949 edition (p. xviii), Amezúa's words were similar: "one of the most monstrous and repulsive works of Spanish literature."

The plot is the following: Casandra, living in Madrid, was to marry her cousin Gerardo; but when he was killed by a rival, Bernardo, she soon married the latter. Later, she gave birth to a son, Félix. When Bernardo died, Casandra rejected all suitors, having conceived an incestuous passion for her own son. One night she took the place of a maid with whom Félix was having an affair, and thus succeeded in satisfying her desire. From this incestuous union, Casandra gave birth to a daughter, Diana, whom she raised in her household as adopted. Félix, meanwhile, after spending many years in Flanders, returned home to fall in love with the fourteen-year-old Diana, his daughter and his sister. Casandra put her in a convent, but since she reciprocated Félix' affection, she refused to become a nun. Employing the ruse that he was embarking for the New World, Félix threw Casandra off guard, and in her absence from home removed Diana from the convent and married her. Casandra did not dare reveal the secret of Diana's parentage, but before dying two years later, she wrote a letter to Félix informing him of the horrible situation.

On learning this fact and being now in "the greatest confusion" and in the depths of despair, Félix sought in his mind what he should do. Leaving Diana, he sought the advice of a Jesuit who, consulting colleagues of his Order and learned professors of Salamanca and Alcalá de Henares, decided that Félix and Diana should continue to live together as man and wife, since neither was guilty of the crime. Félix returned home, and he and Diana lived happily ever after, loving each other very dearly for many reasons, "not the least being that they were so closely united in blood, for their children were brothers and sisters and cousins: brothers and sisters because they were children of Diana and Félix, and cousins because they were the children of brother and sister" (see Dixon, "*La mayor confusión*," p. 21).

Caroline Bourland had believed the source of this short novel to be Francesco Sansovino or Giovanni Brevio, sixteenth-century Italian writers of *novelle*, but Dixon offers other possibilities: Marguerite de Navarre, Matteo Bandello, some other novel, native or foreign, or some real happening. Montalván himself argues, in his dedication of the novel to Lope de Vega (Amezúa edition, p. 129), that the source was neither Italian nor any other foreign one, but a real case ("*La mayor confusión*, whose case has a great deal of reality in it . . ."); but Montalván was known in such statements to be singularly inaccurate (cf. his "Life" of Lope de Vega). In any event, the story did not cease with Montalván, but various versions of it have run through literature, not necessarily having been inspired by the Montalván account.

The ending of *The Greatest Confusion* (as well as Casandra's preceding acts) makes the modern reader agree with Victor Dixon that in the pen of a future Doctor of Theology and Apostolic Notary of the Holy Office the dénouement is to say the least "shocking" (Dixon, p. 21). For the first edition (1624), the enthusiastic "approval" by Lope de Vega found nothing contrary to the Faith or to Good Morals, but by 1626, 1629, 1630, violent objection to the story had arisen on the part of ecclesiastical censorship,[5] and several changed endings are found, one (Seville, 1633, for example) having Félix die within twenty days of reading his mother's letter and having Diana retire to a convent. Another, an ambiguous ending of Tortosa, 1635, says that Félix followed for the rest of his life the advice of learned men, but does not record what that advice was!

It is clear that Amezúa in his writings on the subject did not have before him the ending of the first edition of *The Greatest Confusion* (supplied to us by Victor Dixon in his article in *Hispanófila*), because he feels that when the *Index librorum prohibitorum* of 1640 expurgated the last pages of the story, leaving the repulsive earlier part, it was removing "precisely the only moral and exemplary ones, since in them the sorrow of the protagonist, caused by the knowledge of his involuntary sin, is so great that, his heart overwhelmed by a moral sadness, he dies" (Amezúa edition, p. xxi). Amezúa was commenting on the later version which he gives us in his edition — the death of Félix; and he can be pardoned for that error of not having the first edition's reading, since not even the Biblioteca Nacional, Madrid, possesses a copy of the first edition of 1624. (The British Museum, London, has one, however.)

IV   La hermosa Aurora *(Beautiful Aurora)*

The other novels of *The Happenings and Prodigies of Love* are a mixed bag. The first of the collection of eight, *Beautiful Aurora*, is the weak production of one who was apparently a beginner in the genre, showing vague reminiscences of Cervantes' *Persiles y Sigismunda*, one of the novels which Montalván had no doubt been reading recently and perhaps studying as a model. In *Beautiful Aurora* are to be found the usual chivalresque adventures and love affairs of gentlemen and ladies of high estate, filled with inverosimilitude and a lack of reality.[6] The ups and downs[7] of the courtship of handsome Prince Ricardo of Poland for the beautiful Aurora of Sicily keep the reader in some suspense for some time, but fortunately at the end of the novel they reach the state of wedded bliss and depart by ship for the groom's distant land:

And after some days [following their wedding], they embarked for Poland, accompanied by all the grandeur of the Court. King Eduardo received them with the pleasure which can be imagined to exist in a father who, having believed his son lost or dead, found him greatly bettered in every way. And seeing himself heavily laden by years and realizing that his ills did not allow him to be the bearer of such burdens, he transferred the crown to his son's head. Also, so that the pleasure of such a great love should be even more fulfilled, Heaven willed within the first year to give him a handsome grandson. Ricardo and Aurora [now king and queen] continued to live in such harmony and love, that it always seemed that they had just been married (Amezúa edition, p. 54).

This concluding paragraph of *Beautiful Aurora* (in my translation) is illustrative of the type of thing these "amazing" novels are, in a prose which is better or worse at times, with an intermingling of an occasional poem or an epistle in prose.[8]

V   La fuerza del desengaño *(The Force of Disillusionment)*

The Force of Disillusionment adds the element of the fantastic and mysterious, and the ending is a less happy one. The student Teodoro, attending the University of Alcalá de Henares, where Montalván himself studied, loses out to the evil Valerio, who,

Prose Writings

through a trick, wins the hand of the unwilling Narcisa, who loves Teodoro. The character Death is present in the story, witchcraft is invoked and inverosimilitude is constantly a characteristic. In the end, poor Teodoro decides to enter a monastery, to become one of the most perfect Franciscans of the whole Community; and another young woman, Lucrecia, who cannot have Teodoro, becomes a nun. From melodrama, this novelistic undertaking reaches compensation, writes Amezúa in his edition, p. xiv, through its "pious dénouement." Indeed it is greatly different from the ending of the first printing of *The Greatest Confusion*.[9]

VI El envidioso castigado *(The Envious Man Punished)*

The third novel in the collection, *The Envious Man Punished*, shows a considerable improvement over the preceding novels, through its character study and realistic description of settings. Scenes of Seville are well presented, and the "Envious Man" is a person of some relief. The title of the novel, writes Montalván in his dedication, is self-explanatory: where there is envy, there must also be virtue; because, though enemies, they are fellow travelers. "The person envied and hated in this novel," continues the moralizing author, "is Carlos, a virtuous youth with all the characteristics required by his station in life. Finally his Fortune grows tired of pursuing him, and rewards him according to his merits; for virtue, although concealed, is like the sun, which however much covered by eclipse always maintains the same rays" (Amezúa edition, p. 92).

The elder brother Alfredo, of less virtue than Carlos, envies his good qualities. Here, Montalván cannot restrain himself from exclaiming: "Oh rigorous infirmity, general vice that thou art, thou art ever present . . . [and] livest among those who are engendered by one very blood." The story is once again a love triangle: Carlos is enamored of the beautiful Estela, and Alfredo tries to take her from him. Indeed Alfredo is so envious that when he does not get his way in the end (after causing Carlos and Estela much suffering) he pines away and dies from profound melancholy. Carlos properly and dutifully mourns his brother, inherits the family estates, and "lives for many years in the company of his beloved Estela, enjoying the fine reputation which his brother lost through so much wrongdoing, for it is certain that only his envy killed him; since no other end is merited by him who is so grieved by good befalling others as if it were his own misfortune" (Amezúa edition, p. 128).

VII La villana de Pinto *(The Peasant Girl of Pinto)*

Skipping the notorious *Greatest Confusion*, already discussed, the fifth novel, *The Peasant Girl of Pinto*, is characterized by Amezúa (his edition, p. xv) as a kind of courtly novel, very nationally Spanish in its atmosphere, and not at all foreign. It was written, according to Montalván's dedication, in Alcalá de Henares. Its opening lines, introducing the reader to the virtuous shepherd Albanio, in love with an equally virtuous shepherdess, remind one of Montemayor's *Diana* or any other novel of the pastoral *genre*. The setting is, as usual, a beautiful valley, through which a rippling brook winds amid its golden sands and flower-bedecked borders.[10] Physical circumstances are comfortable, but the psychological sufferings, as is usual in these novels, are many.

Albanio rescues a disconsolate lady of high lineage, who has just given birth to a baby girl in secret. The lady had been forced through unhappy circumstances to absent herself from her lover, who wanted to marry her, and she is now alone and unprotected. As the mother departs, the baby girl, Silvia, is left with the shepherds. She grows into a beauty, and later on a gentleman from Madrid, Don Diego de Osorio, falls in love with her, changes his name to Cardenio (echoes of Cervantes!) and pours forth beautiful poetry of love, appealing to Nature as he declares his mental sufferings (echoes of Garcilaso de la Vega!). After the usual trials and tribulations (in appearance it is a case of a courtier enamored of a peasant girl), anagnorisis, or the recognition of true lineage, is employed: Don Diego (Cardenio) can marry his now noble Silvia, and there is spread about this marvellous story of true love, amid the celebration of Diego's good Fortune and Silvia's divine beauty. She is now a leading lady of the Court, "although for some years a humble peasant girl of Pinto" (Amezúa edition, p. 208).

Cervantes' exemplary novel *La Gitanilla* (The Little Gypsy Girl) is just one preceding example of the idea that blood will tell. The dramatic convention of recognition in the dénouement had been used many times in novel or in play,[11] and Montalván's case has in its favor a certain simple attractiveness, amid its good prose and occasional verse, combined with a psychological treatment of some insight. "In short," declares Amezúa, pp. xiv-xv, "[there are to be found] the qualities which the reader of the day asked for in the novel in general and which rendered popular the novels of Juan Pérez de Montalbán."

VIII La desgraciada amistad *(The Unfortunate Friendship)*

The next novel, *The Unfortunate Friendship*, which contains among other Cervantine reflections an Algerian episode, brings us very close to Cervantes' *Novela del cautivo* (The Captive), interpolated in *Don Quijote*. The ending, in Montalván's hands, is a tragic one, for the heroine, Rosaura, after very many difficulties, dies, following the unfortunate double murder, through error in the dark of night, of her beloved Don Felisardo and his very close friend Don Fadrique. Before this unhappy outcome, there is a great deal of the usual mental suffering; Rosaura, for example, becomes the captive on a ship near Mallorca of a corsair, who presents her to the North African Lord Celín Hamete. There is also interspersed throughout the whole story much of the lyricism usual in these novels; for instance, Felisardo sings a love ballad to the accompaniment of a harp. The descriptions of nature are, as is customary, idealized, in the tradition of the pastoral novel.

In this case once again, Amezúa (his edition, pp. xv-xvi) complains very rightly of the licentious character of Montalván's novelistic writing in general. "In this aspect," he writes, p. xvi, "the novels of Montalbán are the most daring of his time, without his feeling any embarrassment in delving deeply into these salacious happenings and events with a great deal of freedom." On the other hand, it is true that the novelist takes care to have an adulterous woman punished through death, after having made her confession to a priest, in the manner of Calderón's *A secreto agravio, secreta venganza* (For a Secret Insult, a Secret Vengeance). In this way a moralizing tone is introduced, as would be expected from our budding theologian.

IX Los primos amantes *(The Lover Cousins)*

The Lover Cousins is based on a real happening, according to the author in his dedication (Amezúa edition, p. 256), and "therefore deserving of being read with more compassion." Laura, the beautiful heroine, is born in Ávila of noble and well-to-do parents, who love her very much as their only child. As she grows up she falls madly in love with her cousin, the impecunious Lisardo, who has been raised with her and who reciprocates her affection. Unfortunately, Laura's father is inclined to another suitor for his daughter — Otavio, the son of a powerful and rich neighbor. When the wedding is arranged, Lisardo, in despair, sets out for Seville to embark for the New World. Laura escapes into hiding, and later, with a trusted friend Alesandro, sets out to look for Lisardo. Also, the father and the jilted Otavio take to the road in search of the runaway pair. At times, in the action of the novel, the various parties are close together, by coincidence; and at times cruel fate snatches them far apart. In the end, all turns out well, however, and Laura and Lisardo are united in marriage through the good graces of Lisardo's father, who arrives unexpectedly from the Americas. Even Otavio is consoled in this happy ending, seeing that his failure to win Laura's hand is not due to any lack of worthiness on his part, "but due to the will of others" (Amezúa edition, p. 297). Montalván ends his novel with one of his usual moralizing phrases: the cousins in love considered it good fortune to have passed through so much travail, "because when what is attempted is accomplished, every adverse circumstance encountered brings about an increase in pleasure."

Montalván himself in his dedication (Amezúa edition, p. 257) mentions the lyric poems which appear from time to time; and these and the prose of the novel have some merit. But once again it is a novel of little substance or depth, a tale of fantastic adventure, full of inverosimilitude and unreality. It is the kind of a story which might appear in serial form in some cheap and popular magazine of today or on radio or television; in short, a soap opera. Here we have the "romantic" Montalván, and the novel is not one to be long remembered nor one to add to the author's posthumous fame.

X La prodigiosa *(The Prodigious Story)*

The last novel of the volume of 1624 is *The Prodigious Story*, one of the usual novels of fantastic adventure. Amezúa's résumé (his edition, p. xvii) describes what it is like: "Wandering princesses of doubtful character; enamored knights; clandestine births; illegitimate children; virgin forests; stormy seas; providential shipwrecks; and other awesome happenings, with all of it enveloped in a vertigo of feverish action, forming the most sombre and semibarbaric composition that can be imagined."

The story begins with the lamentations of an enamored "savage" (in dress) as he beholds the portrait of his absent Policena, for he has been away from his native Albania for twelve years on her account. This Gesimundo uses words, phrases and references to past worthies which give the lie to his rustic appearance. At that moment a beautiful shepherdess, Ismenia, singing a ballad, interrupts his mournful meditation. Struck by her resemblance to the long-absent

Policena, there enters into him a sudden concern which astonishes him. Poor Ismenia relates that she is fleeing from the man whom she is to marry at her parents' command. Although she was apparently born in the wilds and is of humble stock, she has thoughts and feelings so noble that it seems to her that she is not inferior to the "King of Armenia or the heir to the throne of Albania" (p. 308).

Following a convention in these novels, Gesimundo in turn relates his story: he is the natural son of the King of Albania and of a duchess of the court. Indeed the king had two sons on the very same day, Gesimundo and the legitimate Flaminio. As they grew up Gesimundo revealed all the good qualities and Flaminio all the bad ones, and the two young men courted the same noble young woman, Policena, who was enamored of Gesimundo. Secretly Policena gave birth to Gesimundo's daughter who, through mischance, as a newborn baby fell into the hands of Flaminio. Flaminio had the baby murdered and sent to Gesimundo on a platter. At that juncture Gesimundo tried to murder Flaminio, but being unsuccessful had to flee the kingdom.

Ismenia, in the wilds, falls in love with a wandering Prince Tancredo, of Armenia, out hunting. To add to the rare happenings of the story, a ship appears on the sea shore, and in it are a dead knight and Policena — after so many years! Policena explains that she had been imprisoned in a tower after Gesimundo's escape. When plotting to get out, she was found out and sent away on a ship with her murdered helper, "so that the anxiety of being with a dead body and the bad odor of decaying flesh would bring her to a miserable end" (Amezúa edition, p. 330).[12]

Since Prince Tancredo, now reciprocating Ismenia's affection for him, refuses to marry his betrothed, a princess of Albania, Gesimundo's father and half-brother Flaminio set about making war on Armenia. Flaminio, to add to the complications, is plotting to kill his father and take the crown of Albania right away. Gesimundo saves the old king, and Flaminio goes to prison. The king reveals, to make all end well, that years ago, to give his illegitimate son the right to the throne, he had switched babies. The legal heir to the throne of Albania is really Gesimundo, and he will now marry Policena, and they will become king and queen of their realm. But the lineage of poor Ismenia has still to be cleared up. She is really the supposedly murdered daughter of Gesimundo and Policena, and through marrying Tancredo will become queen of Armenia. She had been saved through a substitution as a baby and taken to Armenia to be raised among peasants. Now what about Flaminio finally? The reader can almost rejoice that it was decreed that this evil prince should die "without illness" (Amezúa edition, p. 345). "So ended" notes Montalván, to conclude his volume of "fantastic" novels, "the prodigious story of Gesimundo and Policena."

As was mentioned for the play *What's Done Can't Be Undone, and the Mountain Prince* (First Volume of plays) and the novel *Beautiful Aurora* (of this collection), we have here in the case of *The Prodigious Story* examples of materials used almost indiscriminantly by Montalván for a play or for a novel, according to the *genre* in which he was working at the time. This closeness of drama to novel, in subject matter, is particularly remarkable in Montalván, and it just seems that the Gesimundo-Policena adventure turned out to be a novel, rather than a play, because the author's mind was on novels at the time.

As for the novel, *The Prodigious Story*, Amezúa (his edition, p. xvii) feels that "So many absurdities and inverosimilitudes seem to hint already at that madness into which, in the final period of his life, Montalván unhappily fell." Yet we must remember that we are still some dozen years before Montalván's end, and these amazing events (found in plays also) seem to be the continuing production of Montalván's vivid and feverish imagination which thought up these "rare" literary products throughout his whole life. This is frequently apparent also in the novels which followed *The Happenings and Prodigies of Love:* the four, mentioned before, which appeared in the compilation of 1632, *For Everybody*.

XI *The Novels of* For Everybody (1632)

In this volume, which is a miscellany of a *Decameron* nature (see next chapter), there are three short novels with distinct titles of their own and one, the first of all, the "Introduction to the Week," which, in the words of its author, is "an exemplary and pleasurable story." The novels with titles of their own form part of the concluding entertainment for the Second, Fourth and Sixth Days. "The four *novelas*," writes Dixon ("*Para todos*," p. 42), "... were very possibly not written for inclusion in *Para todos.*" They were probably materials which Montalván had composed some time previously, and gathered together for publication at this time. "Even the one which constitutes the frame, *Introducción a la semana*, may only have been adapted for that purpose. Any *novela cortesana* which ended with a wedding — as almost all do — would have served our author's turn." "The three novels so far mentioned [*Introduction to the Week, At the End of One Thousand Years*, and *The Compassionate Bandit*] are sufficiently indistinguishable in style and content from those in *Sucesos y prodigios de amor* to have been written well before *Para todos* appeared. Only the one related on the Fourth Day, *El palacio encantado* [The Enchanted Palace], which recalls his late, spectacular plays on chivalresque themes, seems less likely to have been an early work" (Dixon, p. 43).

XII Introducción a la semana *(Introduction to the Week)*

Introduction to the Week "has a plot, an action of its own, independent of its function of cradling" the rest of *For Everybody*.[13] As Dixon continues, "It is still not an integral part of the work; it offers only a reason for the diversions of which that work is supposed to consist" (Dixon, p. 39). This novel's plot begins with the arrival of the Zaragozan Don Francisco in Madrid, after dark. In front of the home of his beloved (Doña Ana) he encounters a mysterious stranger serenading a lady; but his initial jealousy is assuaged when the two men are united in battle to drive off a group of robbers who fall upon Francisco. After the scuffle which ensues, successful for Don Francisco and his companion in need, Don Francisco realizes that his "rival" at his lady's window is none other than his best friend, Don Pedro, who is revealed to be the suitor of Ana's cousin, Doña María. Then a good many pages of the short novel are devoted to Don Pedro's story of his courtship, including the rivalry of an evil intriguer, Don Rodrigo. A satisfactory explanation is provided for María's being in Ana's home. A happy ending to the complications of love then comes about, with a double wedding (Don Francisco: Doña Ana; Don Pedro: Doña María); and Don Pedro invites his many friends to celebrate the occasion with an "academic" week of festivity on his estate on the bank of the River Manzanares. Doña María sets about assigning rôles to the participants, and among these is one Montano, who must represent Montalván himself. As Willard F. King points out *(Prosa novelística*, p. 135), a "courtly novel" is thus used to lead into the framework of *For Everybody* with its week's entertainment of plays, novels, philosophical-theological-scientific discussions, sonnets, etc.

XIII Al cabo de los años mil *(At the End of One Thousand Years)*

At the End of One Thousand Years (part of the Second Day's entertainment of *For Everybody*) relates the story of the beautiful, rich and noble Lisarda, a resident of Ciudad Real. Lisarda, at sixteen, is in love with the talented Ricardo — Ricardo's participation in a fiesta is described in realistic detail — and the future seems rosy for them. However, through a misunderstanding, Lisarda finds Ricardo in a compromising situation with another woman, and in her jealousy agrees to marry another man, Don Flugencio. Ricardo, in despair, goes to Barcelona and embarks for Italy. On board is a despondent nobleman from Barcelona, Don Enrique, who tells his own sad story at great length: married happily for ten years, his wife Estefanía granted him two weeks to go to the Capital to seek a reward for services to the Crown. ("Since she did not know Madrid's ways of doing things, she thought that this period of time would be sufficient for his purpose!") The king granted Enrique membership in the Order of Santiago; and on his way home Enrique had to take refuge from a storm in an inn. There he fell in with another traveler, who had expected to spend a pleasurable night with an Estefanía in Barcelona. Enrique believed that this Don Federico was having an affair with his wife; and while riding with him next day, ran his sword into him. When others arrived to help Federico, Enrique rode off and decided to embark for Italy, like Ricardo.

Enrique and Ricardo, on reaching Italy, travel around together for two years. Back in Spain once again, they go to Montserrat; and, through coincidence, run into Federico, Estefanía and her sister Angela. The "Estefanía" of Federico's experience was really Angela, whom he married after he recovered from Enrique's attack. Estafanía was innocent all the time, and Enrique joyfully rejoins her. By further coincidence, Estafanía knows Lisarda well, and she is now living in Barcelona. Lisarda had married Don Flugencio, but on their wedding night, before the marriage was consummated, he fell suddenly ill and died. She is now a widow, and still a virgin, richer than ever and still as beautiful. So Ricardo and Lisarda are married, fulfilling the old proverb that "at the end of one thousand years, the waters return to where they used to run."

"The suspense of the novel, the purity of its language, the variety of its verse" writes Montalván in *For Everybody*, "brought forth congratulations [from those hearing it]." Perhaps the audience of *For Everybody* and the popular readers of the day were fond of this type of escape from the reality of everyday life. Montalván seems to be following and providing what was wanted in prose fiction, to achieve success and popularity, but such a novel as *At the End of One Thousand Years* does not make him remembered among the superior novelists of Spain's Golden Age.

XIV El palacio encantado *(The Enchanted Palace)*

The Enchanted Palace, again told or read by one of the participants in the entertainment of its day (the Fourth) of *For Everybody*, brings us, according to Montalván, an "exemplary, pleasing and entertaining novel." The opening pages find Prince Cloridano on a Grecian island, listening to the complaints of a damsel in distress, Ismenia, tied hand and foot and blindfolded. This predicament diverts the purposes of Cloridano, who was on his way to court the beautiful Princess Fénix of Tracia, with whom he is in love through a portrait. Cloridano saves this dolorous maiden, and rides hurriedly away with her to a shepherd's hut "in a green and pleasant meadow." There a shepherd is lamenting *his* unhappy love affair!

Ismenia, it turns out, is the cousin of Princess Fénix, and she was on the point of being put to death for having loved the valiant Aristeo. The eldest child of King Eduardo of Dalmatia, she has the right of succession to the throne, but her younger brother, Arnaldo, is favored by the king, who is trying to abrogate the law of succession. The father has been trying to get rid of her in various ways, including an attempt to marry her off to a foreign prince; but she is madly in love with her cousin, Aristeo, and he with her. Cloridano now takes Ismenia with him to Tracia, and they find cousin Fénix in her Enchanted Palace. Fénix has by this time decided to accept one of her many suitors, and after a year of trial and testing, Cloridano, as part of his courtship, is required to give a discourse on "The Perfect Prince." This he does in great detail, describing the fine qualities found in such a man.[14]

Naturally Princess Fénix decides on Prince Cloridano, and they are married amid much rejoicing, feasting and festivity. Poor Ismenia's problem is solved rapidly, almost as an anticlimax. In the jousting at the wedding celebration, Ismenia's other suitor, Meleandro, is killed, and her brother and her father repent of their evil intentions. Ismenia will ascend the throne which is rightly hers, and her prince consort will be Aristeo.

Dixon ("*Para todos*," p. 43), as noted previously, has mentioned that *The Enchanted Palace* recalls Montalván's "late, spectacular plays on chivalresque themes"; and we are reminded of *Don Florisel of Nicaea* and *The Children of Fortune*, of Volume Two, and *Palmerín of the Olive Tree*, of *Parte XLIII, Comedias de diferentes autores*. *The Enchanted Palace* seems to include something of all the novelistic types Montalván had read — books of chivalry, courtly romances, pastoral novels, and what have you.

XV El piadoso bandolero *(The Compassionate Bandit)*

In *The Compassionate Bandit*, the noble, rich and handsome Don Vicente, from Valencia, is in love with the noble, beautiful and virtuous Doña Camila, whom he has been courting chastely for two years. A trouble-maker and slanderer, Don Claudio, casts aspersions on Camila's character, declaring that he has been enjoying her favors. Vicente naturally challenges him to a duel, but Claudio has no intention of endangering his life. Moreover, he is the brother-in-law of the Governor, and the Viceroy, at the Governor's request, insists that Vicente make peace with Claudio.

This Vicente does, although swearing in his heart to avenge the insult to his lady. To make matters worse, Camila's relatives, abetted by financial aid from the Viceroy, would marry Claudio to the damsel, to put an end to gossip. This leads to an exchange of letters between the two lovers, and an arrangement for a midnight rendezvous at her window. But Claudio is there before Vicente, and in an ensuing scuffle, Vicente kills Claudio. Vicente and Camila run away together that night, but as chance would have it they meet the Governor and his men, and amid sword play, Camila is captured and Vicente takes refuge in a monastery.

Later, Vicente tries to see Camila again, but is captured and seems to be in an impossible situation. However, he escapes to the wilds where, before long, he is elected the leader of a group of bandits. Vicente sets down strict rules for the gang: not to harm women, nor the poor, nor murder for gain; to keep careful account of all stolen; to treat peasants well. Plotting against his "friends," he has them come twelve by twelve to a hermitage (the hermit interrupts the main action to tell *his* story), and they are captured group by group. Vicente is so compassionate that he has his former companions spared the death penalty and only condemned to life-long service in His Majesty's galleys. Pardoned by the Viceroy for his good job in cleaning up the countryside of criminals, Vicente and Camila are married, to live happily ever after. And so in the Sixth Day's entertainment of *For Everybody* there comes to an end the story of the compassionate bandit, "who was a bandit in dress only and who in his actions reflected in all ways his noble blood."

At the beginning of this short novel there is a very good and realistic description of the city of Valencia; just as there are several other realistic descriptions of places and events from time to time in the stories of *For Everybody* or *The Happenings and Prodigies of Love*. In *The Compassionate Bandit* there is promise of more character study and of a story somewhat better and more logical than in the other novels generally speaking. Unfortunately Montalván's burning imagination gets the better of him, and the good qualities in embryo fall by the wayside, resulting in many of the usual fantastic and unlikely happenings. It is no wonder that after the publication of 1632 Quevedo's scorn should fall upon Montalván's novels like a sharp knife: "Montalván's novels," Quevedo proclaimed in *Teetotum*, "are neither fables, nor plays, nor stories, nor novels at all . . . being so bad that they have neither head nor tail" and are "both long-winded and boring" *(Obras completas*, ed. Buendía, I: 452). Yet, as Amezúa points out (p. xxiv), *The Happenings and Prodigies of Love* ran through fifteen editions in the seventeenth century, with translations into English, Dutch, French and Italian;[15] and *For Everybody*, with all its contents, was extremely successful too. "With Cervantes, Céspedes, Castillo Solórzano and doña María de Zayas," writes Amezúa, pp. xxvi-xxvii, "although he may be esthetically inferior to all of them, Montalbán shares the novelistic popularity of his century. We have already noted the causes of this success, definite causes without doubt, although they may not be of the best kind. But the common people continued for many years to be solaced by them, and their vogue was propagated into the eighteenth century, to be extinguished entirely in the nineteenth century, in which their oblivion was so complete that they are not reprinted once, and only two of his novels achieve partial reception in the *Biblioteca de Autores Españoles*" (i.e., *The Peasant Girl of Pinto* and *The Lover Cousins)*.

There were novels of Montalván's day which did have enduring characteristics: a penetrating vision of Spanish society, subtle and deep theses and ideologies, a good depiction of character, a psychological insight, and a logical and well-developed plot, but those apparently were novels which did not receive the popular acclaim of contemporary readers and did not go beyond the first printing. It is difficult to know whether Montalván consciously or unconsciously sought to follow the path to "popularity," as he did, or whether his only mediocre results arise from his inability to grasp the necessities of good prose. Like those of his mentor Lope de Vega, his literary abilities no doubt lay in the dramatic and the poetic. Novelistic prose was a *genre* which he might better have avoided. He seems to stand, unfortunately, at that stage of the Spanish Golden Age novel which is described by Peter Dunn for Castillo Solórzano: "We noticed in our analysis of the plots of these novels that there is a distinct movement towards a type of literature which is amoral and which cultivates adventure and the primary feelings — love, curiosity, the desire for action — for their own sakes. These were the popular fiction, the best-sellers of seventeenth-century Spain with all that that implies — wish-fulfilment, action, 'romance,' 'glamour' and the clumsy handling of delicate matters (religion, honour, love) which we call popularization. The novels of Castillo were nothing more nor less than commercial . . ." (p. 128).

XVI Vida y purgatorio de San Patricio
(Life and Purgatory of St. Patrick)

In 1627 Montalván announced in a prefatory note to Alonso de Castillo Solórzano's *Tiempo de regocijo y carnestolendas de Madrid* (Time of Rejoicing and Carnival in Madrid) that he was about to publish a treatise on St. Patrick of Ireland.[16] In that very same year the intention was fulfilled with the completion and publication of *The Life and Purgatory of St. Patrick*, which Montalván calls in words to the reader a *"novela a lo divino*, to cause thought and to provide a warning lesson."[17]

One might ask why Montalván would be interested in things Irish; but it is to be remembered that facts and legends about the famous St. Patrick of Ireland were widespread in Europe. Also, Montalván was keenly interested in the lives of the saints, and the Spaniards in general looked upon Ireland as a bastion of Catholicism in the faraway North. In 1592 Philip II founded an Irish college in Salamanca, and surely part of the aspirations of the Invincible Armada (1588) had been to carry support and solace to the Catholic brethern in that distant land, which was valiantly battling the heretics from England who were trying to oppress it and lead it astray from the True Faith. Furthermore, Montalván was in an ideal position to put his hands on source materials, for his father's greatly in vogue bookstore and publishing business was *au courant* of all the contemporary possibilities.

XVII Sources of the Purgatory of St. Patrick

Antonio G. Solalinde has given us his opinion of source materials which were available to Montalván.[18] The main source for the *Purgatory* seems to be the account of the Catalan Ramon de Perellós (who is supposed to have visited St. Patrick's cave in Ireland in 1397), which was translated into Latin by the Irishman, Philip O'Sullevan, and published in Lisbon in 1621.[19] "With the *Viatge* of

Perellós," writes Solalinde (pp. 253-54), "the Peninsular literature now possesses a novelistic outline easy to develop: all the elements are laid down; they exist in a book printed in Latin and they soon will be picked up by some imaginative writer. This man is Juan Pérez de Montalván, the well-known author of plays and the biographer of Lope de Vega. His *Vida y purgatorio de San Patricio* achieves numerous editions in Spain and is translated into several languages."

Montalván's vivid imagination soon went to work on the Latin version before him — he always believed in the superiority of poetic to historical truth — and, supplementing it with other readings,[20] he brought forth a brief prose account: the life of the saint (including the period of slavery and the miracles), the "founding" of St. Patrick's "Purgatory" on an Irish island, and its practical application as illustrated by the case of Ludovico Enio, who made a successful trip through this "purgatory" and entertained the vision of sinners' torments and the redeemed's reward.

XVIII *The Contents of the* Purgatory

Montalván's *Life and Purgatory of St. Patrick* is a small volume of prose of about 25,000 words, divided into nine chapters. Chapter One tells the story of "the admirable life of the glorious St. Patrick, archbishop and primate of Hibernia [Ireland]." His father was Irish and his mother, French. A very devout couple, in later years they separated and became a priest and nun respectively. Miracles were associated with their son, Patrick, even from babyhood: a blind man was cured of his blindness, floods abated, etc. At sixteen, Patrick was captured by pirates and, like the Old Testament Joseph, was sold into slavery to work as a shepherd on a very distant Irish island. Fortunately, his guardian angel, Victor, visited him frequently and, after a while, showed him gold in a cave, with which Patrick was able to ransom himself. Patrick's stay among the barbarians was not wholly without fruit: he had been able, in secret, to convert to Christianity and baptize his master's daughters.

On his way home to the more civilized part of Ireland, Patrick made a detour via France (after all, his mother was French), where he studied for eighteen years with Bishop St. Germain and was ordained to the priesthood. He also had the opportunity to visit his mother's brother, St. Martin, the archbishop of Tours. Thinking that he should stay a while in Rome before beginning his labors in Ireland, he made a further detour; and in the Holy City Pope

Celestino I made him a bishop and commissioned him to undertake the propagation of the Faith in Ireland (his guardian angel Victor had impressed the same point upon him). On the trip to Rome he had had a miraculous experience: coming upon a group of penetential hermits living in caves, Patrick was received with great joy. The explanation was that some time previously a pilgrim (who turned out to be Jesus Christ himself) had left his staff with the hermits to be presented to "Patrick of Ireland" on his arrival among them!

During the return journey, from Rome to Ireland, Bishop Patrick was attacked by evil men, and was saved from certain death by the Lord's sending fire and earthquake. This supernatural phenomenon caused many to rush for baptism and confounded those who did not. At home, the king and queen of Ireland were soon converted; and through Patrick's ministry on many Irish islands, amid many miracles such as the raising of the dead and the healing of the sick, Christianity became firmly established and widespread in the Emerald Isle. In all, St. Patrick, in Montalván's version, lived one hundred thirteen years: sixteen years at home as a youth, six years in slavery, eighteen years with Bishop St. Germain in France, fifteen years in Rome, thirty-five years preaching in Ireland and twenty-three final years in retirement and contemplation in a monastery.

In the second chapter of the *Life and Purgatory*, Montalván, the theologian, provides the reader with "some qualities of the soul so as to provide a better understanding of St. Patrick's Purgatory." The soul, writes Montalván, has three attributes: Memory, Understanding and Will (connected with the Trinity: the Father, the Son and the Holy Ghost). The soul, incorporeal, at man's death goes to one of four places: Heaven (those dying without any venial sin), Purgatory (with venial sin, to be purified), Limbo (the unbaptized, who will not suffer but will be forever deprived of the Divine Vision) and Hell (those dying in mortal sin go to eternal punishment). The consequences of going to Hell are recorded at great length: eternal fire, great cold, great noise, smoke, the smell of sulphur, the vision of fearful devils, hunger, thirst, tight quarters and the general sorrow at seeing oneself naked and treated like a slave. There is also some discussion, from the young Montalván, in a theological-philosophical way, of the soul's connection or lack of connection with the body.

Chapter Three introduces the reader to St. Patrick's "Purgatory," situated in a cave on an Irish island, into which one can enter in life, in the proper state of grace, and return to life on earth. In spite of his overwhelming success in his missionary work, at one time at least Patrick became very annoyed at the stubbornness of many whom he encountered and he asked God to enlighten the incredulity of the "barbarians" by a special miracle — to put the fear of the Lord into them, so that their souls should not be lost. In response to this plea, Christ himself appeared to Patrick and led him to a cave, and explained to him how the "Purgatory" in a cave was to be used for the propagation of the True Faith. Christ's words were these: "Anyone who, having made a true and contrite confession, and being firm in the Faith, entered therein, would be absolved of all the penalty which he merited for his sins, and not only would he see the suffering and the punishment meted out to sinners, but the reward and the glory experienced by the good; for a period of one day. However, the warning was to be heeded that if anyone entered only through vain curiosity without being in a state of grace through confession, or when inside believing the deceits and blasphemies of the devils found there, failed to trust in God's infinite mercy, he would be condemned to never come out again." In other words, this miracle would provide incontrovertible proof of the existence of an afterlife of reward or punishment.

Patrick was able to spread this marvellous news around, to the increasing benefit of Christianity in Ireland; and many went into the cave, honestly, and came out at the end of twenty-four hours much enlightened, to relate to others the wonders they had seen and experienced. Needless to say, they led extremely virtuous lives thereafter, so that future time in Purgatory would be lessened. Some, on the other hand, went into the cave dishonestly, and disappeared forever. The results of the phenomenon were outstanding, and the True Faith spread rapidly.

In Chapter Four, Montalván "proves" the certainty of the existence of St. Patrick's "Purgatory" in the Irish cave: tradition maintains it; many authors say so (these are cited by Montalván and include Perellós, who entered therein after the death of his King Juan of Aragon whom he loved dearly, "to see for himself whether the king was on his way through Purgatory to salvation"); Catholic piety gives credence to the cave's existence; and, according to Montalván, some lines from an Irish hymn ("in my opinion one of the proofs and authorities of most weight") confirm the truth of the matter:

> Magni Patris sunt miranda Patricii,
> Cui Dominum ostendit locum Purgatorii,
> Qui viventes se expurgent delinquentes filii.

Chapter Five returns to a discussion in some detail of questions relating to the cave: such as, What are the fruitful results of entering this "Purgatory"? Is permission granted to all? What must a man do who proposes to enter? These questions were really answered some time previously in the *Life and Purgatory*, but the answers are repeated at greater length, to drive the points home. The great spiritual preparation for the proposed journey is stressed, and this preparation is carefully supervised by the monks in the adjoining monastery. Not everyone can meet this testing of faith, the steadfastness required, and the fasting, prayer and penance. The fruits of the undertaking are repeated many times in the book: a lesson for the "traveler," and those around him, to ready himself for future punishment, and everlasting reward, after death.

In Chapters Six to Nine, we seem to return to the Montalván of the exemplary novels. Giving the reader a concrete example of one of the many who had had this experience of the "Purgatory" in the cave, Montalván provides once again, as he develops a novel of devotion, a fantastic tale of a fantastic hero. The Perellós account contained the story of a sinner who was redeemed through his experience in the cave; but Montalván must make his example one of the most extreme possible. Montalván's "hero," Ludovico Enio, was born in Ireland but raised in France. When grown up, he squandered his large inheritance in loose living, like the Prodigal Son. Fleeing from Justice for repeated crimes of the worst nature, he took refuge in a convent, where he persuaded his niece, the nun Teodosia, to steal the convent treasures and accompany him to Valencia. There he got her working as a prostitute, and lived on her earnings for ten years. Fortunately she was able, after that period of time, to flee from him, to enter the lowliest of convent service, and to die six years later, a most saintly death. As for Ludovico, for eight more years he continued his gambling, his thievery, his rape and his murders, and finally returned to France where he joined the army, not with the purpose of serving king and country, but to be able more easily to engage in his evil deeds. In due time, for three successive nights a mysterious paper floated in the air above him. When after much effort he was finally able to read the message contained in the note, he read of his own death.

Overwhelmed by sorrow for his sins, he meditated upon this sign of his approaching demise, and felt that he could never be pardoned by God. However, in Rome he heard a famous preacher say "never despair of the God's infinite mercy"; and after a long period of confession and penance he became filled with an overwhelming desire

to participate in the "Purgatory" of St. Patrick, about which he had heard. In brief, Ludovico Enio went home to Ireland, was thoroughly prepared and tested by the monks at the cave's entrance, and passed through the twenty-four-hour "Purgatory" successfully. Becoming a monk on the spot, his Prior asked him to tell of his experience in the cave, "to move the faithful to open their eyes and look upon the terrible punishments which await those who do not fulfill their obligations."

In the seventh chapter of the *Life and Purgatory*, Ludovico Enio begins his story of his "Visit to Hell," with his experiences in "the dangerous cave of St. Patrick": the darkness, the thunder, the battle with Hell and its ministers, the torments, the temptations of the devils, the fire, the ice, etc., but in all he is protected by his Faith and his steadfastness. In Chapter Eight the devils lead him through all the sufferings of Purgatory, and he sees many who are beleaguered by all the horrors of that place. But some, who are in great distress, have the light of hope in their eyes; they know that they are being purged of their sins committed on earth, for a future dwelling place in Heaven. Ludovico sees many whom he knows: his Roman confessor, well along his way in this fearful journey, and his saintly niece, being purged of her vanity. Out of this experience the message Enio has for all mankind is: Purge yourselves all ye on earth, to avoid so much purging later on in Purgatory. The devils continue to attack him at every moment, to show him horrors and to urge him to turn back in despair. But steadfast in the Faith and certain of God's infinite mercy, he has only one more terror to overcome: the crossing of a fearful bridge. This he crosses successfully, to find himself (the devils gone) in a beautiful, peaceful valley, a real Garden of Eden. Here are marvellous edifices, with doors of gold and precious jewels, perfumed air, white-clothed figures, a choir of angels, celestial music, Light and Great Joy. All except him (for Enio is still in the flesh) are beholding the Divine Presence. Among the Blessed is the glorious patriarch St. Patrick, who praises Ludovico Enio for his constancy and Faith and promises him that he too will see God in Heaven, in the afterlife.

Ludovico Enio had to return to life's usual activities via the same road through the cave of "Purgatory," but now the devils had no power over him and his passage was rapid and painless. As Montalván wrote previously, when Enio came forth from the cave he decided to become a monk in the adjacent monastery of St. Patrick, in the certainty that his story and the story of others would be "a brake on our follies" and an exhortation to lead good lives in preparation for that which would come after.

XIX The Success of the Purgatory and Its Followers in Spanish Drama

It has been noted by several critics that the *Life and Purgatory of St. Patrick* ran through many editions in the seventeenth and eighteenth centuries ("at least thirty-one," Solalinde, p. 254, note 1) and enjoyed translations into French, Dutch and Italian (Solalinde, p. 254, note 2). No doubt, in addition to its strong theological message, the popularity of the *Life and Purgatory* arose from some of the same reasons that the novels were popular: Montalván was providing his readers with an entertaining story of adventure.[21] Ludovico Enio's experiences, similar to those of the heroes and heroines in the novels of the 1624 and 1632 collections, were an escape from life's dull realities. As Solalinde wrote (p. 255), "A novel more to the liking of the epoch cannot be produced." The theater took up the story of the converted and repentent malefactor, and at times leaving out the early chapters on the life of St. Patrick, gave the audience Ludovico Enio, his depths of depravity and his heights of redemption.

El mayor prodigio o el purgatorio de la vida (The Greatest Prodigy or Purgatory in Life) bears the name of "Lope de Vega Carpio" but is considered to be of doubtful authorship by Morley and Bruerton (*Cronología*, pp. 507-08); in fact, it is rejected from the Lope de Vega canon, at least in its present form, on account of its versification. The play presents the experiences of Ludovico, his nun niece Teodosia, and a third leading person, Lupercio, who helps her to escape from her uncle. It is a play of slight literary value, and is a poor one of the type of the evil hero redeemed, such as Cervantes' *El rufián dichoso* (The Happy Ruffian); Lope de Vega's *La fianza satisfecha* (The Outrageous Saint); Tirso de Molina's(?) *El condenado por desconfiado* (The Man Condemned for Lack of Faith); Mira de Amescua's *El esclavo del demonio* (The Devil's Slave); Calderón's *La devoción de la Cruz* (Devotion to the Cross); and Moreto's *San Franco de Sena* (St. Franco of Siena).

The most famous and most worthy descendent of Montalván's treatise is Calderón's *El purgatorio de San Patricio* (The Purgatory of St. Patrick).[22] It would seem that Calderón had both the Montalván *Life and Purgatory* and the previously mentioned play (*The Greatest*

Prose Writings

Prodigy) before his eyes when he set about composing. From his sources, which may have gone beyond these two works, Calderón brought forth a very good drama, which incorporates this time both the life of St. Patrick and the life of Ludovico Enio.[23] "By boldly transporting [the evil soldier] back to the earlier days of St. Patrick" wrote E. J. Hasell,[24] "and by making him not only a contemporary but a chance companion of the saint, Calderón gained at once a foil whose trancendent wickedness might make his comrade's holiness look brighter still, and at the same time [bring about] as great an approach to unity of interest and design as was possible from the nature of his subject." The case of good overcoming evil is well handled by this mature dramatist, Calderón de la Barca, who produces a work of theater which "on several accounts may be regarded as a good specimen of Calderón's sacred drama" (Hasell, p. 320). Indeed, in the opinion of one critic of distinction (Solalinde, p. 256), Calderón has written, at least partly inspired by Juan Pérez de Montalván, "the best production of the whole cycle of our legend in Spain."

CHAPTER 8

Para todos *(For Everybody)*

I *The Contents of the Work*

MONTALVAN'S *For Everybody* (1632) is a literary, philosophical and theological, as well as "scientific," miscellany, in the tradition of Boccaccio's *Decameron*. Within a frame of seven days' entertainment for a wedding, Montalván gives his reader a great deal indeed, following recent Spanish examples before him and imitating the sessions of contemporary "academies," with which he was well acquainted.[1] The complete title of the work gives an idea of what this seven days' entertainment is made up of: "*For Everybody*, moral, human and Divine examples, in which are treated diverse sciences, matters and faculties, divided into the seven days of the week."[2] It is, according to Montalván in his foreword, "an apparatus of various matters," and it would seem that a translation of the "table of contents" would provide a good guide to what *For Everybody* contains:

Table of all the matters, examples and moralities which are treated in this Book.

The Introduction to the whole week, which is an exemplary and pleasurable story, in prose and verse.

The Play concerning Philip II and Prince Charles.

The Division into Days, in imitation of the academies.

The First Day

The Number of things which God made on Sunday, with their definitions, particularly the celestial spirits, the Empyreal Heaven, time, chaos and light of day.

The Fable of Apollo, according to the opinion of all the Greek and Latin poets.

The Influence and characteristics of the Sun, considered as a planet.

The Definition of Philosophy, its divisions, the names of the first

Para todos (For Everybody) [107]

philosophers in the world; the number of the sybils; and the honors which the princes have conferred upon the professors of good letters.

The Play, No hay vida como la honra (There Is No Life Like Honor).

[A sonnet.]

The Second Day

The Explanation of the Firmament, and the position of the superior waters.

The Fable of the Moon.

The Characteristics of this Planet, place, quantity, effects and dominion.

The Mysteries of the Mass, meaning of its words and an account of its robes and ceremonies.

The Novel which is entitled Al cabo de los años mil (At the End of One Thousand Years), in prose and verse.

[A sonnet.]

The Third Day

The Discourse on the waters of the sea and on the mountains, proving that the earth is superior to water.

The Fable, birth and name of Mars, with everything else that deals thereof.

The Characteristics of this Planet.

The Treatise on military matters, their beginning, the inventors of arms, their need, their divisions, their apparati, their instruments, the action of the prince and the obligation of the soldier.

The Play, De un castigo dos venganzas (For a Punishment a Double Vengeance).

[A sonnet.]

The Fourth Day

The Magnitude of the greatest stars, the size of the earth and water; the size of the Sun and the Moon; and the reason why God first created the grass and the stars.

The Fable of Mercury, his names, pictures, his women and children.

The Characteristics, influence and dominion of this Planet.

The Discourse on good and bad angels, their division, their number, their differences, their names, their occupations, the sins of the bad, their punishment, the places where they are, the evil they do us, their power; all the kinds of bewitchment which

exist in the world; whether witches, magi, hobgoblins, ghosts, enchanters, phantoms, the bewitched, the possessed, and the remedies those on earth and in heaven try to employ.
The Novel, El palacio encantado (The Enchanted Palace), in prose and verse.
[A sonnet.]
The Fifth Day
The Treatment together of the birds and fishes, which God commanded the waters to bring forth; their perfection and their differences.
The Fable of Jupiter, his names, birth, upbringing, pictures, his acts of vengeance and love affairs.
The Influence and meaning of this Planet.
The Discourse of the Preacher, his greatness, his occupation, his holiness, his knowledge, his wisdom, his teaching and choice of books.
The Fable of Polyphemus.
The "auto sacramental," Polifemo (Polyphemus).
The Story of Jorge Castrioto. Introduction to *Skander Beg.*
The "auto sacramental," Escanderbech (Skander Beg).
[A sonnet.]
The Sixth Day
The Discourse on the animals which the earth brought forth, and what is understood by asses; what stature and appearance the first man had; what age Eve was; whether there were giants, and other pertinent matters.
The Fable of Venus, her names, her love affairs, her pictures, and temples.
The Characteristics of this Planet.
The Discourse on the Arts, determining according to their definition and divisions what ones are liberal and what ones are mechanical.
The Novel, El piadoso bandolero (The Compassionate Bandit), in prose and verse.
[A sonnet.]
The Seventh Day
What the Scripture means when it says that God rested on the seventh day. Why Saturday (the Sabbath) is called the Lord's Day. Why God brought about Creation in six days. Why Moses did not treat of the angels in them.
The Fable of Saturn.

Para todos (For Everybody) [109]

The Characteristics of this Planet.
The Discourse on the best of all things, divided into one hundred conclusions, with some curious details.
The Play, La más constante mujer (The Most Devoted Fiancée).
A Catalogue of the eminent authorities in the diverse arts, sciences and natural professions in Madrid.
A Listing of those who write plays in Castile only.
An Epilogue on those whom Antiquity celebrates as the greatest in various fields of learning.
[A sonnet.]

II *The Intention of* For Everybody

Victor Dixon's résumé of *For Everybody*, in his previously mentioned article on the work,[3] gives a very clear picture of what this is all about (p. 38): "A romantic adventure (the short novel *Introducción a la semana*) ends happily with a double wedding; and at the celebrations, which are held at a *quinta* on the banks of the Manzanares (and which include a performance of the play *El segundo Séneca de España*), each of seven gentlemen of Madrid — Fabio, Silvio, Lisardo, Anfriso, Montano, Celio and Valerio — is invited to afford a day's entertainment for a 'cortesana Academia.' Their contributions all follow the same pattern: 1) A commentary on the part of Creation which we are told in Genesis was performed on the day of the week in question, and a discussion of the planet and pagan god associated with that day. 2) A learned discourse on some serious subject. (The topics are Philosophy, the Mass, Arms, Angels, Preaching, the Arts and 'lo mejor de lo mejor.') 3) An entertainment — a *novela*, a *comedia* or a pair of *autos*. 4) A sonnet, supposed to have been sung. (Before this, on the last Day, the well-known *Índice de los ingenios de Madrid* and *Memoria de los que escriben comedias en Castilla solamente* are said to have been recited.)"

III *The Lists of Contemporary Learned Men and Women*

The plays and *autos* contained in *For Everybody* have been discussed previously in this book, as have the novels. The theological-philosophical-scientific discourses are old-fashioned and in general have little more than an historical interest.[4] The lists of writers and other learned men and women of the day are not the source of information that one would like them to be. Yet they are sufficiently pertinent to our purposes to include a sampling of both the first list (eminent authorities of Madrid) and the second list (dramatists of

Castile). The lists are alphabetically arranged under the person's given name, as the following names, selected from the lists, will show:

I. From the *Índice de los ingenios de Madrid* (Index of the Eminent Authorities of Madrid):

A. Don Antonio Coello, whose youth gives the lie to his many achievements and of whom it can be truly said that he begins where others leave off, wrote in octaves a prayer for the dedication of the church of the Jesuit Order, and in addition many other verses on diverse subjects which he has composed with great profundity and vigor, and among them two or three *comedias*.

F. Don Francisco Gómez de Quevedo y Villegas, Knight of the Order of St. James, ... [wrote] *La política de Dios*, published by Pedro Taza in Madrid, and *Los sueños*, also printed in Madrid, ... which in all are eighteen books; [this being] a fine opportunity to be able to say much concerning the ability and learning of their author, if by having mentioned his name everything had not been said.

G. El padre maestro Fray Gabriel Téllez, of the Order of Mercy, preacher, theologian, poet and always great, has printed and written, under the pseudonym of Master Tirso de Molina, many very excellent *comedias* and *Los cigarrales de Toledo*, and has ready for publication some exemplary novels which, when one says they are his, are sufficiently praised and held in high esteem.

G. Don Gerónimo de Villaizán y Garcés, famous man of letters and most lucid poet, because his genius is like manna, "which is agreeable to every taste" ("que sabe a todo lo que quiere") *[Wisdom*, XVI: 20-21], and of whom it can be truly said that in him Fortune and Merit have joined hands. In addition to other verse on various subjects, he has written three *comedias*, which have received the greatest applause ever seen.

J. El doctor Juan Pérez de Montalván, priest, presbyter, apostolic notary of the Inquisition, a graduate in philosophy and theology, has written verses for all the academies and poetic contests of Spain and has written thirty-six *comedias* and twelve *autos sacramentales*. He has published the *novelas ejemplares*, the *Orfeo en lengua castellana*, the *Purgatorio de San Patricio* and this last book which he calls *Para todos*. He is about to bring forth the prodigious life of Malhagas the trickster, without mentioning many other books which are not listed so as not to waste time.

L. Frey Lope Félix de Vega Carpio, of the Order of St. John, Officer of the Holy Inquisition and of the Apostolic Chamber, "swan," "phoenix," Virgil, Apollo and prodigious "thunderbolt" of our Spain, has written and published forty-two books, [such as] *La Arcadia, La Dragontea, El Isidro de Madrid, Las rimas humanas*, with *El arte de escribir comedias*, ... *La Dorotea*, a play in prose; twenty volumes of printed *comedias* and fifteen hundred which have been performed, not to mention *autos* and mis-

Para todos (For Everybody) [111]

cellaneous works, whose number is almost infinite; which being calculated result in five gatherings of paper for each day this great man has lived up until now. Let his name be his greatest renown, let his fame be his greatest praise, and let the respect in which he is held be his greatest glory.
M. Doña María de Zayas, tenth muse of our century, has written for the poetic contests with great success, and has completed a *comedia* containing excellent verse, and a book of eight exemplary novels in prose and verse about to be printed.
P. Don Pedro Calderón, select, gallant, heroic, lyric, comic and rare poet, has written many *comedias, autos* and miscellaneous works, with the general acceptance of the learned. In the academies he has held the foremost place; in the poetic contests he has won the best prizes, and in the theaters the most secure reputation; and he has begun also to write for printing a most elegant poem which he entitles *El diluvio general del mundo*.

The above eight entries, out of a total of three hundred and two, are, as mentioned before, only a sampling. From name to name we find some concrete information, but above all a repetition of flowery phrases and praise of the person being dealt with. It is to be noted that most of these people of this List One are writers, of a wide variety of *genres*, some are in the Church or in science, and a few only are dramatists. Indeed there is some repetition of a few persons in the two lists, but Montalván must have considered those of his first listing to be wider in their literary contributions than those who appear in the *List of Those Who Write Plays in Castile Only*.

II. From the *Memoria de los que escriben comedias en Castilla solamente:*
Álvaro Cubillo, rare poet, . . . writes excellent *comedias*, as has been the case in this Capital and all of Spain, two of his plays being about Mudarra.
El doctor Don Antonio de Mira de Mescua, a great master of this most noble and scientific art, both in the divine and in the human. His *autos sacramentales* are singularly successful as are his human comedies.
Don Antonio de Solís wrote [first edition: is writing] *La Gitanilla*, an excellent play, and the one who knows his outstanding spirit, talent and learning, will believe that just as in this he excelled, in the rest he will do so too.
Don Diego Jiménez de Enciso, Knight of the Order of St. James, needs no praise here, on account of his renown and the fact that he wrote *Los Médicis de Florencia*, which has been a guide and example for all great plays.
El doctor Felipe Godínez has a very great facility, knowledge and subtlety for this kind of poetry, especially in the divine *comedias*, for there he has wide scope to make use of his knowledge, erudition and doctrine.
Don Francisco de Quevedo has been successful with plays to such an extent that it would seem that he were writing them continuously, such is his universal, select and sovereign genius.

El maestro José de Valdivielso brought forth his plays, like all the rest of his writings, with singular success and glory, for indeed in the *autos sacramentales*, since things divine are most suited to his mind, he has never had a rival.

Don Juan Ruiz de Alarcón writes plays with such novelty, skill and rarity that there is no play of his which does not contain much to be admired and none has reason to be criticized, for his having written so much is proof of his most fertile production.

El licenciado Luis [Quiñones] de Benavente has not written *comedias*, but has brought forth so many *bailes* ("dances") and *entremeses* (interludes) for the presentation with *comedias* that we can say with great certainty that to him are due the production and success of many plays and the lightening and adornment of all; because in this he has been unique through the natural grace, excellent talent, spirited wit and continuous acuteness with which Heaven has endowed him.

Luis Vélez de Guevara has written more than four hundred plays, and all of them are of subtle thought, poetic thrust and most excellent and rare verse, in which his valiant spirit has no competition.

. . . .

Here I make no mention of the past dramatists, for princes, lords and men of great importance and position have written plays, both laymen and men of the Church; because Frey Lope de Vega Carpio, with the great knowledge he has in the field, has written copiously and scientifically a treatise only in praise of this most illustrious Art and Exercise, to the revised version of which that will soon be published I refer, and also so as not to provide boredom by dwelling too long on one subject. And I do not know whether this subject has been agreeable to all, because there are many who are offended by praise to others just as if it were insult to themselves.

The above ten entries, out of a total of twenty-eight names (plus an enumeration in a sentence or two of some fifty additional dramatists) reveal that the second list, like the first, is on the whole of little value, so filled is it with generalities and repetitious statements. However, it does stress to us the great participation of writers, and the public, in drama in Montalván's time, and it does show what names were uppermost in Montalván's mind. Some of the persons mentioned, like Mira de Amescua, Ruiz de Alarcón, Quiñones de Benavente, Vélez de Guevara — to mention only a few — are still today what one could call household words in Spanish drama, but many have sunk into oblivion. (Calderón, Tirso de Molina, Lope de Vega and some others, it is to be remembered, are in the first list, and are treated there at some length.) The second *Memoria* is very short (twenty-eight names plus the long listing following in a prose paragraph), and is presumably not to repeat the

Para todos (For Everybody)

previous "Ingenios de Madrid"; but it does repeat, for example (through error?), Quevedo: "Don Francisco Gómez de Quevedo y Villegas" and "Don Francisco de Quevedo." Only occasionally does the *Memoria* give us some real information or hit the mark; for instance, when it points out that Luis (Quiñones) de Benavente has made a fine contribution to the theatrical art, not in *comedias*, but in the *género chico:* the *bailes* and *entremeses* (used before, between and following the acts of a three-act *comedia*, to help provide the audience with a performance of total entertainment). This "Luis de Benavente" is well remembered in the twentieth century for his contribution in the way mentioned by Montalván, as continuing studies of him demonstrate.[5]

It seems strange that Montalván should speak of Ruiz de Alarcón's having written a great deal in drama, for the general opinion held by critics in the twentieth century is that Alarcón wrote a limited number of plays,[6] and this statement may be some of Montalván's misinformation, which is misleading. Also puzzling, for example, is the reference to Lope de Vega's forthcoming revised version of the *New Art of Writing Plays*, which has not come down to us. On the other hand, Montalván's listings can be useful to the twentieth-century investigator, as has been noted in the discussion of *The Little Gypsy Girl* (chapter on Problems of Authorship). Montalván wrote, we remember, in the first (1632) edition of *For Everybody*, that "Don Antonio de Solís is writing a play which he calls *La Gitanilla* . . . ", whereas the statement in editions from 1635 on is that "Don Antonio de Solís wrote *La Gitanilla*. . . . " Some declarations are, as mentioned before, significant for authorship and chronology. A few other changes from edition to edition in these listings of writers and other persons in *For Everybody* would seem to provide additional clues to fact or attitude; cf. Victor Dixon's reference to such changes in his important study of the work (*"Para todos,"* p. 58 and p. 58n65).

IV Montalván's Models for Writing *For Everybody*

In writing *For Everybody*, taken as a whole, Montalván was following a favorite literary device of his day and he had many Spanish models before him. The chief model, which Montalván probably had on his desk, would seem to be Tirso de Molina's *Cigarrales de Toledo* (The Country Estates of Toledo), published in 1624 (with "aprobación" of 1621).[7] The *Cigarrales* is within a frame of imagined literary festivals celebrated by several gentlemen at their country homes on the bank of the Tagus near Toledo, during a period of five sessions, at certain intervals of time. This compilation of Tirso's, which is chiefly remembered for its brilliant defense of Lope de Vega's dramatic system,[8] is made up of poetry, plays and short novels, in line with the arrangement of several miscellaneous collections which appeared in the 1620's, authored by writers such as Salas Barbadillo and Castillo Solórzano. Montalván may very well have been inspired by the popularity and success of this type of literary endeavor to try his hand at it also, in competition with other Golden Age men of letters. "They had for instance," writes Victor Dixon, "*Para todos*," p. 38, "included plays as well as novels within the frame, although never as many as Montalbán included in *Para todos*. They had imagined the sections into which the contents were divided as sessions of *academias* like those of the time — opportunities for retailing verses, discourses and witticisms; but they had never offered those academies such a bulk of erudite information. Certainly they had never attempted to embrace in one frame-story such a diversity of literary forms."

V *Montalván's Reasons for Writing* For Everybody

The popularity and success of such compilations around him may have encouraged Montalván to prepare a similar work also, as mentioned above. Furthermore, he may have accumulated on his desk or in his cupboards, for some years, a good deal of the material which he brought together for the volume of 1632. Certainly many of the pages of *For Everybody* had been written some time before the "compilation." Also, Montalván makes it very clear in his preface to the reader that around 1631 he had grown tired of writing plays and sought literary diversion of another sort. ("The truth is that plays had made me so weary that I undertook this measure not to enter into the writing of any more for some months.") And Edward Glaser has added another reason: Montalván had a burning desire "to achieve recognition as an accomplished scholar in many fields" ("The *Auto del Polifemo*," p. 103). Strengthening this idea, Dixon adds ("*Para todos*," p. 43) that the discourses and the commentaries of the days of the week (a great show of erudition!) "argue a desire on Montalbán's part to impress his readers by a display of ability in the field of popular scholarship, on which he had to some extent already ventured in *Vida y purgatorio de San Patricio* (1627)."[9]

VI *Literary Polemics*

There seems to be at least one additional very important reason for Montalván's preparation and publishing *For Everybody*: literary

Para todos (For Everybody)

polemic. In 1951, Amezúa paid a great deal of attention to the bitter quarrels surrounding the work, focussing upon Quevedo's burning hatred of Montalván as expressed in his subsequent *Teetotum* (1632), dedicated to "Dr. Juan Pérez de Montalván, graduated it is not known where, nor is it known in what, nor does he himself know."[10] This *Teetotum* (Perinola), called "one of the most ferocious diatribes written in Spanish" by Amezúa in his "Polémicas" (p. 73),[11] has seemed to many critics to indicate that a Quevedo-Montalván controversy was the reason for the composition of *For Everybody*. Yet it is to be remembered that Quevedo was mentioned twice in the work's listings of writers in friendly terms; and Edward Glaser recently warned us to be cautious in reaching a false conclusion: "so clever and scathing is Quevedo's satire against the alleged folly and pedantry of Montalván that later critics have been taken in by his statements. . . . The accepted views on the controversy stand in need of modification" ("The *Auto del Polifemo*," p. 104). Victor Dixon has taken up this suggestion very thoughtfully: "And if we investigate the circumstances of its composition, we may decide that its publication was not so much an early move in the war with Quevedo, as a late sortie in a struggle which has almost escaped attention until now, between Montalbán and Jerónimo de Villaizán" ("*Para todos*," p. 37).

Quevedo, in his *Teetotum*, had already made this point. Asking the rhetorical question why Montalván wrote *For Everybody*, Quevedo answers: "In a word I shall tell you. Well it was only to speak ill, in a very nasty way, of Villaizán" (*Obras completas*, ed. Buendía, I, p. 450). Jerónimo de Villaizán had written a flattering preliminary poem to the *Orpheus in the Castilian Language* (1624); so it seems that in the mid-twenties "all was quiet on the Western front." But later on some trouble apparently began. Quevedo in *Teetotum* accused Montalván of having "lifted" a play of Villaizán's, but plays in existence do not corroborate this charge. Victor Dixon has noted a manuscript in the Biblioteca Nacional which hints at some differences (Villaizán-Montalván) concerning the play *For a Punishment a Double Vengeance*. Dixon has brought forth various statements of the day which lead him to believe that it is possible that Montalván's play "was deliberately modelled on one by Villaizán, and could be regarded, according to one's allegiances, as a parody, as an original *refundición* or as a shameless piece of plagiarism" ("*Para todos*," p. 48). There has been attributed to Villaizán a "lost" *De un agravio tres venganzas* (For an Insult a

Triple Vengeance), which could have been the source of Montalván's play of the slightly different title. Also, the king, Philip IV, seems to have shown special favor towards Villaizán, and Montalván does complain in *For Everybody* (preface to the reader) that "the success of a play is due more to a patron's favor than to the dramatist's skill." In this rivalry for royal applause and theatrical success, Villaizán seems to have written *Sufrir por querer más* (To Suffer Through Greater Love), 1630 or 1631, Dixon suggests, and Montalván, *The Most Devoted Fiancée*, "to vindicate his reputation at a time when it was menaced by the machinations of jealous rivals" (Dixon, p. 51), in the Spring of 1631.

Victor Dixon finds throughout *For Everybody* in "Montalbán's high-minded moralizing" (p. 53) many possible attacks on his enemies, especially Villaizán. The evil Rodrigo of the first novel of *For Everybody* ("Introduction to the Week") may have symbolized Villaizán, and Montalván "may have had the upstart Villaizán in mind" (Dixon, p. 55) on several other occasions in the book, including the Sixth Day's Discourse on the Arts. The entry for Villaizán in Montalván's listing of the worthies of Madrid (translated above) seems to have been favorable, but may have contained some malice — at least it did in Quevedo's interpretation; and Antonio Restori may have been wrong when he found no irony in the treatment of Montalván's rival in *For Everybody*.[12] On the other side, Dixon is no doubt completely on the right track when he says regarding *For Everybody* that "Montalván seems to have taken the opportunities its publication offered to 'decir mal' [speak ill], consistently if obliquely, of Villaizán and his allies in their rivalry. But that rivalry was also, surely, the book's immediate *raison d'être*" (p. 56). Villaizán died in 1633, and it is gratifying to know that before that early demise mutual friends, such as Lope de Vega and José de Pellicer, apparently achieved a reconciliation. Editions of *For Everybody* of 1633 introduce amendments and deletions, and possible slurs on Villaizán are removed. (It is to be noted that Montalván slightly revised several of his books in subsequent editions, influenced by criticism encountered.)

VII *The Success of* For Everybody

For Everybody was highly appreciated by many readers, and after the first edition of 1632 it ran through a number of subsequent ones. Restori describes in detail sixteen editions, from that of Madrid, 1632, to that of Seville, 1736, attesting to the book's success.[13] Mon-

Para todos (For Everybody)

talván had been annoyed and upset by the storm of criticism which had fallen upon him and by the disturbing controversy, but he was greatly encouraged by the positive reception of his work (in his prologue to the first volume of plays, 1635, he noted specifically the several editions which had appeared in two years' time). He was so much encouraged that he had in mind a second part to *For Everybody*, and he mentioned this intention in both the above-mentioned prologue to the First Volume of plays and also in the prologue to *Fama póstuma* (Posthumous Fame), 1636, in memory of Lope de Vega: "After this I promise you the Second Part of *For Everybody*, in spite of the fact that I might have been discouraged by so much satire, calumny and controversy ..." (First Volume of Plays), and "I plan to give you very soon in print the Second Part of *For Everybody* ..." *(Posthumous Fame)*. Needless to say, no Second Part has come down to us, as has been mentioned previously.

VIII Recent Studies of For Everybody

Victor Dixon's important article on *For Everybody (Hispanic Review*, 1964) has been quoted extensively. Another recent study, that of Willard F. King, previously mentioned *(Prosa novelística y academias literarias en el siglo XVII*, 1963), is very helpful also. King notes (pp. 135-39 especially) that the introductory "novel" leads logically into the week's literary festivities, when Don Pedro invites the others to spend seven days with him on his estate on the bank of the Manzanares. The very serious Montalván, observes King — he seems to have taken himself too seriously all his life — is not without some shred of humor when he speaks of the rôles of the ladies present. They were allowed to leave the "dull" academic presentations for the freedom of the countryside if they wished. And Montalván mentions — a reflection of the female taste of the times — that they were present for the short novels and the plays, or when the weather was bad, as happened on the Fourth Day. Some of them, however, who were really learned, or wanted to appear so, attended all of the sessions. Willard F. King finds that the majority of pages containing the discourses and the philosophical-theological-"scientific" materials are pedantic, heavy and "in general, tolerable only as curiosities" (p. 137). The novels and theatrical pieces, however, have merit, according to King. King makes a rather strong plea in favor of Montalván's novelistic writing ("His great talent resides, in reality, in the construction of novels"): that it contains originality of plot, narrative agility, simplicity of language, and characters who are unusually coherent. In fact, Willard King's very strong statement that "Some of his novels can be counted among the best of the century" (p. 137) is hardly borne out by our discussion in the chapter on Montalván's prose.

Amezúa ("Las polémicas literarias") had found *For Everybody* as a whole to be a confused mass of odds and ends ("un cajón de sastre") and had considered most of the erudition contained in the work to be second-hand, superfluous, pedantic and impertinent (p. 70). Montalván seemed to have been attempting to pick up "learning" from many sources in a desire to impress, as mentioned before. Bacon ("Life," p. 15) had previously considered *For Everybody* to be a "hodge-podge," and Quevedo, several centuries before that, for reasons which are not very clear,[14] had pounced upon the work for its mixture of everything in an apparently undisciplined confusion. Yet this "variety" was a keyword of the day, and Lope de Vega, in his *New Art of Writing Plays*, of the early 1600's, had come out strongly for this characteristic: "For this variety gives great pleasure. Of this Nature gives us a good example, for she is beautiful on account of her variety." And Victor Dixon points out (p. 37) that "Montalbán's answer would have been, in the first place, that diversity of style and content had been his main intention in the work, and was its principle merit." It was his desire to entertain, instruct and edify every possible reader, and Dixon protests rightly against the critics who have condemned the work for this very feature of variety: "Despite this deliberate diversity, *Para todos* cannot justly be said to lack continuity and cohesion. Its formal construction is the reverse of disorderly . . ." (p. 38). We must agree, I am sure, with the World's leading *Montalvanista* when he concludes his article by saying (p. 59) that "*Para todos*, from its pretentious title to the pious *Si quid dictum* . . . of its close, is a work worthy, with all its oddities, of an unquiet but always colourful epoch, and an erratic but always exuberant author."

CHAPTER 9

The First Biography of Lope de Vega: Fama póstuma (Posthumous Fame)

I An Exaggerated Encomium

FÉLIX de Vega and Francisca Fernández, he noble by decree and she noble by birth, and residents both of the illustrious city of Madrid, were the most happy parents of Dr. Frey Lope Félix de Vega Carpio, portent of the orb, glory of the nation, lustre of the motherland, oracle of the tongue, center of fame, prince of verse, Homer of the heroics, Pindar of the lyricists, Sophocles of the tragedies, and Terence of the comic art; unique among the greatest, greatest among the great, and magnificent in every aspect and in all ways.[1]

These very flowery words which begin the *Posthumous Fame* in memory of Lope de Vega establish the tone for the exaggerated "Life" which Montalván set about writing after Lope died in 1635. The volume in Lope de Vega's honor which Montalván prepared for the press includes in addition to this first biography of the dramatist some one hundred fifty-three contributions in praise of Lope de Vega by various of his contemporaries. The date of publication, as noted, is 1636.

II Montalván's Lope de Vega

According to Montalván's *Posthumous Fame*, Lope de Vega was throughout his life a paragon of virtue. During his years of schooling he was always at the head of his class. Before he could even write, he was dictating verse, which his fellow students wrote down for him in exchange for a share of his lunch. Later, to prove that he was "modern" and "human," Lope set out, as a youth, to see the world with a traveling companion. They hiked to Segovia from Madrid, and rode on horseback as far as Astorga. But there, repentant of this departure from home, the two young men tried to change some coins and pawn some jewelry for the return journey. However, on the

[119]

complaint of a suspicious silversmith, they were arrested. But all ended well: they were soon released and sent back home.

Shortly after this escapade, Montalván credits Lope de Vega with having written a play, *La pastoral de Jacinto* (Jacinto's Pastoral), "which was the first he composed in three acts." This statement is just one of Montalván's many very questionable ones, for the play, in its present form at least, is not particularly early.[2] After this composition, Montalván declares, Lope de Vega went on writing in great abundance, in addition to attending the University of Alcalá de Henares for four years before becoming secretary to the Duke of Alba, for whom he wrote the *Arcadia*. Mention is made in this *Posthumous Fame* of Lope's marriage to Isabel de Urbino, and later to Juana de Guardo; but no hint is allowed concerning his many amours and later amorous escapades. To believe Montalván, it would seem that the life of the flesh ended for Lope with Juana's death and that he took Holy Orders to spend the rest of his life in a most exemplary way. There *is* reference to early exile in Valencia, for writing satirical verse against an individual who had slandered him, and to Lope's enlisting in the Invincible Armada. But a great deal of the *Posthumous Fame*, in addition to the repeated compliments, is devoted to Lope's last, three-day illness and his pious death (and the preparations for it), his elaborate funeral and his will, which bequeathed, among specific gifts to others, "to me, his pupil and humble servant, a picture in which he was portrayed as a youth, sitting in a chair and writing at a table, surrounded by dogs, monsters, hobgoblins, monkeys and other animals, some making faces at him and others barking at him, while he went on writing without paying any attention to them."[3]

The second half of the *Posthumous Fame* is devoted to out and out praise: "Lope Félix de Vega Carpio was.... Oh how the mention of his name alone impedes the possibility of properly praising him!" And the praise pours forth filled with embroidered exaggeration. As was the custom of the times, there is much show of erudition on Montalván's part and the comparisons are ever abundant, especially to the great worthies of the past: in Lope are the greatness of Alexander, the knowledge of Ptolmey, the justice of Numa Pompilius, the clemency of Julius Caesar, the wit of Ulysses, the strength of Hercules, the poetry of Virgil, the gravity of Cato, the poverty of Curius, the truthfulness of Trajan, the patience of Augustus, the piety of Antonius, the temperance of Constantine, the humility of Teodosius, etc. "What will not be the merit of him who had all these fine qualities and many more? — this most illustrious man known to both worlds, Europe and America. Indeed, in full support of his great reputation are Felipe IV, the Duque de Sesa and his mother city Madrid itself."

III *The* Posthumous Fame *as a Source of (Mis)information*

A perusal of the *Posthumous Fame* indicates very clearly that the rather short essay is the source of, or in some cases the recording of, quaint ideas, true or untrue, concerning Lope de Vega.[4] His super-precociousness — and we know that he was precocious — has already been referred to, and must be taken with some modification. Montalván moves forward to state boldly that Lope's *comedias* performed "reach eighteen hundred." Lope de Vega himself used the phrase "one thousand five hundred," but the critics have taken this to be a vague round number, subject to drastic reduction.[5] The statement that Lope de Vega wrote "more books in number and quality than all the ancient and modern poets" reveals Montalván's naïveté or constant over-enthusiasm in the way he proposes to prove his point: put all the volumes of the ancients and moderns in a balance against Lope's, for Montalván declares that they have all of those books, ancient and modern and presumably Lope's too, in the bookstores of Madrid! It is possible that all the homes of thoughtful men had a portrait of the master, and that in addition to pointing him out to strangers, the *madrileños* ran after Lope in the streets. It is possible too, as Montalván puts it, that foreigners came from abroad to see whether Lope de Vega really existed; and it is plausible that good things came to be associated with Lope's name as an adjective, to the extent that a woman witnessing the funeral said wittily that "without doubt this funeral is Lope's, since it is so good." But it is strange that Montalván should believe that Lope de Vega stopped writing plays many years before his death, asking the Duke of Sesa for support, when we know that *Las bizarrías de Belisa* (The Gallantries of Isabel) belongs to 1634 (dated autograph MS) and *La mayor virtud de un rey* (The Greatest Virtue of a King) may be even closer to Lope's date of death.[6]

It is an error of omission and a glossing over for Montalván to write that Lope's funeral procession passed in front of the convent of the Discalced Trinitarians because one of the nuns, Sister Marcela de Jesús, "a very near relative of the deceased," requested it; when it was well known that Sister Marcela was the illegitimate daughter of the dramatist and his beloved mistress Micaela de Luján, who bore him at least seven children. Montalván is suppressing, it can be clearly seen, any information that would make Lope de Vega anything less than the above-mentioned paragon of virtue, throughout his whole life.

IV *The Interest of the Work*

Much of the interest of the *Posthumous Fame* resides in the fact that it was written by a younger man (35) who had been closely related to the older man (72) over a period of a third of a century. It is a first-hand biography, and the first on the great Lope de Vega, but as has been said many times, in generalities it contains a good deal of truth, but in particulars a good deal of error. Montalván's reminiscences, accurate or not, remind us that he and the subject of his biography were living people, and when he speaks of something he experienced himself or of somebody he knew well, he is at his best. The *Posthumous Fame* cannot be called an important elegy in prose; it rather resembles a funeral eulogy by a person who knew the subject of his remarks very well. It contains a very sincere and deep emotion at the loss of one who was dearly beloved, and a deference to the deceased (and to the living too when Montalván addresses the Duke of Sesa directly and King Philip IV indirectly) which seems overdone. That Montalván had been raised to glorify the master and to hang upon his very words is clear enough, and here may be an indication of Montalván's constant dependence on others and a weak character. But in Lope de Vega's case it is also clear that the master loved and expected a reverence and deference from the younger. As Castro and Rennert wrote (*Vida*, p. 333), "Without doubt [Lope de Vega] thought that he had the right to demand a display of deference from the younger generation, and when he received it — as in the case of Montalván — he showed himself to be paternally amiable and generously liberal." The closeness of the older man to the younger and their intimate literary experience are vividly revealed by Montalván's pen as he performs this last, sad task to honor his mentor.

V *Montalván's Father*

Montalván's father, Alonso Pérez, the bookseller and publisher, is mentioned several times in the *Posthumous Fame:* as the heir to a religious picture (Our Lady, St. Joseph and the child Jesus), as one present at Lope de Vega's death, and before that, as the dear friend and host who invited the elderly dramatist to dine in the last year of

The First Biography of Lope de Vega

his life on the Day of the Transfiguration. This last act on Alonso's part was an effort to cheer up Lope de Vega, who had recently suffered two misfortunes ("disgustos") which Montalván does not identify. These, however, may very well have been the abduction of his beloved daughter Antonia Clara by Cristóbal Tenorio, late in 1634, and the earlier death of his son, Lope Félix, drowned the same year on a pearl-hunting expedition off the coast of the Island of Margarita. In the conversations at this intimate dinner, as Montalván describes it in the *Posthumous Fame*, Juan is the third member of the group, and Juan's exhortations to Lope de Vega concern continuing on in life with good cheer: "Don't think about [the end of life], for I trust in God and in your good constitution that your state of depression will pass, and that we shall see you in your usual good health for twenty more years." This exhortation, however, was fruitless, for as Montalván sadly reports: "Lope was to die very shortly after." Nevertheless, the father's contacts with the great Lope de Vega, according to the son, were constant and always very close; and there may be something boastful in Montalván as he has himself and his family reflect in the glory of the great.

VI An "Immediate" Biography

As an observer of the daily scene, Montalván relates in the *Posthumous Fame* that he saw year after year Lope de Vega's name in a prominent position on the billboards on the street corners of Madrid; and he attempts to give us a listing of some of Lope's published works, such as *La Jerusalén conquistada* (Jerusalem Conquered) and *La Dragontea*, etc., adding *Rimas nuevas* (New Rhymes), still in an unpublished state. One of Montalván's most vivid literary memories, which he recounts, is his writing in collaboration with Lope the play *The Third Order of St. Francis* (previously mentioned), with Lope composing the first act, Montalván the second and the two of them sharing the third.[7] To get at the writing of Act III, Montalván declares that he rose at 2 a.m., and finished his part at 11. Lope, he found, had started at 5 a.m., and was finished at 10, and while waiting for his younger collaborator he had had a snack, written a fifty-tercet letter and watered his whole garden!

VII Customs of the Day

A few ideas and comments on contemporary society, and Lope de Vega's own customs in particular, appear from time to time in the

Posthumous Fame: concerning processes of law (which were protracted and costly); concerning good habits (Lope de Vega felt that he owed his constant good health to temperance and to walking, and according to Montalván, "exercise is Nature's most useful remedy"); concerning medical practices (in his final illness, Lope de Vega was given a purgative and bled); and concerning travel (masters sent their servants on ahead to reserve lodgings and have them ready). As to the solaces of the Church, it is noted that Extreme Unction has the dual purpose of comforting him who is leaving this world and also healing him who is to recover; and as to religious practices, Montalván records that Lope de Vega was wont to scourge himself in private, to atone for his sins, to the point of spattering the walls of his room with blood. Finally, declared Lope de Vega, according to Montalván, real fame is that of being good; and Lope is supposed to have said too that he would have gladly exchanged all worldly honors received to have performed one additional virtuous deed.

VIII *Other Panegyrics in the* In memoriam

Following the "Life" of Lope de Vega in this volume of 1636, Montalván included the above-mentioned laudatory contributions of one hundred fifty-three writers and some lines of verse of his own. The contents of these panegyrics are usually vague generalities; sometimes specific works are mentioned, but again in general terms. "Although little," writes José María de Cossío, "I believe that something can be gleaned from that enormous poetic farrago, in which the panegyric contents are repeated to the point of satiety."[8] Something can be gleaned too from Montalván's account of Lope, as has been noted, but it is often difficult to separate the wheat from the chaff. The "Life" by Montalván has the distinction, at any rate, of being the first in the long line of "lives" which continue to pay homage to the Phoenix of Writers up until the present day. In rendering tribute to his master, Juan Pérez de Montalván could assure himself and his readers that Lope de Vega's honor and glory would continue long into the future:

And I who loved you best will give a beginning to your praises, so that sonorous poets with more felicitous words and more expressive pens will take up the torch.[9]

CHAPTER 10

Miscellaneous Poetry

IN addition to the thousands of lines in his plays, all in verse, Montalván wrote occasional, or incidental, poetry for poetic contests, as has been seen; poetry to be interspersed amid the narrative prose of his novels;[1] elegiac verse for the death of Lope de Vega in the *Posthumous Fame;* and other miscellaneous poetic contributions for various purposes. G. W. Bacon printed a group of Montalván poems early in this century;[2] Joaquín de Entrambasaguas has noted two preliminary *décimas* to a Lope de Vega work;[3] in recent years José Simón Díaz has been able to add several poetic items to the Montalván canon;[4] and Edward M. Wilson has found a 52-line ballad by Montalván in a seventeenth-century *Cancionero*.[5]

Bacon's transcriptions of materials in the Biblioteca Nacional (and these are repeated by Ada Godínez de Batlle in her "Labor literaria") are of a miscellaneous nature. Most frequently these poems are eulogistic "preliminary" poems in a certain contemporary author's work, and only rarely are they contributions to poetical collections. There is a preliminary *décima*, for example, in praise of the author, in Part II of Pedro Díaz Morante's *Arte nueva* [sic] *de escribir* (New Art of Writing), Madrid, 1624, and another eulogistic *décima* to Part III, Madrid, 1629 (this is reprinted by Simón Díaz, his item No. 6, pp. 288-89). There is another *décima*, again praising the author, in the preliminaries to Miguel Colodrero de Villalobos' *Varias rimas* (Several Rhymes), Córdoba, 1629 (reprinted by Simón Díaz, item No. 5, p. 288). Ana de Castro Egas' *A la eternidad del Rey Felipe tercero* (To the Eternal Life of King Philip III), Madrid, 1629, was the occasion for a preliminary poem of four *décimas* addressed to the authoress, in praise of her work and in praise of the deceased (reprinted by Simón Díaz, item No. 4, pp. 287-88). A royal *fiesta* of October 13, 1631, in which King Felipe IV tangled with a bull, brought about *elogios* published by José Pellicer de Tovar *(El an-*

[125]

fiteatro de Felipe el Grande [The Amphitheater of Philip the Great] which contain an *espinela* by Montalván.

The *Compendio de la ortografía castellana* (Compendium of Castilian Orthography) by Nicolás Dávila, Madrid, 1631, includes a preliminary *décima* by Montalván, as usual in praise of the author (reprinted by Simón Díaz, item No. 13, p. 292); and to the *Poesías dirigidas al Monte Vesuvio por varios ingenios* (Poems Addressed to Mount Vesuvius by Several Poets), collected by Juan de Quiñones, Madrid, 1632, Montalván contributed a very appropriate sonnet beginning "Ya es humo, polvo, incendio, lodo . . ." ("Smoke, dust, fire, mud . . .") (reprinted by Simón Díaz, item No. 16, p. 293). Rodrigo Fernández de Ribera's *Mesón del mundo* (Inn of the World), Madrid, 1632, has an introductory contribution by Montalván (a *décima*), which declares that this "inn" should really be called a literary academy, for its great merits (reprinted by Simón Díaz, item No. 15, pp. 292-93). In Francisco de las Cuevas' *Experiencias de Amor y Fortuna* (Experiences of Love and Fortune), Barcelona, 1633, Montalván's preliminary sonnet is, as is to be expected in such a case, filled with classical mythological allusions. In Valencia, 1634, Luis de Arellano compiled *Avisos para la muerte, escritos por algunos ingenios de España* (Warnings for Death, Written by Some Poets of Spain), and for this Montalván provided a long poem in ballad meter, confessing his sins, like a lost sheep seeking its Shepherd, and asking, through the Crucifixion of our Lord and the Redemption of Mankind, the aid of Jesus Christ and his Blessed Mother and the Saints. Pedro Gutiérrez de Arévalo's *Práctica de boticarios, guía de enfermos, remedio para pobres* (Practice of Apothecaries, Guide for the Sick, Remedy for the Poor), Madrid, 1634, includes a preliminary poem (four octaves) of dedication to the "most worthy Pedro"; and Jerónimo de Porras' *Rimas varias* (Varied Rhymes), Antequera, 1639, contains as part of its introductory material a sonnet in praise of the author by Montalván. Bacon prints another Montalván ballad "A una boca" ("To a Mouth"), which begins "Clavel dividido en dos . . ." ("Carnation rent in two . . ."), from José Alfay's *Poesías varias de grandes ingenios españoles* (Varied Poetry of Great Spanish Writers), Zaragoza, 1654.[6] Bacon, in his article (p. 460, note 1), also makes mention of a satiric *décima* on the description ("Elogio descriptivo") prepared by Ruiz de Alarcón of the *fiestas* in honor of Prince Charles Stuart and Princess María of Austria, Madrid, 1623.[7]

To the miscellaneous collection of poems printed by Bacon — to repeat, usually of an eulogistic kind, as a preliminary poem to some contemporary's writings — José Simón Díaz has added several new ones: a preliminary *décima*, in praise of the author, for José de Valdivielso's *Exposición parafrástica del Psalterio y de los Cánticos del Brevario* (Paraphrastic Exposition of the Psalter and the Canticles of the Breviary), Madrid, 1623; another, this time in praise of Miguel de León Suárez who, in Madrid, 1624, translated and published the Italian Roberto Belarmino's *Oficio del Príncipe Cristiano* (Office of the Christian Prince); two introductory *décimas* to Lope de Vega for his *Corona trágica. Vida y muerte de la serenísima reina de Escocia María Estuardo* (Tragic Crown. Life and Death of Her Serene Highness Queen Mary Stuart of Scotland), Madrid, 1627; another preliminary *décima* to Martín de Hermosilla's *La degollación de San Juan Bautista* (The Beheading of St. John the Baptist), Madrid, 1630; a preliminary *décima* "to the author" in praise of Manuel de Ocampo's *Copia de una carta moral escrita a un amigo suyo* (Copy of a Moral Letter Written to a Friend of His), Madrid, 1630; still another preliminary *décima*, of the usual laudatory nature, for Salvador Jacinto Polo de Medina's *Academias del Jardín* (Garden Academies), Madrid, 1630; and another preliminary *décima* for the same writer's *El buen humor de las Musas* (The Good Humor of the Muses), published in the same city in the same year.

The next "new" poem brought from oblivion by Simón Díaz is still another preliminary *décima* which lauds the "científico" and "discreto" José Camerino for his *Discurso político sobre estas palabras: "A fee de hombre de bien"* (Political Discourse on These Words: "On the Word of an Honest Man"), Madrid, 1631; and Pedro de Castro y Anaya was similarly praised in a preliminary *décima* to his *Auroras de Diana* (Dawns of Diana), Madrid, 1632. For Gabriel Bocángel [y] Unzueta's *Retrato panegírico de Carlos de Austria* (Panegyric Portrait of Charles of Austria), Madrid, 1633, Montalván chose a longer and more sonorous form of metric as he provided a laudatory, introductory *silva* in the Italianate eleven- and seven-syllable line to proclaim, along with this librarian to His Royal Highness, the excellences of an Infante of Spain. Three *décimas* forming one poem are the preliminary praise of "La Virgen de la Humildad, que está en una pared pintada en el Real Convento de San Filipe de Madrid" ("The Virgin of Humility, who is painted on a wall in the Royal Monastery of St. Philip of Madrid") to preface Hernando de Camargo y Salgado's *La Virgen de la Humildad y la humildad de la Virgen* (The Virgin of Humility and the Humility of the Virgin), Madrid, 1634. A *décima* praises the "salón del Buen Retiro" in *Elogios al Palacio Real* (Praises of the Royal Palace) gathered by Diego [de] Covarrubias y Leiva, Madrid, 1635. Finally, in the verse entries in this Simón Díaz contribution to Montalván scholarship are a preliminary *décima* to Luis Pacheco de Narváez for his *Historia ejemplar de las dos constantes mujeres españolas* (Exemplary History of the Two Constant Spanish Women), Madrid, 1635, and three quatrains *(cuatrillos)* for Fray Pedro Beltrán's *Ramillete de flores de la Retama* (Bouquet of Flowers of the Broom), published in Madrid, 1648.

The first impression received from these many short poetic compositions is that Montalván was very fond of the 10-line, 8-syllable *décima*, a stanza form with a rhyme scheme of *abbaaccddc*, which lent itself very well for his purpose: a short, unified tribute. A second, more important conclusion is that while he had many enemies in the literary field, Montalván was also very closely associated with many writers and was definitely in the "literary swim" for a period of a good many years. Of course it is well known that books of the day were brought forth from the press preceded, as introductory and prefatory material, by the usual series of laudatory compositions by other writers; some close friends, it is true, but some not so close, and perhaps seeking publicity for themselves.[8] However sincere or not such compositions were, and however trite they tended to be in their repetitions, Montalván was quite busy with them. It is apparent, as noted before, that he rarely contributed to an "anthology" of verse and that his main contribution to poetry (not excluding verse portions of the novels) was made in drama, which as mentioned several times previously, was a verse drama throughout.

"While for men as learned and of such good judgment as Don José Pellicer" writes Godínez de Batlle, "Labor literaria," p. 53, "Montalván is an elect of the Muses, for others less just, like Schack, he is an author of slight poetic success, in whom is lacking an energetic and powerful inspiration to take possession of the soul, to move it, to inspire it and persuade it to action."[9] "Certainly," continues Batlle, "Montalván has his defects and like his great master is uneven and careless; on occasions his style is rhetorical and ostentatious and he has the failing of amplifying and repeating the same thing in several ways, taking pleasure frequently in the contemporary bad taste. Nevertheless, often rising above unjust and impassioned judgments,

Miscellaneous Poetry

Montalván reveals himself to be a great poet distinguished by the facility and beauty of his verse."

The words of Ada Godínez de Batlle, to put Montalván in a middle category, as neither one of the greatest poets of his day, nor one of the worst, seem to hit the mark. Montalván did appear to have poetic inspiration, from a very early age, and that poetic ability is best judged in Montalván's lyric dramas, into which he put most of the effort of his short, active and feverish life.

CHAPTER 11

Conclusion

IT has already been pointed out several times that Montalván's incidental poetry made only a minor contribution to the *genre;* indeed the bulk of it, we remember, beyond the entries in poetic contests, is made up of repetitious praise on behalf of the writings of some friend or other, which may or may not be of merit. In the *Orpheus in the Castilian Language* (if it was Montalván's), to mention the longer, "epic" poem, there was little to place the work alongside the good compositions on the theme which have come forth from the pens of world authors up until the twentieth century.[1] In the novel, as is very evident, Montalván, generally speaking, is a follower of the most popular and violent elements in his predecessors and contemporaries,[2] and he achieved a resounding success in his lifetime, but not an enduring success, except in the rarest of cases. The *Life and Purgatory of St. Patrick*, as prose, has some value, but it is not outstanding, and is historically interesting. To use Esther Sylvia's words, "derived from old historical works, it forms part of that body of Spanish literature which kept alive Spain's pride in her Celtic influences."[3] *For Everybody,* from which the novels and plays can be extracted as self-supporting entities, is a worthy work of its kind and of historical interest also. Lope de Vega's *Posthumous Fame* is an unreliable "first" among the biographies of Spain's most distinguished dramatist.

If we remove these writings from outstanding praise and relegate them to a side position (without discarding them, however), there is left the drama of our precocious author, who "lived and died forcing time."[4] And it is in this dramatic output that we have found, as several chapters of this study have declared, a considerable amount of solid substance. Montalván's few *autos sacramentales*, written for Madrid's annual Corpus Christi celebrations, are not impressive, but many of his three-act *comedias*, always in verse as was the custom,[5]

Conclusion

are. Intent on providing entertainment above all, and to some extent a moral lesson, Montalván's main weakness was that he tried to imitate Lope de Vega in fecundity, taking less care and pause in writing than he should have done. Listed in favorable terms by the late seventeenth-century Nicolás Antonio,[6] and in the Neo-classical eighteenth century still having his plays performed,[7] Montalván caught the attention of critics in the nineteenth century, and in the journals they made mention of him, sometimes in glowing words and sometimes with a more moderate assessment.[8] Ramón de Mesonero Romanos, in writing of dramatists contemporary to Lope de Vega, was high in praise of Juan Pérez de Montalván, awarding him "perhaps the first place among our dramatists of second rank."[9] For Mesonero Romanos those of first rank were six: Lope de Vega, Calderón de la Barca, Moreto, Tirso de Molina, Rojas Zorrilla and Ruiz de Alarcón (modern critics would probably make them four: Lope, Calderón, Tirso and Alarcón); but however one looks at it, Mesonero Romanos was holding Montalván very high. Among his many complimentary words he says emphatically that "with the exception of Tirso de Molina and Moreto, perhaps from no other author of our theater could one extract so many very beautiful passages of elocution, so many lofty thoughts, tender or satiric, clothed in correct verses, which are inspired and full of the most excellent poetry."

The German critic of the same century, von Schack, is less flattering, however: "Montalván's dramas have, no doubt, their beauties, but not sufficient, neither for their importance nor for their brilliance, to be assigned first rank in this literary *genre*.... His works do not excel for any individual characteristic feature, not for any, at least, worthy of praise, and perhaps nothing else can be said of them except that their most notable characteristic is that of an insipid and swollen loquacity, on account of their rhetorical and ostentatious style and on account of their lack of substance and of life."[10]

Surely Montalván's worth in drama lies between the overly enthusiastic opinion of Mesonero Romanos and the overly severe declaration of von Schack. *The Lovers of Teruel*, for example, has been shown to have very positive qualities; and indeed Esther Sylvia insists (p. 470) that "[Montalván's] dramatic interpretation of the romantic tale was not to be surpassed until the nineteenth century." The Cloak-and-Sword plays, so much the essence of the *Comedia*, are clearly at times among the best of their day, rivalling Calderón's in all the features pertaining to them. *The Waiting Maid, The Cap*

Seller of Biscay, Like a Lover and *Like an Honorable Woman*, to mention only three, contain all the entertaining characteristics desirable, including psychologically true characters. As to character depiction, Philip II of *The Second Seneca of Spain*, Don Juan of Austria, of the play of the same title, or the steadfast Isabel of *The Most Devoted Fiancée*, stand out as superior in Golden Age production. In the "comedia lopesca" tradition, *There Is No Life Like Honor* is an excellent play, and it is not surprising that when first put on the boards it enjoyed simultaneous performances in both public theaters of Madrid, and was one of Montalván's plays which in the Americas was far more successful than even Lope de Vega's plays. Likewise as an example of an honor play — and honor, advocated by Lope de Vega in his *New Art of Writing Plays*, was the most common theme in Golden Age drama — *For a Punishment a Double Vengeance* is a very good one, and here the dénouement is unconventional in that a jilted young woman kills both her former lover and an adulterous wife.

"Montalván" wrote Esther Sylvia, p. 470, "is frequently called a transition dramatist, one of those who bridged the gap between Lope de Vega and Calderón; but the position has not been made very clear. Neither is it logical to couple this with the conclusion that Montalván's place is that of an imitator who fell short of his model, Lope. He must have possessed characteristics which connected him with Calderón too, who accepted him as a collaborator." Maria Grazia Profeti notes this collaboration with Calderón as evidence of their ever increasing closeness in their manner of writing, and she mentions various characteristics in Montalván which are Calderonian: such as the repetition of motifs and situations in plays and the use of parallel constructions (see *Montalbán*, p. 58, p. 61). In *The Children of Fortune* (a spectacular play, probably late, 1634-35?), for instance, Profeti feels that we are "quite far from the *Comedia nueva* of Lope de Vega," and finds in such a play an "intellectual and refined art" and "motifs and techniques" which are Calderón's unmistakeably. In fact, Profeti makes strong claim for a "progressive stylization" ("progressivo stilizzarsi") in Montalván, an evolution to Calderón which is evident, through promise of things to come, even in the early and middle Montalván productions. However, Dixon, in the review of the Profeti monograph (p. 187) warns that such a possible evolution or progression in dramatic style "can hardly be studied without some attempt at a better chronology of the plays than we at present possess" and that "Montalbán's con-

Conclusion

tribution to the changes in styles cannot be clarified without reference to the part played by Tirso, Alarcón, Mira, the later Lope. . . ."

Victor Dixon would not agree with the idea that Montalván became a member of the Calderón camp out and out; but he does see his progress beyond the immediate cycle of Lope de Vega. For Dixon, Montalván falls "between two schools"; and in a survey of Spanish studies, 1971, Drama, in *The Year's Work in Modern Language Studies*,[11] Dixon commended Profeti for her monograph, saying that "her attempt, through Juan Pérez de Montalbán, to trace 'un itinerario della commedia dei primi anni del Seicento' is a welcome corrective to interpretations of its development in terms merely of two sharply differentiated personalities." Indeed, Montalván's position in the history of Spanish drama is well put by Esther Sylvia. "Montalván had neither Lope's gift for depicting life, nor Calderón's aptness for converting philosophy into presentable drama; he met the requirements of his public, and in so doing mirrored the changing trends. In his attempts at character delineation, especially of heroines, in his choice and range of subjects, and in his fight against elaborate expression he was following Lope. But in his lack of emotional quality, in his use of stock characters, in his portrayal almost exclusively of the upper classes, and in his lapses into 'culteranismo' he was approaching the unreal, ornamental and witty drama [of the Calderón school]" (pp. 470-71).

Montalván, then, does not belong to Lope de Vega, nor to Calderón de la Barca. He does not have Lope's *acierto* nor Calderón's *cerebralismo*, and only in a limited sense does he possess a *diligencia* so far as it pertains to keeping at the job. While Montalván has not that characteristic in the Calderonian application of a "capacity for careful calculation," he does anticipate Calderón's intellectualism and refinement while still retaining a freshness and a spontaneity which was Lope's.[12] Juan Pérez de Montalván is, as Profeti would insist (and Dixon points out this insistence in his review, p. 186), "a dramatist in his own right and a figure of significance in the development of the *comedia*."

Notes and References

Preface

1. Montalván (or Montalbán), a surname which came from the paternal grandmother's family, was not added until about 1620. This addition may be part of the reason for Quevedo's attack on Juan for assuming aristocratic airs, which included a satiric verse (at least attributed to Quevedo, if not actually written by him):

> The "Doctor" you assume,
> The "Montalván" you presume;
> Taking the "Don" from your names,
> Naught but "Juan Pérez" remains.

(This translation is given by Esther Sylvia, "A Dramatist of Spain's Golden Age," *More Books* [Boston Public Library], XIII [1938]: 469. Juan Pérez was the name of a stage buffoon.) Since the continuing surname, Pérez (that of the father), is a very common one, modern critics usually refer to the dramatist as Montalván (or Montalbán).

Regarding the spelling "Montalván" or "Montalbán": In the seventeenth century there was inconsistency between "b" and "v" (or "u"). Montalván's own spelling of his name in the signature at the end of the partially autograph MS of *The Most Sacred Host of Alcalá* (Biblioteca Nacional, Madrid) clearly has a "v"; although the autograph MS of *The Knight of Phoebus* (Biblioteca Palatina, Parma) has a "b." I prefer the "v", which is found in many printings of the name in Montalván's time. Montalván himself was apparently inconsistent, and modern critics employ both spellings of the surname.

We possess three portraits of the author: Montalván at 23 (reproduced in the first edition of *Orpheus in the Castilian Language* and of the Novels, both dated 1624); Montalván at 29 (reproduced in the first edition of *For Everybody*, 1632, and in the First Volume of plays, 1635); and Montalván at 36 (in the *Panegyric Tears*, 1639).

2. Victor Dixon, "Juan Pérez de Montalbán's *Para todos*," *Hispanic Review*, XXXII (1964): 59.

3. Maria Grazia Profeti, *Montalbán: un commediografo dell'età di Lope* (Pisa: Università di Pisa, 1970), p. 79.

4. Victor Dixon, *Bulletin of Hispanic Studies*, XLIX (1972): 186.
5. Edward Glaser, "Quevedo versus Pérez de Montalván: The *Auto del Polifemo* and the Odyssean Tradition in Golden Age Spain," *Hispanic Review*, XXVIII (1960): 120.
6. Joaquín de Entrambasaguas, *Estudios sobre Lope de Vega*, II (Madrid: CSIC, 1947), p. 74, note 49.

Chapter One

1. George William Bacon, "The Life and Dramatic Works of Doctor Juan Pérez de Montalván (1602-1638)," *Revue Hispanique*, XXVI (1912): 1-474. This supersedes the briefer treatment by Bacon which had appeared previously in his *An Essay upon the Life and Works of Juan Pérez de Montalván* (Philadelphia: University of Pennsylvania, 1903). Ada Godínez de Batlle's "Labor literaria del Dr. Juan Pérez de Montalván," *Revista de la Facultad de Letras y Ciencias*, Universidad de la Habana, XXX (1920): 1-151, adds little to Bacon except a few pages on "Montalván lírico" and "Montalván novelista."
2. Constant references will be made to Dixon's findings as presented in his important articles on Montalván. Unfortunately Dixon's doctoral dissertation of Cambridge University, 1959, *The Life and Works of Juan Pérez de Montalbán, With Special Reference to His Plays*, has not been published.
3. See the Profeti monograph (already mentioned in the Preface), *Montalbán: un commediografo dell'età di Lope* (Pisa: Università di Pisa, 1970), and other studies which will be cited later.
4. Victor Dixon, "Juan Pérez de Montalbán's *Segundo tomo de las comedias*," *Hispanic Review*, XXIX (1961): 96, note 22. The article covers pages 91-109.
5. See Cristóbal Pérez Pastor, *Bibliografía madrileña*, III (Madrid: Los Huérfanos, 1907): 451-53.
6. Francisco Maldonado de Guevera, "El incidente Avellaneda," *Anales Cervantinos*, V (1955-56): 41-62. (The article had been previously published in *Revista de Ideas Estéticas*, VIII [1950]: 243-71). Rafael Sánchez Mariño adds a note, "Sobre Alonso Pérez de Montalbán y el falso *Quijote*," in the same number of *Anales Cervantinos*, pp. 274-75, to support Maldonado's theory. This note is from the former's unpublished thesis (see note 22).
7. Bacon ("Life," p. 29) explains the choice of the title: "That Quevedo should have employed so odd a title is due to the fact that the author is supposed to be a teetotum, which has seen and heard what it narrates."
8. Edward Glaser, op. cit., 105. Glaser points particularly on this occasion to the article by José Simón Díaz, "Los *Sucesos y prodigios de amor* de Pérez de Montalbán vistos por la Inquisición," *Revista Bibliográfica y Documental*, II (1948), Suplemento No. 2, pp. 1-6.
9. ". . . Pérez de Montalván, in spite of his origin, identified himself completely with Catholic values." — Edward Glaser, "*El divino portugués*

San Antonio de Padua," in *Estudios Hispano-portugueses: Relaciones literarias del Siglo de Oro* (Valencia: Editorial Castalia, 1957), p. 177.

10. See Victor Dixon's previously mentioned review of Maria Grazia Profeti's 1970 monograph in *Bulletin of Hispanic Studies*, p. 187.

11. Dixon, "Segundo tomo," p. 95, note 19.

12. Pérez Pastor, op. cit., III: 451.

13. For information on this Peruvian benefactor, see Irving A. Leonard, "Pérez de Montalbán, Tomás de Gutiérrez and Two Book Lists," *Hispanic Review*, XII (1944): 275-87.

14. *Justa poética y alabanzas justas que hizo la insigne Villa de Madrid al bienventurado San Isidro en las fiestas de su Beatificación, recopiladas por Lope de Vega Carpio* (Madrid: Viuda de Alonso Martín, 1620). An index to this and other *Justas poéticas* has been published by José Simón Díaz and Luciana Calvo Ramos in *Siglos de Oro: Índice de justas poéticas* (Madrid, CSIC, 1962).

15. *Relación de las fiestas que ha hecho el Colegio Imperial de la Compañía de Jesús de Madrid en la Canonización de San Ignacio de Loyola y S. Francisco Xavier. Por don Fernando de Monforte y Herrera* (Madrid: Luis Sánchez, 1622).

16. *Relación de las fiestas que la insigne Villa de Madrid hizo en la Canonización de su bienaventurado hijo y patrón San Isidro, con las comedias que se representaron y los versos que en la Justa Poética se escribieron* (Madrid: Viuda de Alonso Martín, 1622).

17. "Textos dispersos de clásicos españoles. VIII. Pérez de Montalbán," *Revista de Literatura*, XVIII (1960): 291, item No. 11.

18. *Las fiestas solemnes y grandiosas que hizo la Sagrada Religión de N. Señora de la Merced, en este su Convento de Madrid, a su glorioso Patriarca y primero fundador san Pedro Nolasco, este año de 1629. Por el Padre Maestro Fray Alonso Remón* (Madrid: Imprenta del Reino, 1630).

19. José Simón Díaz has printed six of these "approvals" in his listing of "Textos dispersos" (Nos. 22, 23, 24, 25, 26, 27), from that of Lope de Vega's *Parte XX de las Comedias* (September 20, 1624) through works of Alonso de Castillo Solórzano, Grabiel Padecopeo, Tirso de Molina and Fernando Pérez Pericón, to Pedro de Oña's *El Ignacio de Cantabria* (undated "aprobación"; work published in 1639).

20. "Montano en Manzanares" is found in the ending of the sacramental play *El caballero del Febo* (The Knight of Phoebus); "Montano," as already noted, is used in *Para todos* (For Everybody); and Montalván is called "Montano" at least twice in the *Lágrimas panegíricas* (Panegyric Tears).

21. For the importance of academies (literary circles) of the day, see, for example, José Sánchez, *Academias literarias del Siglo de Oro español* (Madrid: Gredos, 1961); and Willard F. King, "The Academies and Seventeenth-Century Spanish Literature," *Publications of the Modern Language Association of America*, LXXV (1960): 367-76; and by the same

author, *Prosa novelística y academias literarias en el siglo XVII* (Madrid: Real Academia Española, 1963).

22. Rafael Sánchez Mariño, *Alonso Pérez de Montalbán: Su importancia en el círculo literario de Lope de Vega.* Unpublished doctoral dissertation, Universidad de Madrid, 1955.

23. See Hugo Albert Rennert, *The Life of Lope de Vega (1562-1635)* (Glasgow: Gowans and Gray, 1904), p. 413.

24. See Entrambasaguas, op. cit., p. 73. Medinilla, a poet from Toledo, born in 1585, was killed in that city on June 28, 1620.

25. Lope de Vega, in the above-mentioned will, speaks of Montalván as one "whom I have loved and held dear as a son."

26. See J. H. Parker, "Lope de Vega and Juan Pérez de Montalván: Their Literary Relations (A Preliminary Survey)," *Hispanic Studies in Honour of I. González Llubera*, ed. Frank Pierce (Oxford: Dolphin, 1959), pp. 225-35.

27. For example, Rubén Darío, in his autobiography (1912): "I realize that I can well be mistaken, from time to time, in matters of date, and may anticipate or postpone the sequence of events . . ." — *Obras completas*, I (Madrid: Aguado, 1950), p. 61.

28. From Lope de Vega's *Laurel de Apolo*, 1630.

29. Antonio Papell, *Quevedo: Su tiempo, su vida, su obra* (Barcelona: Barna, 1947), p. 130.

30. Satire on obscurity was the crux of the matter in Montalván's (?) *Orfeo en lengua castellana* (Orpheus in the Castilian Language), 1624. See the later discussion.

31. Cayetano Alberto de la Barrera y Leirado, *Catálogo bibliográfico y biográfico del teatro antiguo español* (Madrid: Rivadeneyra, 1860), p. 265.

32. Maldonado de Guevara, op. cit., p. 62.

33. Victor Dixon reminds us that in *For Everybody* Montalván speaks of a "crisis" which overtook him before he turned to compile that book, around 1631, a strange disinclination to write any more plays. Dixon, referring to the later polemic centering around *For Everybody*, has written: "The added strain of this new rivalry, following closely on the crisis which had produced *Para todos*, must have been among the causes of the mental affliction which was soon to overtake him and bring him to an early grave." See Dixon, "*Para todos*," op. cit., p. 59.

34. *Lágrimas panegíricas a la temprana muerte del gran poeta y teólogo insigne Doctor Juan Pérez de Montalván . . . Lloradas y vertidas por los más ilustres ingenios de España. Recogidas y publicadas por el licenciado don Pedro Grande de Tena* (Madrid: Imprenta del Reino, 1639).

35. Luis Astrana Marín, *La vida turbulenta de Quevedo*, 2nd ed. (Madrid: Gran Capitán, 1945), p. 471.

36. Ruth Lee Kennedy, *The Dramatic Art of Moreto*, Smith College Studies in Modern Languages, XIII (Northampton, Mass., 1931-32), p. 23. Moreto's "neighbor" in the panegyric volume, Gaspar Buesso de Arnal, is the subject of an article by Titus Heydenreich, "Gaspar Buessos poetischer

Notes and References

Nachruf auf Juan Pérez de Montalbán (1638/39)," *Romanische Forschungen*, 84 (1972): 45-76. Buesso de Arnal reminds us, in a later work, of his "Canción" to the memory of Montalván, and mentions that Juan, his reason gone, "died in the arms of his father."

Chapter Two

1. General information on the Spanish *comedia* may be found in many places. For example, the characteristics of the *comedia*, including the *autos sacramentales*, have been given to us by Everett W. Hesse in his volume on *Pedro Calderón de la Barca* (Twayne, 1967); the stage of Montalván's day and the staging of plays have been described by Francis M. Hayes in *Lope de Vega* (Twayne, 1967); and the historical background to the Montalván period, the first third of the seventeenth century, is discussed by Donald W. Bleznick in *Quevedo* (Twayne, 1972). Among other very useful studies might be mentioned: Charles Vincent Aubrun, *La Comédie espagnole (1600-1680)* (Paris: Presses Universitaires de France, 1966); H. J. Chaytor, *Dramatic Theory in Spain* (Cambridge: The University Press, 1925); J. P. W. Crawford, *Spanish Drama Before Lope de Vega*, rev. ed. with a Bibliographical Supplement by Warren T. McCready (Philadelphia: University of Pennsylvania Press, 1967); Cyril A. Jones, "Some Ways of Looking at Spanish Golden Age Comedy," in *Homenaje a William L. Fichter: Estudios sobre el teatro antiguo español y otros ensayos*, ed. A. David Kossoff and José Amor y Vázquez (Madrid: Castalia, 1971), pp. 329-39; Sturgis E. Leavitt, *An Introduction to Golden Age Drama in Spain*, Estudios de Hispanófila, vol. 19 (Chapel Hill: Romance Languages, University of North Carolina, 1971); Alexander A. Parker, *The Approach to the Spanish Drama of the Golden Age*, colección Diamante, No. 6 (London: The Hispanic and Luso-Brazilian Councils, 1957), reprinted in *Tulane Drama Review*, IV (1959): 42-59; Alexander A. Parker, *The Allegorical Drama of Calderón. An Introduction to the "Autos sacramentales"* (Oxford: Dolphin, 1968); Arnold G. Reichenberger, "The Uniqueness of the *Comedia*," *Hispanic Review*, XXVII (1959): 303-16; followed by Eric Bentley, "The Universality of the *Comedia*," *Hispanic Review*, XXXVIII (1970): 147-62, and in the same number, Reichenberger's "The *Comedia*: Universality or Uniqueness?", pp. 163-73; Gerald E. Wade, "The Interpretation of the *Comedia*," *Bulletin of the Comediantes*, XI, No. 1 (1959): 1-6; Bruce W. Wardropper, *Introducción al teatro religioso del Siglo de Oro: Evolución del Auto sacramental antes de Calderón* (Salamanca: Anaya, 1967); Edward M. Wilson and Duncan Moir, *A Literary History of Spain. The Golden Age: Drama 1492-1700* (London: Ernest Benn; New York: Barnes and Noble, 1971); and Margaret Wilson, *Spanish Drama of the Golden Age* (Oxford: Pergamon, 1969). For the technicalities of the Stage and Staging, the monographs by Rennert and Shergold are standard works (see notes 12 and 21, below).

2. Dixon has made good progress in a laudable intention: "I had hoped

— I still hope — to determine so far as possible which of the hundred-odd plays attributed to Juan Pérez de Montalbán were in fact written by him" ("*Segundo tomo*," p. 91).

3. Walter Poesse, *Juan Ruiz de Alarcón* (New York: Twayne, 1972), p. 36.

4. Jack Horace Parker, "The Chronology of the Plays of Juan Pérez de Montalván," *Publications of the Modern Language Association of America*, LXVII (1952): 186-210.

5. A modern printing of the play — and Montalván's drama generally speaking has not been printed in modern times — can be found in Federico Carlos Sainz de Robles, *El teatro español: Historia y antología (Desde sus orígenes hasta el siglo XIX)*, IV (Madrid: Aguilar, 1943), pp. 509-80. Sainz de Robles characterizes this play as Montalván's "most perfect and moving work" (p. 509, note).

6. Federico Carlos Sainz de Robles, "El ciclo dramático de Lope de Vega," *Historia general de las literaturas hispánicas*, ed. Guillermo Díaz-Plaja, III (Barcelona: Barna, 1953): 264-95. Montalván: pp. 281-85. Quotation: p. 282.

7. On the three plays of the Philip II cycle, see Profeti, *Montalbán*, pp. 86-89; also, Angel Valbuena Prat, "El tema de Felipe II en el teatro de Montalbán," *Historia de la literatura española*, 3rd ed., II (Barcelona: Gili, 1950): 382-86.

8. G. W. Bacon, "The *comedia El segundo Séneca de España* of Dr. Juan Pérez de Montalván," *Romanic Review*, I (1910): 64-86, and "Life," pp. 358-67.

9. Noël Salomon, *Recherches sur le thème paysan dans la "Comedia" au temps de Lope de Vega* (Bordeaux: Institut d'Études Ibériques et Ibero-Américaines de l'Université de Bordeaux, 1965), pp. 94, 126, 152, 807.

10. Text can be found in *Comedias escogidas del Dr. Don Juan Pérez de Montalván*, I (Madrid: Ortega, 1827): 273-394; in *Teatro escogido desde el siglo XVII hasta nuestros días*, I (Paris: Baudry, 1838): 161-89; in Eugenio de Ochoa, *Tesoro del teatro español desde su origen (año de 1356) hasta nuestros días*, IV (Paris: Baudry, 1838): 161-89; in *Colección selecta del antiguo teatro español* (Paris: C. Denné Schmitz, 1854): 432-53; and in *Biblioteca de Autores Españoles*, XLV (Madrid: Rivadeneyra, 1858): 477-94.

11. Victor Dixon has remarked correctly ("*Segundo tomo*," p. 108): "Now the fully-developed *gracioso* is found in every authentic play by Montalbán."

12. For an account of this famous actress, see Hugo Albert Rennert, *The Spanish Stage in the Time of Lope de Vega* (New York: Hispanic Society, 1909), pp. 421-22.

13. Romualdo Álvarez Espino, *Ensayo histórico-crítico del teatro español* (Cádiz: Rodríguez y Rodríguez, 1876), pp. 145-49.

14. See J. H. Parker, "A Possible Source of a *jeu de scène* in Molière's *École des maris*," *Modern Language Notes*, LV (1940): 453-54. Leonor

gives her hand, behind her back, to Carlos to kiss while she greets Fernando at their first meeting. Molière's action is similar.

15. See Rodrigo de Carvajal y Robles, *Fiestas de Lima por el nacimiento del Príncipe Baltasar Carlos (Lima, 1632)*, ed. Francisco López Estrada (Seville: Escuela de Estudios Hispano-Americanos, 1950), pp. 51-52.

16. See Irving A. Leonard, "Montalbán's *El valor perseguido* and the Mexican Inquisition, 1682," *Hispanic Review*, XI (1943): 50, note 11; and Victor Dixon, "*La mayor confusión*," *Hispanófila*, No. 3 (1958), p. 24, note 16.

17. For an account of the famous theatrical director (*autor de comedias*) Roque de Figueroa, see Rennert, *Spanish Stage*, pp. 473-74.

18. Available in Montalván, *Comedias escogidas*, II (Madrid: Ortega, 1831): 119-232; and in *Biblioteca de Autores Españoles*, op. cit., XLV: 495-511.

19. In the dedication of *Cumplir con su obligación*, First Volume of plays, to Gaspar Alonso de Guzmán el Bueno.

20. See Guillermo Lohmann Villena and Raul Moglia, "Repertorio de las representaciones teatrales en Lima hasta el siglo XVIII," *Revista de Filología Hispánica*, V (1943): 325.

21. For a description of Corpus Christi processions and the staging of the *autos* (as well as *comedias* in general), see N. D. Shergold, *A History of the Spanish Stage from Medieval Times until the End of the Seventeenth Century* (Oxford: Clarendon Press, 1967); in addition to Rennert, op. cit.

22. *Polyphemus*, in Spanish, is available in *Piezas maestras del teatro teológico español*, ed. Nicolás González Ruiz, 3rd. ed., I (Madrid: Biblioteca de Autores Cristianos, 1968): 778-98.

23. The Glaser discussion is to be found in his article on "Quevedo versus Pérez de Montalván," op. cit. Glaser notes (p. 105) that Quevedo was entirely serious: "Quevedo's remarks are not merely entertaining gibes. The author affirms in all earnestness that he is concerned with gross errors that warrant Inquisitorial intervention."

24. See also Profeti's discussion of Montalván's *autos* in *Montalbán*, pp. 107-10.

25. Maria Grazia Profeti, "Il manoscritto autografo del *Caballero del Febo* di Juan Pérez de Montalbán" *Miscellanea di Studi Hispanici* (Pisa: Università di Pisa, 1966-67), pp. 218-309. This *auto* was listed by Antonio Restori in his description of "La collezione CC* IV.28033 della Biblioteca Palatina-Parmense," *Studj di Filologia Romanza*, VI (1893): 86-87.

Chapter Three

1. The "Prólogo largo" is reproduced, from the *Primero tomo de las comedias*, Alcalá, 1638, by Alberto Porqueras Mayo in *El prólogo en el Manierismo y Barroco españoles* (Madrid: CSIC, 1968), pp. 155-57. In "Una nueva aprobación de Tirso de Molina," *Estudios*, VI (1950): 349-52, G. Placer López reproduces Tirso's approval of Montalván's first volume of

plays, although the author of the article speaks only of the 1638, Alcalá, printing.

2. For this and other examples of materials used from play to play or in novel to play, or vice versa, see Dixon, "*Para todos,*" pp. 42-43. Other dramatists were wont to make use of this process also. A striking example is that of Tirso de Molina: Gerald E. Wade, "Tirso's Self-Plagiarism in Plot," *Hispanic Review,* IV (1936): 55-65.

3. See, for example, Florence L. Yudin, "The *novela corta* as *comedia:* Lope's *Las fortunas de Diana,*" *Bulletin of Hispanic Studies,* XLV (1968): 181-88.

4. For example, in *Orpheus:*

> Canté, lloré, mové tu Reina hermosa,
> gané, tuve, gocé mi prenda amada . . . ;

in *The Son of the Seraphim:*

> Amé, pené, sufrí su tiranía,
> Canté, lloré, temí su rigor fiero. . . . .

5. The text may be found in *Comedias escogidas* of Montalván, op. cit., I: 3-142; and in *Biblioteca de Autores Españoles,* op. cit., XLV: 551-70.

6. Mendoza's characteristics are noted by Charles David Ley, *El gracioso en el teatro de la Península (Siglos XVI-XVII)* (Madrid: Revista de Occidente, 1954), pp. 172-73.

7. For the importance and popularity of this kind of "disguised" rôle in the *Comedia,* see Carmen Bravo-Villasante, *La mujer vestida de hombre en el teatro español (Siglos XVI-XVII)* (Madrid: Revista de Occidente, 1955).

8. The text is in *Teatro antiguo español* (Madrid: D. F. Grimaud de Velaunde, 1837); and in *Biblioteca de Autores Españoles,* op. cit., XLV: 587-604.

9. Francisco de Quevedo, *Obras completas. I. Obras en prosa,* ed. Felicidad Buendía (Madrid: Aguilar, 1961), p. 457(b).

10. Winifred Smith, "The Maréchal de Biron on the Stage," *Modern Philology,* XX (1923): 301-38.

11. The text is available in *Comedias escogidas* of Montalván, op. cit., I: 143-272; in *Teatro escogido desde el siglo XVII hasta nuestros días,* op. cit., I: 189-219; in Eugenio de Ochoa, *Tesoro del teatro español desde su origen (año de 1356) hasta nuestros días,* op. cit., IV: 189-219; and in *Biblioteca de Autores Españoles,* op. cit., XLV: 513-31.

12. Raymond R. MacCurdy, *Spanish Drama of the Golden Age: Twelve Plays* (New York: Appleton-Century-Crofts, 1971), p. 268.

13. See Françoise Capdet and Jean-Louis Flecniakoska, "Le Bâtard Don Juan d'Autriche personnage de théâtre," in Jean Jacquot, Elie Konigson and Marcel Oddon, eds., *Dramaturgie et société. Rapports entre l'oeuvre*

théâtrale, son interprétation et son public aux XVIe et XVIIe siècles (Paris: Centre National de la Recherche Scientifique, 1968), pp. 125-32.

14. Emilio Cotarelo y Mori, "Sobre el origen y desarrollo de la leyenda de los Amantes de Teruel," *Revista de Archivos, Bibliotecas y Museos*, VIII (1903): 347-77. See also Caroline B. Bourland, "Boccaccio and the *Decameron* in Castilian and Catalan Literature," *Revue Hispanique*, XII (1905): 1-232 (especially pp. 99-114).

15. For example, Jaime Caruana y Gómez de Barreda, an historian of the region, makes a special point of rejecting Cotarelo's assertion in *Los Amantes de Teruel*, 3rd. ed. (Valencia: Ecir., 1963).

16. Tirso de Molina, *Obras dramáticas completas*, I (Madrid: Aguilar, 1946): cxxxii.

17. See, for example, Hildegart Rodríguez Carballeiro, *Tres amores históricos: Estudio comparativo de los amores de Romeo y Julieta, Abelardo y Heloisa y los Amantes de Teruel* (Teruel: Ediciones de la Diputación, 1930). The author, writing under the name "Hildegart," analyses Montalván's play, pp. 223-47.

Chapter Four

1. The key study — already mentioned several times previously — to this Second Volume is Victor Dixon's "Juan Pérez de Montalbán's *Segundo tomo de las comedias*," *Hispanic Review*, XXIX (1961): 91-109.

2. En Madrid. En la Imprenta del Reino. Año 1638. A costa de Alonso Pérez de Montalván, Librero de Su Majestad, y padre del Autor.

3. In Glaser, "*El divino portugués San Antonio de Padua*," op. cit., pp. 133-77.

4. *El sufrimiento premiado. Comedia famosa. Atribuida en esta edición, por primera vez, a Lope de Vega Carpio, con prólogo y notas de Victor Dixon* (London: Tamesis Books, 1967).

5. Mabel M. Harlan, *The Relation of Moreto's "El desdén con el desdén" to Suggested Sources*, Indiana University Studies, XI (Bloomington, Indiana, 1924), pp 85-86.

Chapter Five

1. The plots of these plays and some notes on them are given by Bacon ("Life").

2. S. Griswold Morley and Courtney Bruerton, *Cronología de las comedias de Lope de Vega* (Madrid: Gredos, 1968). (A revision of *The Chronology of Lope de Vega's "Comedias"* [New York: Modern Language Association, 1940].)

3. Alberto Porqueras Mayo and Federico Sánchez Escribano, "Las ideas dramáticas de Pellicer de Tovar," *Revista de Filología Española*, XLVI (1963): 137-48. Quotation: pp. 137-38.

4. Maria Grazia Profeti, "Il Pellicer e la sua *Idea de la Comedia de Castilla deducida de las obras cómicas del doctor Juan Pérez de Montalbán*,"

Miscellanea di Studi Ispanici (Pisa: Università di Pisa, 1966-67), pp. 170-217. Quotation: p. 198.

5. The 1635 treatise, "one of the most original and systematic treatises of dramatic theory possessed by the Spanish Golden Age" (Porqueras Mayo and Sánchez Escribano, op. cit., p. 137), can be found in Sánchez, *Academias literarias*, pp. 82-89; or in Federico Sánchez Escribano and Alberto Porqueras Mayo, *Preceptiva dramática española del Renacimiento y el Barroco*, 2nd. ed. (Madrid: Gredos, 1971), pp. 263-72. For a further comparison of the two treatises, see Jean Canavaggio, "Réflexions sur l'*Idea de la Comedia de Castilla*," in *Mélanges de la Casa de Velázquez*, II (1966): 199-223.

Chapter Six

1. Let me repeat Dixon's words on the problem: "I had hoped — I still hope — to determine so far as possible which of the hundred-odd plays attributed to Juan Pérez de Montalbán were in fact written by him" ("*Segundo tomo*," p. 91). Maria Grazia Profeti, in her monograph of 1970 *(Montalbán)*, discusses some forty plays.

2. See Raúl A. Del Piero, "La respuesta de Pérez de Montalbán a la *Perinola* de Quevedo," *Publications of the Modern Language Association of America*, LXXVI (1961): 46. The article, which gives the text of *The Trumpet*, covers pp. 40-47.

3. Raymond R. MacCurdy, *Francisco de Rojas Zorrilla* (New York: Twayne, 1968), p. 25.

4. Profeti *(Montalbán)* skilfully examines Montalbán's characters. See p. 148 passim.

5. Coats of arms, mentioned in several Montalbán plays, are carefully studied by Warren T. McCready in *La heráldica en las obras de Lope de Vega y sus contemporáneos* (Toronto: Private, 1962), pp. 319-28. "Victor Dixon," writes McCready, p. 325, "in his recent article on Pérez de Montalbán's *Segundo tomo* has convinced us that the text *El sufrimiento premiado* attributed to Montalbán is in reality Lope de Vega's play."

6. "Now the fully-developed *gracioso* is found in every authentic play by Montalbán; but he has notoriously not yet appeared in Lope's early plays — in all those before 1593, and many of those before 1604" (Dixon, "*Segundo tomo*," p. 108). Also in the edition of 1967, pp. xviii-xix: "the lack of a full-fledged *gracioso* would be very notable in a play [later than the turn of the century] by Lope or another author." For further light on the subject, see J. H. Arjona, "La introducción del gracioso en el teatro de Lope de Vega," *Hispanic Review*, VII (1939): 1-21.

7. The Morley and Tyler study referred to is S. Griswold Morley and Richard W. Tyler, *Los nombres de personajes en las comedias de Lope de Vega. Estudio de onomatología*, University of California Publications in Modern Philology, No. 55 (Berkeley-Los Angeles: University of California Press, 1961). Although Montalbán is not one of the five dramatists treated

specifically, very useful is Juana de José Prades, *Teoría sobre los personajes de la Comedia Nueva, en cinco dramaturgos* (Madrid: CSIC, 1963). (Anejos de la *Revista de Literatura*, 20.)

8. See the previously mentioned J. H. Parker, "*La Gitanilla* de Montalván: Enigma literario del siglo XVII," op. cit., pp. 409-14. A short résumé of a paper read at the Congress, Oxford University, September, 1962.

9. Eduardo Juliá Martínez, ed., Antonio de Solís, *Amor y obligación* (Madrid: Hernando, 1930), p. lxiii.

10. Note the common confusion of titles: *La Gitanilla*, *La Gitanilla de Madrid;* for Antonio de Solís y Rivadeneyra (1610-86) has a very well known *Gitanilla de Madrid*.

11. Aubrun, p. 72: "[Montalván] put on the stage Cervantes' *La Gitanilla* . . ."; Alborg, II: 349: "Montalbán also cultivated . . . the novelesque *comedia*, putting on the stage Cervantes' *La Gitanilla*."

12. J. H. Parker, *La Gitanilla*, an edition, unpublished Ph.D. thesis, University of Toronto, 1941.

13. See Emilio Cotarelo y Mori, "*La Estrella de Sevilla* es de Lope de Vega," *Revista de la Biblioteca, Archivo y Museo del Ayuntamiento de Madrid*, VII (1930): 13: "a *suelta*, with indications of being from Seville . . . on account of the excessive size of the letters of the word *Comedia*, a common occurrence for printings of *sueltas* produced in Seville, different from those of Madrid, in which the word did not differ from the others of the title."

14. Everett W. Hesse, in reviewing the H. C. Heaton edition of *La cruz en la sepultura*, in *Hispanic Review*, XVIII (1950): 185, speaks of the "Gran Memoria," "who was unable to recall all the lines and hence in several places composed his own verses."

15. Francisco A. Icaza, *Las novelas ejemplares de Cervantes* (Madrid: Sucesores de Rivadeneyra, 1901), p. 251.

16. *La Gitanilla* ("M"): red. 30.6%; rom. 50.3%; Ital. 13.2%. *La Gitanilla de Madrid* ("S"): red. 24%; rom. 66.8%; Ital. 4.2%. Plays of Lope de Vega of the early 1630's (see Morley-Bruerton, *Cronología*) are not far from *La Gitanilla* ("M"). Plays of Calderón de la Barca of the mid-century (see H. W. Hilborn, *A Chronology of the Plays of Don Pedro Calderón de la Barco* [Toronto: University of Toronto Press, 1938]) are not far from *La Gitanilla de Madrid* ("S"). The general tendency of seventeenth-century Spanish drama — to use fewer *redondillas* and Italianate lines and to increase the *versos de romance* — is very clear in a comparison of the versification of "M" and "S". See J. H. Parker, "The Versification of the *Comedias* of Antonio de Solís y Rivadeneyra," *Hispanic Review*, XVII (1949): 308-15.

17. Fredson Bowers, "Some Relations of Bibliography to Editorial Problems," *Studies in Bibliography*, III (1950-51): 52.

18. See Albert E. Sloman, *The Dramatic Craftsmanship of Calderón: His Use of Earlier Plays* (Oxford: Dolphin, 1958), pp. 250-77.

19. See Wade and Mayberry, *Bulletin of the Comediantes*, XIV, No. 1

(1962): 1-16; and María Rosa Lida de Malkiel, *Hispanic Review*, XXX (1962): 275-95. In his edition of *Tan largo me lo fiáis* (Madrid: Revista Estudios, 1967), Xavier A. Fernández vigorously declared his belief in the textual priority of *El Burlador*, which declaration is reiterated in "En torno al texto de *El burlador de Sevilla y Convidado de piedra*," *Segismundo*, Nos. 9-14 (1969-71): 1-417 (see p. 105 especially).

20. See his above-mentioned review of Bacon, *Modern Language Review*, IX (1914); 557.

21. *Comedias escogidas* (Madrid: Imprenta de Ortega, 1828), pp. 505-06.

22. Juan Pérez de Montalván, *El Orfeo en lengua castellana* (Madrid: Por la viuda de Alonso Martín, a costa de Alonso Pérez, mercader de libros, 1624).

23. William L. Fichter, "The Present State of Lope de Vega Studies," *Hispania*, XX (1937): 349.

24. Miguel Romera-Navarro, "Lope y su defensa de la pureza de la lengua y estilo poético," *Revue Hispanique*, LXXVII (1929): 296.

25. See J. H. Parker, "Lope de Vega, the *Orfeo* and the *estilo llano*," *Romanic Review*, XLIV (1953): 3-11.

26. See Maria Grazia Profeti's chapter on "Il problema dell'*Orfeo* ed il cultismo," where she speaks (*Montalbán*, p. 33) of the "'vexata quaestio' della paternità del poemetto, che tuttora si continua a dibattere."

27. Eustaquio Fernández de Navarrete, *Biblioteca de Autores Españoles*, XXXIII (Madrid: Rivadeneyra, 1871): xcv.

28. In the previously mentioned *Estudios sobre Lope de Vega*, op. cit., II: 168, note 12.

29. Pablo Cabañas, *El mito de Orfeo en la literatura española* (Madrid: CSIC, 1948), p. 180: "All the indications and a whole tradition point to the fact that Lope wrote the *Orpheus in the Castilian Language* signed by his pupil Juan Pérez de Montalbán." See also the Cabañas edition of the *Orfeo en lengua castellana* (Madrid: CSIC, 1948).

30. S. Griswold Morley, *The Pseudonyms and Literary Disguises of Lope de Vega*, University of California Publications in Modern Philology, XXXIII, No. 5 (Berkeley-Los Angeles: University of California Press, 1951), pp. 479-80.

31. "Little circumstances," such as the dedication of the *Orpheus in the Castilian Language* to Lope de Vega's friend, the Décima Musa, Doña Bernarda Ferreira de la Cerda, a Portuguese poetess, have been used by critics in favor of the Lope de Vega authorship. But it is to be noted that the "Décima Musa" was not named as "Doña Bernarda Ferreira de la Cerda" on the title page until the 1638 edition. Dixon ("*Segundo tomo*," p. 94, note 15) would identify the "Décima Musa" otherwise: "I suspect that the 'Décima Musa' of 1624 may have been Lope's 'Amarilis', Marta Nevares Santoyo. . . ."

32. Gerardo Diego, "El virtuoso divo Orfeo," *Revista de Occidente*, XIV (1926): 183.

33. *La trompa*, which exists in one manuscript only, a copy made in 1688 or 1689, in the British Museum, London, was printed for the first time in the previously mentioned article by Raúl A. Del Piero, in *Publications of the Modern Language Association of America*, LXXVI (1961): 40-47.

34. Note Victor Dixon's remark ("*Para todos*," p. 36, note 2): "We cannot show to the best of my knowledge, . . . that Montalbán had anything to do with the prohibition of Quevedo's works by the Inquisition. . . ."

35. In *Opúsculos histórico-literarios*, II (Madrid: CSIC, 1951): 64-94. Also published in *Estudios dedicados a Menéndez Pidal*, II (Madrid: CSIC, 1951): 409-53.

Chapter Seven

1. *La villana de Pinto* and *Los primos amantes* are available in *Biblioteca de Autores Españoles*, XXXIII (Madrid: Rivadeneyra, 1871): 525-50. Agustín González de Amezúa edited the *Eight Exemplary Novels* of 1624, with a good introduction, in 1949 (Madrid: La Sociedad de Bibliófilos Españoles). Amezúa's introduction was reprinted in his *Opúsculos histórico-literarios*, II (Madrid: CSIC, 1951): 48-63, as "Juan Pérez de Montalbán novelista." Fernando Gutiérrez published Montalván's *Novelas ejemplares* (containing *La villana de Pinto, La desgraciada amistad, Los primos amantes* and *Al cabo de los años mil*) in 1957 (Barcelona: Selecciones Bibliófilas). The Amezúa introduction is the best treatment available of the novels of Montalván; but they have also been referred to from time to time in various studies of Montalván, such as Godínez de Batlle's "Labor literaria," pp. 54-72; Profeti's *Montalbán*, pp. 17-31; and Wolfram Krömer's "Gattung und Wort *novela* im spanischen 17. Jahrhundert," *Romanische Forschungen*, LXXXI (1969): 381-434 (Montalván specifically, pp. 418-22).

2. Caroline B. Bourland, *The Short Story in Spain in the Seventeenth Century* (Northampton, Mass.: Smith College, 1927), p. 13 and pp. 15-16.

3. In the previously mentioned "*La mayor confusión*," *Hispanófila*, No. 3 (1958): 17-26.

4. Agustín González de Amezúa, *Formación y elementos de la novela cortesana* (Madrid: Tipografía de Archivos, 1929), p. 91.

5. See the previously mentioned article by José Simón Díaz, "*Los Sucesos y prodigios de amor* de Pérez de Montalbán vistos por la Inquisición," *Revista Bibliográfica y Documental*, II (1948), Suplemento No. 2, pp 1-6.

6. Edward C. Riley, in *Cervantes's Theory of the Novel* (Oxford: Clarendon, 1962), p. 196, refers to "the credibility of the event." "Credibility" did not seem to concern Montalván very much in his novels.

7. Joaquín Casalduero, in his *Sentido y forma de las novelas ejemplares*, 2nd ed. (Madrid: Gredos, 1969), p. 219, speaks of these trials and tribulations: "In all the love novels we have seen peripetias, struggles, sufferings . . ."

8. Caroline Bourland, in her above-mentioned monograph on *The Short*

Story in Spain in the Seventeenth Century, writes, p. 19, that "Letters, usually love letters, quoted in extenso are often introduced, as well as verses, which may be texts of serenades or of songs sung in social gatherings, poems recited for the entertainment of friends or used by lovers as vehicles to express their feelings of joy or of despair." Professor Bourland correctly speaks of the delaying and interruptive tactics such devices are.

9. Jean F.-A. Ricci, in *Cardenio et Célinde: Étude de littérature comparée* (Paris: Corti, 1947), discusses this novel in a section on "La nouvelle espagnole de Montalván (1624)," pp. 1-24, noting its philosophizing and moralizing: "The text is adorned with aphorisms which the reader is clearly invited to meditate upon" (p. 12). Ricci also mentions that this is the only story of the road to sainthood in the 1624 collection, as Teodoro relates how the road of love, with its prodigious happenings and here, supernatural interventions, leads him to his decision to become a monk.

10. Note the words of Juan Bautista Avalle-Arce, in his study of *La novela pastoril española* (Madrid: Revista de Occidente, 1959), p. 66: "The setting, in its special expression idealized. . . ."

11. Recognition ("agnición, conocimiento o reconocimiento") is discussed by Alfredo Hermenegildo in *Los trágicos españoles del siglo XVI* (Madrid: Fundación Universitaria Española, 1961), p. 51.

12. Ludwig Pfandl notices in Montalván's novels "the tendency towards horror" ("la tendencia a lo tremebundo") in his *Historia de la literatura nacional española en la Edad de Oro*, trans. Jorge Rubió Balaguer, 2nd ed. (Barcelona: Gili, 1952), p. 367. Twentieth-century horror movies could find inspiration in many of Montalván's scenes.

13. Dixon ("*Para todos*," p. 39 and note 12) is quoting Peter N. Dunn's *Castillo Solórzano and the Decline of the Spanish Novel* (Oxford: Blackwell, 1952), p. 17, as Dunn refers to the introduction to *Fiestas del jardín* (1634).

14. "A curious feature of this novel" writes Dixon, "*Para todos*," p. 43, "is the discourse on the Perfect Prince which is introduced on the pretext that the heroine required her suitor to prepare and deliver it. One is tempted to picture Montalbán discovering that he has one more little learned treatise than he needs for *Para todos*, and casting anxiously around for a place to 'work it in'."

15. For the Dutch translations, see J. A. van Praag, "Nederlandsche vertalingen van novellen van Juan Pérez de Montalbán," *Neophilologus*, XVI (1930): 9-11; with information also given in his review of Bourland, *Revista de Filología Española*, XVIII (1931): 267.

16. See *Colección selecta de antiguas novelas españolas*, VII (Madrid: Bibliófilos Españoles, 1907): 190.

17. *Vida y purgatorio del glorioso S. Patricio, arzobispo y primado de Hibernia* (Madrid: Luis Sánchez, a costa de Alonso Pérez, mercader de libros, 1627). Aprobación, January, 1627. Modern scholarship is indebted to Maria Grazia Profeti for providing a recent edition: Juan Pérez de Montalbán, *Vida y Purgatorio de San Patricio*. Introduzione, testo critico e note di M. G. Profeti. Istituto di Letteratura Spagnola e Ispano-Americana. Serie

Bibliografica, 23. (Pisa: Università di Pisa, 1972). Dr. Profeti points out that the *editio princeps* has disappeared (with no manuscript existing) and that the 1628 printings (Barcelona; and Madrid, definitively amended by Montalván) are the earliest available. Victor Dixon has prepared, for *Bulletin of Hispanic Studies*, a review of the Profeti edition and also an article on "Montalbán's *Vida y purgatorio de San Patricio*: Its Early Textual History." J. Eric Diehl promises a doctoral dissertation on the work: "Juan Pérez de Montalbán y el *Purgatorio de San Patricio*" (University of North Carolina, directed by J. B. Avalle-Arce) — *Hispania*, LVI (1973): 394.

18. Antonio G. Solalinde, "La primera versión española de *El purgatorio de San Patricio* y la difusión de esta leyenda en España," *Homenaje ofrecido a Menéndez Pidal*, II (Madrid: Editorial Hernando, 1925): 219-57.

19. *Historiae catholicae Hiberniae compendium*, Tome I, Book II (Lisbon: Craesbeeck, 1621).

20. Perhaps Richard Stanhurst, *De vita S. Patricii Hiberniae apostoli, libri duo* (an edition of Antwerp: Christophe Plantin, 1587); Fray Dimas Serpi, *Tratado de purgatorio* (Madrid. Luis Sánchez, for Alonso Pérez, 1617); and Thomas Messingham, *Florilegium insulae sanctorum* (Paris: Sébastien Cramoisy, 1624). See Léo Rouanet, *Drames religieux de Calderón* (Paris: A. Charles, 1898), p. 285.

21. George Philip Krapp, *The Legend of Saint Patrick's Purgatory: Its Later Literary History* (Baltimore: John Murphy, 1900), has commented (p. 11): "In Spanish literature the legend of the Purgatory took an interesting and original course of development. It was first given popular form by a writer of power and imagination: Juan Pérez de Montalván." More recently, Beatriz Elena Entenza de Solare, "Notas sobre *El purgatorio de San Patricio*," *Filología* (Buenos Aires), IV (1971): 31-52, has stated (p. 31) that Montalván's *Life and Purgatory* "popularized a theme which already possessed a very rich tradition."

22. Dated as probably 1634 (or 1633-35) by the previously mentioned H. W. Hilborn, *A Chronology of the Plays of D. Pedro Calderón de la Barca* (Toronto: University of Toronto Press, 1938), p. 25. In his study "Sobre la difusión de la leyenda del Purgatorio de San Patricio en España," *Nueva Revista de Filología Hispánica*, II (1948): 195-96, Avalle-Arce relates the two plays to their main source: Montalván's prose account.

23. Translated into English verse by Denis Florence MacCarthy, in *Calderón's Dramas* (London: H. S. King, 1873), pp. 235-348.

24. E. J. Hasell, "Calderón's Sacred Dramas. *The Purgatory of St. Patrick*," *The Saint Paul's Magazine*, XIII (July-Dec., 1873): 313-31. Quotation, pp. 329-30. Calderón's play is also discussed by E. J. Hasell in her book on *Calderón* (Edinburgh-London: Blackwood, 1879), pp. 85-90.

Chapter Eight

1. See three previously mentioned studies: Willard F. King, "The Academies and Seventeenth Century Spanish Literature," *Publications of the Modern Language Association of America*, LXXV (1960): 367-76; José

Sánchez, *Academias literarias del Siglo de Oro español* (Madrid: Gredos, 1961); Willard F. King, *Prosa novelística y academias literarias en el siglo XVII* (Madrid: Real Academia Española, 1963).

2. *Para todos* (Madrid: Imprenta del Reino, for Alonso Pérez, 1632). For some years Georg Olms Verlag, Hildesheim, Germany, has promised a reprint of the Madrid, 1635, edition.

3. Victor Dixon, "Juan Pérez de Montalbán's *Para todos*," *Hispanic Review*, XXXII (1964): 36-59. Novels in English based on those of *For Everybody* appeared in 1710 (London: J. Woodward) as *A Week's Entertainment at a Wedding*.

4. Karl-Ludwig Selig in the article listed below has found material of value in Montalván's presentation of "the basic library" of the Preacher (Fifth Day, "The Discourse of the Preacher"), pointing out that Montalván offers us "an almost complete catalogue of mythographies and emblem books" (p. 85). "What we have here is a list of authorities and reference works, a genuinely international list" (p. 86). See "Three Spanish Libraries of Emblem Books and Compendia," in *Essays in History and Literature Presented by Fellows of the Newberry Library to Stanley Pargellis* (Chicago: The Newberry Library, 1965), pp. 81-90.

5. For example, Hannah E. Bergman, *Luis Quiñones de Benavente y sus entremeses* (Madrid: Castalia, 1965); Eugenio Asensio, *El itinerario del entremés desde Lope de Rueda a Quiñones de Benavente* (Madrid: Gredos, 1965); and Hannah E. Bergman, *Luis Quiñones de Benavente* (New York: Twayne, 1972).

6. Cf. the previously mentioned Walter Poesse, *Juan Ruiz de Alarcón* (New York: Twayne, 1972), "Preface": "his slender output (small even when compared with the more modest achievements of his day)...."

7. For a discussion of this probable source, see Ludwig Pfandl, *Historia de la literatura nacional española en la Edad de Oro*, 2nd. ed. (Barcelona: Gili, 1952), p. 398.

8. See J. H. Parker, "Tirso de Molina, defensor de la Comedia Nueva," *Universidad de San Carlos* (Guatemala), No. 12 (1948): 39-48.

9. Speaking of "the bitterness and disillusionment betrayed throughout *Para todos* in Montalbán's allusions to the theatre," Dixon (p. 57) goes on to say: "He turned his back therefore, temporarily, on the writing of new plays, and determined to discountenance all his competitors by demonstrating in print his brilliance not only as a dramatist but in a variety of other rôles — as a poet, a novelist, a scholar. He embarked on the compilation of *Para todos*, and spared no effort until it was completed to his satisfaction."

10. See the previously mentioned Agustín González de Amezúa, "Las polémicas literarias sobre el *Para todos* del doctor Juan Pérez de Montalbán," in *Opúsculos histórico-literarios*, II (Madrid: CSIC, 1951): 64-94; also published in *Estudios dedicados a Menéndez Pidal*, II (Madrid, CSIC, 1951): 409-53. Quevedo's words may be found in Quevedo, *Obras completas*, ed. Felicidad Buendía, I (Madrid: Aguilar, 1961): 446. We have

Notes and References

referred to the bitter Quevedo-Montalván quarrelling from Chapter I ("Life of Montalván") on, and bibliography is very rich on the subject. For example, still another interesting discussion of the matter is to be found in Segundo Serrano Poncela's "Los enemigos de Quevedo," *Anuario de Filología* (Universidad del Zulia), II-III (1963-64): 235-51.

11. And previously in the same author's *Las almas de Quevedo* (Madrid: Aguirre, 1946), p. 44: "the most truculent personal diatribe which our letters know."

12. Antonio Restori, *Piezas de títulos de comedias* (Messina: V. Muglia, 1903), p. 29, note 1.

13. Antonio Restori, "Il *Para todos* di Giovanni Pérez de Montalván," *La Bibliofilia*, XXIX (1927): 1-19. Caroline B. Bourland *(The Short Story in Spain in the Seventeenth Century)* gives good bibliographical information on *For Everybody* also. The book was taken up in translation, and Maria Grazia Profeti has looked at the French situation in "La traduzione francese del *Para todos* di Juan Pérez de Montalbán,*" Prohemio*, I (1970): 109-19, describing the translation in two volumes of Paris: Guillaume de Luyne, 1684.

14. Dixon's words *("Para todos*," p. 36, note 2) are worth repeating. "We cannot show, to the best of my knowledge, that the references to Quevedo in *Para todos* contain anything but sincere praise; that Alonso Pérez was ever responsible for a pirated edition of the *Buscón*; that Montalbán had anything to do with the prohibition of Quevedo's works by the Inquisition; or that he attacked the *Política de Dios* in his *Como padre y como rey*...."

Chapter Nine

1. *Fama póstuma a la vida y muerte del doctor Frey Lope Félix de Vega Carpio y elogios panegíricos a la inmortalidad de su nombre. Escritos por los más esclarecidos ingenios. Solicitados por el doctor Juan Pérez de Montalván*. En Madrid, en la Imprenta del Reino. Año 1636. A costa de Alonso Pérez de Montalván, librero de su Majestad. To be found in Lope de Vega, *Obras sueltas*, XX (Madrid: Antonio de Sancha, 1779): 27-60; in *Biblioteca de Autores Españoles*, XXIV (Madrid: Rivadeneyra, 1853): ix-xvii; and in modern printings, such as that of México: R. Peregina, 1966.

2. "1595-1600," according to the Morley-Bruerton, *Cronología*, p. 228.

3. This portrait was mentioned in Lope's first will. See Américo Castro and Hugo A. Rennert, *Vida de Lope de Vega (1562-1635)*, with "Notas adicionales" by Fernando Lázaro Carreter (Salamanca: Anaya, 1969), p. 396.

4. Montalván, it is very clear, suppressed and altered facts to shield his hero's reputation and to enhance his presentation. Unfortunately, as Profeti puts it *(Montalbán*, p. 12), "the exhuberant figure . . . comes out falsified and debased, deprived of his true relief and character." The Castro-Rennert *Vida* refers repeatedly to "the little precision of [Montalván's] account" (p. 327, note 2); as do many critics, such as Joaquín de Entrambasaguas, in

Estudios sobre Lope de Vega, I (Madrid: CSIC, 1946), etc.

5. See, for example, Morley and Bruerton, "How Many *comedias* Did Lope de Vega Write?," *Hispania*, XIX (1936): 217-34; and S. Griswold Morley, "Lope de Vega's Prolificity and Speed," *Hispanic Review*, X (1942): 67-68.

6. See Joseph H. Silverman, "Lope de Vega's Last Years and His Final Play, *The Greatest Virtue of a King*," *The Texas Quarterly*, Spring, 1963, pp. 174-87. (P. 174: "some time after August 12, 1634.")

7. Morley-Bruerton, *Cronología*, p. 566: "According to Montalván (not a trustworthy witness)..."

8. José María de Cossío, "Notas de un lector. Algunos datos sobre Lope de Vega, contenidos en su *Fama Póstuma*," *Boletín de la Biblioteca Menéndez Pelayo*, XI (1929): 51-55. (Quotation, p. 51.)

9. Montalván's *Fama póstuma* was followed in the same year by the Venice *Essequie poetiche, ovvero lamento delle muse italiane in morte del signor Lope de Vega* (compiled by Fabio Franchi). See description in Castro-Rennert, *Vida*, p. 331, note 11.

Chapter Ten

1. Edward M. Wilson has shown that a sonnet ("A Ladie Weeping"), translated by Thomas Stanley from Montalván, is from the play *Don Juan of Austria* and not (in another version) from the novel *The Enchanted Palace*, as believed by Henry Thomas in an earlier discussion. See Edward M. Wilson, "*Polyphemus* and Other Translations from Spanish," pp. 548-51, in Wilson and E. R. Vincent, "Thomas Stanley's Translations and Borrowings from Spanish and Italian Poems," *Revue de Littérature Comparée*, XXXII (1958): 548-56. Fifty years ago Ludwig Pfandl dealt with a poem ("Listen, Shepherds of Henares...") from a Montalván novel, *The Force of Disillusionment*, in "Eine angeblich unbekannte spanische Romanze," *Archiv für das Studium der neueren Sprachen und Literaturen*, CXLVI (1923): 122-23. This ballad had been previously associated with Lope de Vega's name by Arthur Ludwig Stiefel in his "Unbekannte spanische Romanze," *Revue Hispanique*, XV (1906): 766-70.

2. G. W. Bacon, "Some Poems of Dr. Juan Pérez de Montalván," *Revue Hispanique*, XXV (1911): 458-67.

3. For Lope's *Triunfos divinos con otras Rimas sacras* (Madrid: Viuda de Alonso Martín, 1625). See Entrambasaguas, *Estudios sobre Lope de Vega*, II (Madrid: CSIC, 1947), p. 176, note 21.

4. In the previously mentioned "Textos dispersos de clásicos españoles. VIII. Pérez de Montalbán," *Revista de Literatura*, XVIII (1960): 285-301.

5. See Edward M. Wilson, "The *Cancionero* of Don Joseph del Corral," *Hispanic Review*, XXXV (1967): 141-60. (A Madrid contemporary of Montalván, born 1596. See also *Poems from the "Cancionero" of Don Joseph del Corral [Phillipps Ms 22216]*, Exeter Hispanic Texts, No. 5, 1973.)

6. This ballad appeared previously in Montalván's novel *The Peasant*

Notes and References

Girl of Pinto, and can be read in *Biblioteca de Autores Españoles*, XVI (Madrid: Rivadeneyra, 1851): 445-46.
   7. This poem, also appearing in Alfay's collection of Zaragoza, 1654, has been reproduced in *Biblioteca de Autores Españoles*, XX (1857): xxxiii, and in LII (1884): 587; as well as in *Museo Universal*, IV (1860): 390.
   8. See Agustín González de Amezúa, *Cómo se hacía un libro en nuestro Siglo de Oro* (Madrid: Editorial Magisterio Español, 1946), p. 37: "the heap, finally, copious or not, of laudatory compositions."
   9. Ada Godínez de Batlle writes on "Montalván lírico," pp. 21-54.

Chapter Eleven

   1. See, for example, the previously mentioned book by Pablo Cabañas, *El mito de Orfeo en la literatura española* (1948) and Eva Kushner, *Le Mythe d'Orfée dans la littérature française contemporaine* (Paris: Nizet, 1961).
   2. We remember that in these novels (as Ricci, *Cardenio et Célinde*, p. 109, puts it), "freed from the restrictions of the stage," Montalván could allow himself the most surprising and extraordinary happenings. Gregorio Sánchez-Puerta, "Ante el centenario de Lope de Vega: Su discípulo Juan Pérez de Montalbán," *Anales de la Universidad de Madrid*, III (1934): 201-15, also speaks of "this tendency to the marvellous and the macabre [which] never abandoned him during his lifetime" (p. 211), giving as an example the case of Lucrecia (of *The Force of Disillusionment*), who, in her attempt to regain Teodoro's affection, snatches the body of a dead suitor from its tomb, cuts the heart out and wishes to have Teodoro drink that heart dissolved in wine.
   3. See the previously mentioned "A Dramatist of Spain's Golden Age," *More Books* (Boston Public Library), XIII (1938): 468.
   4. Fernando Gutiérrez, edition of the *Novelas ejemplares* (Barcelona: Selecciones Bibliófilas, 1957), p. 9. Selected works of our precocious author were edited for children in the early 1930's by Julio de Ugarte, in a series of children's "classics": *Juan Pérez de Montalbán. Sus mejores obras al alcance de los niños* (Madrid: Juan Ortiz, no date [1933?]).
   5. My previously mentioned "Chronology" (1952) discusses the variety of verse forms used by Montalván in his plays. See also Dorothy C. Clarke, "A Chronological Sketch of Castilian Versification Together with a List of Its Metric Terms," *University of California Publications in Modern Philology*, XXXIV (Berkeley, 1952), No. 3: 279-382.
   6. In his *Bibliotheca hispana nova*, published in Madrid by J. de Ibarra, 2 vols., 1783, 1788. See the edition of Mario Ruffini, I (Torino: Bottega d'Erasmo, 1963): 757.
   7. "Throughout the [seventeen] eighties the commonest features of the playbills were still the dramas of Calderón, Moreto, Matos Fragoso, Montalbán, Cañizares, and Zamora." — I. L. McClelland, *Spanish Drama of Pathos 1750-1808*, I (Toronto: University of Toronto Press, 1970): 221. See

also, John A. Cook, *Neo-Classic Drama in Spain, Theory and Practice* (Dallas: Southern Methodist University Press, 1959).

8. Examples are R. de Mesonero Romanos, "Teatro de Montalván," *Semanario Pintoresco Español*, XVII (1852): 50-51, and E. Serrano Fatigati, "Juan Pérez de Montalván," *El Museo Universal*, V (1861): 45-47.

9. Ramón de Mesonero Romanos, "Dramáticos contemporáneos de Lope de Vega," *Biblioteca de Autores Españoles*, XLV (Madrid: Rivadeneyra, 1858): xxxii.

10. Aldolf Friedrich von Schack, *Historia de la literatura y del arte dramático en España*, trans. Eduardo de Mier, III (Madrid: Tello, 1887), p. 377.

11. Volume 33 (Cambridge, England: The Modern Humanities Research Association, 1972), p. 275.

12. In the *Posthumous Fame* (see *Biblioteca de Autores Españoles*, XXIV, p. xvi), Montalván himself speaks of Lope de Vega's *acierto* (which might be interpreted as hitting the mark in an undertaking) and his own *diligencia* (which might be interpreted as steadfastly keeping one's nose to the grindstone) re their collaboration in writing the play *The Third Order of St. Francis:* "Seeing then that I could not equal him in his skill (acierto), I wanted to attempt it on the side of diligence (diligencia), and to achieve that I got up at two a.m. and at eleven completed my part [of the play]."

Selected Bibliography

PRIMARY SOURCES

1. Collections of Plays (in order of publication dates)

Para todos (Madrid: Imprenta del Reino, 1632). This miscellany, written and prepared for the press by Montalván, contains four three-act *comedias* and two *autos sacramentales*, the former being *El segundo Séneca de España; No hay vida como la honra; De un castigo dos venganzas;* and *La más constante mujer;* and the latter: *El Polifemo* and *Escanderbech.*

Primero tomo de las comedias (Madrid: Imprenta del Reino, 1635). Prepared for the press by Montalván, it contains twelve of his plays: *A lo hecho no hay remedio, y príncipe de los montes; El hijo del serafín, San Pedro de Alcántara; Cumplir con su obligación; Los templarios; La doncella de labor; El mariscal de Virón; La toquera vizcaína; El fin más desgraciado y fortunas de Seyano; Olimpa y Vireno; Lo que son juicios del cielo; El señor don Juan de Austria;* and *Los amantes de Teruel.*

Segundo tomo de las comedias (Madrid: Imprenta del Reino, 1638). Prepared for the press by Juan's father, Alonso Pérez de Montalván, and published at his expense very soon after the dramatist's death, this collection contains what are apparently nine authentic plays and three spurious ones, the former being *Como amante y como honrada; Segunda parte del segundo Séneca de España; Don Florisel de Niquea; La deshonra honrosa; El valiente Nazareno, Sansón; Los hijos de la Fortuna, Teágenes y Clariquea; Despreciar lo que se quiere; La ganancia por la mano;* and *El valiente más dichoso, Don Pedro Guiral;* and the latter: *Amor, lealtad y amistad; El divino portugués, San Antonio de Padua;* and *El sufrimiento premiado.*

Comedias escogidas del Dr. Juan Pérez de Montalván. 2 vols. (Madrid: Ortega, 1827 and 1831). Vol. I contains: *Cumplir con su obligación; La toquera vizcaína;* and *No hay vida como la honra;* as well as *Ser prudente y ser sufrido* (at times attributed to Montalván). Vol. II contains: *La más constante mujer,* as well as *Como padre y como rey* (attributed to Montalván).

Teatro escogido desde el siglo XVII hasta nuestros días. Vol. 1 (Paris: Baudry,

1838) contains *No hay vida como la honra* and *La toquera vizcaína* (and plays by other dramatists). With the same pagination, also published in Eugenio de Ochoa, *Tesoro del teatro español desde su origen (año de 1356) hasta nuestros días*, IV (Paris: Baudry, 1838).

MESONERO ROMANOS, RAMÓN DE. "Dramáticos contemporáneos de Lope de Vega. El Doctor Juan Pérez de Montalván." Vol. XLV of the *Biblioteca de Autores Españoles* (Madrid: Rivadeneyra, 1858). This volume contains: *No hay vida como la honra; La más constante mujer; La toquera vizcaína; Cumplir con su obligación*; and *La doncella de labor*; as well as the attributed *Como padre y como rey* and *Ser prudente y ser sufrido*.

2. Individual Plays

Authentic (presumably) individual plays, including plays in collaboration and suppositious dramas (many in number) have been listed in Chapter Five. There are few printings of Montalván plays in the twentieth century, exceptions being *El segundo Séneca de España*, in Sainz de Robles, *Teatro español*, IV (Madrid: Aguilar, 1943), pp. 509-80; the *auto sacramental*, *Polifemo*, in Nicolás González Ruiz, *Piezas maestras del teatro teológico español*, 3rd ed., I (Madrid: Biblioteca de Autores Cristianos, 1968), pp. 778-98; and the *auto sacramental, El caballero del Febo*, in Maria Grazia Profeti's contribution to *Miscellanea di Studi Hispanici* (Pisa: Università di Pisa, 1966-67), pp. 218-309.

3. The *Orpheus in the Castilian Language*

El Orfeo en lengua castellana (Madrid: Viuda de Alonso Martín, 1624). At times attributed to Lope de Vega, this epic poem has been edited in this century by Pablo Cabañas (Madrid: CSIC, 1948).

4. Collections of Novels

Sucesos y prodigios de amor en ocho novelas ejemplares (Madrid: Juan González, 1624). It contains *La hermosa Aurora; La fuerza del desengaño; El envidioso castigado; La mayor confusión; La villana de Pinto; La desgraciada amistad; Los primos amantes*; and *La prodigiosa*. These eight exemplary novels have been edited, with a good introduction, by Agustín González de Amezúa (Madrid: La Sociedad de Bibliófilos Españoles, 1949).

Para todos (Madrid: Imprenta del Reino, 1632). This miscellany contains four novels: *Introducción a la semana; Al cabo de los años mil; El palacio encantado*; and *El piadoso bandolero*.

FERNÁNDEZ DE NAVARRETE, EUSTAQUIO. "Bosquejo histórico sobre la novela española." Vol. XXXIII of the *Biblioteca de Autores Españoles* (Madrid: Rivadeneyra, 1871). This volume contains *La villana de Pinto* and *Los primos amantes*.

GUTIÉRREZ, FERNANDO (ed.). *Juan Pérez de Montalbán, Novelas ejemplares* (Barcelona: Selecciones Bibliófilas, 1957). The volume contains *La villana de Pinto; La desgraciada amistad; Los primos amantes*; and *Al cabo de los años mil*; as well as useful introductory words.

5. The *Life and Purgatory of St. Patrick*

Vida y purgatorio de San Patricio (Madrid: Luis Sánchez, 1627). This book

Selected Bibliography

has been edited recently by Maria Grazia Profeti (Pisa: Università di Pisa, 1972).

6. *For Everybody*
Para todos (Madrid: Imprenta del Reino, 1632). A reprint of the Madrid, 1635, edition has been promised by Georg Olms Verlag, Hildesheim, Germany.

7. The *Posthumous Fame*
Fama póstuma a la vida y muerte del doctor Frey Lope de Vega Carpio (Madrid: Imprenta del Reino, 1636). This "In memoriam" to Lope de Vega has been printed several times throughout the years, in Lope de Vega's *Obras sueltas*, XX (1779); in the *Biblioteca de Autores Españoles*, XXIV (1853); and in several twentieth-century editions, for example.

8. The *Panegyric Tears*
Lágrimas panegíricas a la temprana muerte del gran poeta y teólogo insigne Doctor Juan Pérez de Montalván (Madrid: Imprenta del Reino, 1639). A tribute to the deceased Montalván, edited by his friend Pedro Grande de Tena.

SECONDARY SOURCES

1. Bibliographies

Barrera y Leirado, Cayetano Alberto de la. *Catálogo bibliográfico del teatro antiguo español, desde sus orígenes hasta mediados del siglo XVIII* (Madrid: Rivadeneyra, 1860). Facsimile editions (Madrid: Gredos, 1969, and London: Tamesis, 1969). A basic work.

McCready, Warren T. *Bibliografía temática de estudios sobre el teatro español antiguo* (Toronto: University of Toronto Press, 1966). For the period 1850-1950. Carefully prepared.

2. Biographies

Mesonero Romanos, Ramón de. "Dramáticos contemporáneos de Lope de Vega. El Doctor Juan Pérez de Montalván," *Biblioteca de Autores Españoles*, XLV (Madrid: Rivadeneyra, 1858), xxx-xxxv. Basic, but outdated in detail by more recent studies.

Bacon, George William. "The Life and Dramatic Works of Doctor Juan Pérez de Montalván (1602-1638)," *Revue Hispanique*, XXVI (1912): 1-474. The old standard study of Montalván; to be used with care and in conjunction with accounts of modern findings.

Godínez de Batlle, Ada. "Labor literaria del Dr. Juan Pérez de Montalván," *Revista de la Facultad de Letras y Ciencias* (Universidad de la Habana), XXX (1920): 1-151. Leans very heavily on Bacon, repeating his information and adding some materials on Montalván as a lyric poet and as a novelist.

Sylvia, Esther. "A Dramatist of Spain's Golden Age," *More Books* (Boston Public Library), XIII (1938): 467-71. A very good short essay on Montalván.

Profeti, Maria Grazia. *Montalbán: un commediografo dell'età di Lope*

(Pisa: Università di Pisa, 1970). The best printed study available. Carefully reviewed by Victor Dixon in *Bulletin of Hispanic Studies*, XLIX (1972): 186-87.

3. Key Articles on Aspects of Montalván's Works

DIXON, VICTOR. "Juan Pérez de Montalbán's *Segundo tomo de las comedias*," *Hispanic Review*, XXIX (1961): 91-109.

———. "Juan Pérez de Montalbán's *Para todos*," *Hispanic Review*, XXXII (1964): 36-59. This article and the preceding one are the results of painstaking research.

4. Unpublished Doctoral Dissertations

SÁNCHEZ MARIÑO, RAFAEL. *Alonso Pérez de Montalbán: Su importancia en el círculo literario de Lope de Vega* (Universidad de Madrid, 1955).

DIXON, VICTOR. *The Life and Works of Juan Pérez de Montalbán, with Special Reference to His Plays* (Cambridge University, England, 1959).

5. Other Documents and Articles Dealing with Montalván

For other critical material, see the Notes and References.

6. The *Comedia* in general and the Staging of the *Comedia*

See the Notes and References, particularly Chapter Two, Note 1.

Index

Works by, or attributed to, Montalván are indexed under the English translation of the title, with a cross reference under the Spanish title. All other literary works are indexed under the original title, with translation and name of author; where no name is given, the work is anonymous.

A la eternidad del Rey Felipe tercero (To the Eternal Life of King Philip III), by Ana de Castro Egas, 125

A lo hecho no hay remedio y príncipe de los montes. See *What's Done Can't Be Undone*

A secreto agravio, secreta venganza (For a Secret Insult, a Secret Vengeance), by Calderón de la Barca, 89

Abélard and Héloise, 51

Academias del Jardín (Garden Academies), by Polo de Medina, 127

Adversa fortuna de don Álvaro de Luna, La (The Adverse Fortune of Don Álvaro de Luna), by Mira de Amescua (?), 47

Aethiopica (The Loves of Theagenes and Charicleia), by Heliodorus, 58-59

Al cabo de los años mil. See *At the End of One Thousand Years*

Alborg, Juan Luis, 73

Alcalde de Zalamea, El (The Mayor of Zalamea), by Calderón de la Barca, 29

Alfay, José, 126

Álvarez Espino, Romualdo, 30, 42, 140n13

Amantes de Teruel, Los. See *The Lovers of Teruel*

Amezúa, Agustín González de, 80, 83, 84, 85, 86, 87, 88, 89, 90, 91, 92, 97, 115, 118

Amor, lealtad y amistad. See *Love, Loyalty and Friendship*

Amor y obligación (Love and Obligation), by Antonio de Solís, 72

Anfiteatro de Felipe el Grande, El (The Amphitheater of Philip the Great), ed. José Pellicer y Tovar, 125

Antonia Manuela (actress), 30

Antonio, Nicolás, 78, 79, 131

Arcadia, La, by Lope de Vega, 61, 110, 120

Arellano, Luis de, 126

Ariosto, Ludovico, 48

Arjona, J. H., 144n6

Art of a Good Death (Arte de bien morir) [not written?], 23

Arte de bien morir. See *Art of a Good Death*

Arte nueva de escribir (New Art of Writing), by Pedro Díaz Morante, 125

Arte nuevo de hacer comedias en este tiempo (New Art of Writing Plays), by Lope de Vega, 43, 67, 110, 112, 113, 118, 132

Astrana Marín, Luis, 23, 80, 81

At the End of One Thousand Years (Al cabo de los años mil), 35, 40, 82, 93-94, 107

Aubrun, C. V., 35, 73

Auroras de Diana (Dawns of Diana), by Pedro de Castro y Anaya, 127

[159]

Avalle-Arce, J. B., 66
Avisos para la muerte (Warnings for Death), ed. Luis de Arellano, 126

Bacon, George William, 15, 17, 18, 19, 20, 21, 24, 27, 28, 30, 31, 32, 34, 36, 37, 40, 42, 44, 46, 47, 48, 50, 51, 53, 54, 55, 56, 60, 65, 73, 74, 118, 125, 126
Bandello, Matteo, 85
Barrera y Leirado, Cayetano Alberto de la, 22, 66, 73
Beautiful Aurora (La hermosa Aurora), 40, 82, *86*, 92
Belarmino, Roberto, 127
Belmonte Bermúdez, Luis, 19, 64
Beltrán, Fray Pedro, 128
Benavides Manrique, Francisco de, 24
Bizarrías de Belisa, Las (The Gallantries of Isabel), by Lope de Vega, 121
Bocángel y Unzueta, Gabriel, 127
Boccaccio, Giovanni, 51, 106
Bouillon, Godefroy de, 42
Bourland, Caroline B., 84, 85
Bowers, Fredson, 76
Brasil restituido, El (Brazil Restored), by Lope de Vega, 31
Bravo-Villasante, Carmen, 64
Brevio, Giovanni, 85
Bruerton, Courtney, 27, 65, 70, 104
Buchanan, Milton, A., 27, 74, 76, 146n20
Buen humor de las Musas, El (The Good Humor of the Muses), by Polo de Medina, 127
Buendía, Felicidad, 97, 115
Burlador de Sevilla, El (The Trickster of Seville), by Tirso de Molina, 76

Caballero del Febo, El. See *The Knight of Phoebus*
Cabañas, Pablo, 78, 79
Cabrera de Córdoba, Luis, 28, 50, 56
Calderón, Rodrigo (courtier), 47
Calderón de la Barca, Pedro, 17, 19, 23, 24, 29, 33, 35, 39, 40, 44, 46, 59, 60, 66, 75, 89, 104, 105, 111, 112, 131, 132
Camargo y Salgado, Hernando de, 127
Camerino, José, 127
Canavaggio, Jean, 144n5
Cap Seller of Biscay, The (La toquera vizcaína), *45-46*, 131

Carlos V, 50, 51
Casalduero, Joaquín, 76
Castillo Solórzano, Alonso de, 23, 24, 97, 98, 114
Castro, Américo, 122
Castro, Guillén de, 19
Castro Egas, Ana de, 125
Castro y Anaya, Pedro de, 127
Cautivo, El (The Captive), by Cervantes, 89
Celestino I (Pope), 100
Centinela del honor, La. See *The Centinel of Honor*
Cervantes, Miguel de, 15, 59, 72, 73, 74, 82, 86, 88, 89, 97, 104
Céspedes y Meneses, Gonzalo, 97
Chaytor, H. J., 139n1
Children of Fortune, Teágenes and Clariquea, The (Los hijos de la Fortuna, Teágenes y Clariquea), *58-59*, 95, 132
Cigarrales de Toledo, Los (The Country Estates of Toledo), by Tirso de Molina, 110, *113-14*
Circe, La (The Circe), by Lope de Vega, 34, 35
Coello, Antonio, 24, 66, 110
Colodrero de Villalobos, Miguel, 125
Como amante y como honrada. See *Like a Lover and Like an Honorable Woman*
Como padre y como rey. See *Like Father and Like King*
Cómo se guarda el honor. See *How Honor is Guarded*
Compassionate Bandit, The (El piadosos bandolero), 82, 93, *96-97*, 108
Compendio de la ortografía castellana (Compendium of Castilian Orthography), by Nicolás Dávila, 126
Condenado por desconfiado, El (The Man Condemned for Lack of Faith), by Tirso de Molina (?), 104
Copia de una carta moral (Copy of a Moral Letter), by Manuel de Ocampo, 127
Corona trágica, La (The Tragic Crown), by Lope de Vega, 127
Cossío, José María, de 124
Cotarelo y Mori, Emilio, 51, 76

Index [161]

Covarrubias y Leiva, Diego de, 128
Crooks, Esther, 73
Cruelty in Innocence, or To Deprive Oneself of Favor (El rigor en la inocencia, o Privarse de privar), 64
Cruickshank, D. W., 64
Cruz, Felipa de la (Mother), 15, 22
Cubillo, Álvaro, 111
Cuevas, Francisco de las, 126
Cumplir con su obligación. See *To Do One's Duty*

Dávila, Nicolás, 126
De un agravio tres venganzas (For an Insult a Triple Vengeance) [lost], by Villaizán, 115
De un castigo dos venganzas. See *For a Punishment a Double Vengeance*
Decameron, The, by Boccaccio, 51, 92, 106
Degollación de San Juan Bautista, La (The Beheading of St. John the Baptist), by Martín de Hermosilla, 127
Del Piero, Raúl, 80, 81
Desdén con el desdén, El (Disdain Conquered by Disdain), by Moreto, 60
Desdicha venturosa, La. See *The Lucky Misfortune*
Desgraciada amistad, La. See *The Unfortunate Friendship*
Deshonra honrosa, La. See *Honorable Dishonor*
Despreciar lo que se quiere. See *To Scorn What Is Liked*
Desprecios en quien ama, Los. See *The Disdain of One Who Loves*
Devoción de la Cruz, La (Devotion to the Cross), by Calderón de la Barca, 104
Diana, La, by Jorge de Montemayor, 88
Díaz Morante, Pedro, 125
Diego, Gerardo, 79
Diluvio general del mundo, El (The Flood), listed for Calderón de la Barca, 111
Discurso político (Political Discourse), by José Camerino, 127
Disdain of One Who Loves, The (Los desprecios en quien ama), 63
Divine Portuguese, St. Anthony of Padua, The (El divino portugués, San Antonio de Padua) [Second Volume of Plays], 53-54, 70
Divine Portuguese, St. Anthony of Padua, The [suelta], 53-54, 63
Divino portugués, San Antonio de Padua, El. See *The Divine Portuguese, St. Anthony of Padua*
Dixon, Victor, 15, 23, 26, 27, 28, 30, 31, 32, 33, 34, 35, 39, 52, 53, 61, 63, 64, 65, 70, 71, 72, 74, 79, 84, 85, 92, 93, 95, 109, 113, 114, 115, 116, 117, 118, 132, 133
Don Filipe el prudente, Segundo de este nombre (King Philip the Prudent, Second By This Name), by Lorenzo Vander Hammen, 28, 56
Don Florisel de Niquea, by Feliciano de Silva, 57
Don Florisel de Niquea. Para con todos hermanos y amantes para nosotros. See *Don Florisel de Nicaea. Brother and Sister to the World and Lovers to Ourselves*
Don Florisel of Nicaea. Brother and Sister to the World and Lovers to Ourselves (Don Florisel de Niquea. Para con todos hermanos y amantes para nosotros), 56-57, 59, 95
Don Juan de Austria, by Lorenzo Vander Hammen, 49
Don Juan of Austria (El señor don Juan de Austria), 28, 49-50, 56, 132
Don Quixote, by Cervantes, 89
Don Quixote (false), 15
Doncella de labor, La. See *The Waiting-Maid*
Dorotea, La, by Lope de Vega, 110
Dos jueces de Israel, Los. See *The Two Judges of Israel*
Dragontea, La, by Lope de Vega, 110, 123
Dunn, Peter N., 97

Elogios al Palacio Real (Praises of the Royal Palace), ed. Diego de Covarrubias y Leiva, 128
Enchanted Palace, The (El palacio encantado), 28, 82, 93, 95, 108
Entrambasaguas, Joaquín de, 78, 125

Envidioso castigado, El. See *The Envious Man Punished*
Envious Man Punished, The (El envidioso castigado), 82, 87
Escanderbech. See *Skander Beg*
Esclavo del demonio, El (The Devil's Slave), by Mira de Amescua, 104
Exodus, Book of, 16
Experiencias de Amor y Fortuna (Experiences of Love and Fortune), by Francisco de las Cuevas, 126
Exposición parafrástica del Psalterio (Paraphrastic Exposition of the Psalter), by José de Valdivielso, 127

Fábula de Polifemo y Galatea, La (The Fable of Polyphemus and Galatea), by Luis de Góngora, 34
Fajardo, Juan Isidro, 72
Fama póstuma, La. See *The Posthumous Fame*
Felipe II, 28, 29, 49, 50, 55, 132
Felipe III, 17, 125
Felipe IV, 116, 122, 125
Fernández de Navarrete, E., 78
Fernández de Ribera, Rodrigo, 126
Fey, Eduard, 73
Fianza satisfecha, La (The Outrageous Saint), by Lope de Vega, 104
Fichter, W. L., 77
Figueroa, Roque de (actor-manager of a theatrical company), 30
Filipe Segundo Rey de España, by Luis Cabrera de Córdoba, 28, 50
Fin más desgraciado y fortunas de Seyano, El, o Amor, privanza y castigo. See *Sejanus' Fortunes and Most Unhappy End, or Love, Favor and Punishment*
First Volume of Plays, The (El primero tomo de las comedias), 17, 18, 26, 27, 28, *39-51*, 52, 56, 62, 69, 77, 92, 117
Fitzmaurice-Kelly, James, 64
For a Punishment a Double Vengeance (De un castigo dos venganzas), *30-32*, 69, 107, 115, 132
For Everybody (Para todos), 16, 18, 19, 21, 23, 32, 40, 45, 52, 56, 69, 77, 79, 80, 81, 82, 97, *106-18*, 130
For Everybody (novels in), *92-98*, 117-18

For Everybody (plays in), 26-38
For Everybody (Part II) [not written?], 23, 53, 117
Force of Disillusionment, The (La fuerza del desengaño), 82, 86-87
Francesilla, La (The Little French Girl), by Lope de Vega, 20
Fuerza del desengaño, La. See *The Force of Disillusionment*

Ganancia por la mano, La. See *Success in One's Plans*
García de la Huerta, Vicente, 72
Garcilaso de la Vega, 88
Gitana de Menfis, Santa María Egypciaca, La. See *The Gypsy of Memphis, St. Mary the Egyptian*
Gitanilla, La. See *The Little Gypsy Girl*
Gitanilla, La (The Little Gypsy Girl) [novel], by Cervantes, 72, 73, 74, 88
Gitanilla de Madrid, La (The Little Gypsy Girl of Madrid), by Antonio de Solís, 65, *73-77*, 111, 113
Glaser, Edward, 16, 34, 35, 53, 54, 114, 115
Godínez, Felipe, 111
Godínez de Batlle, Ada, 27, 73, 125, 128, 129
Góngora, Luis de, 21, 34, 68, 77, 78, 80
González de Amezúa. See Amezúa
Grande de Tena, Pedro, 24
Gravedad en Villaverde. See *Vanity in Villaverde*
Greatest Confusion, The (La mayor confusión), 63, 65, 82, *84-86*, 87, 88
Gregory XV (Pope), 17, 18, 40
Gutiérrez, Fernando, 83
Gutiérrez de Arévalo, Pedro, 126
Gutiérrez de Cisneros, Tomás, 16
Gypsy of Memphis, St. Mary the Egyptian, The (La gitana de Menfis, Santa María Egypciaca), 63

Hainsworth, George, 73
Happenings and Prodigies of Love, in Eight Exemplary Novels, The (Los sucesos y prodigios de amor, en ocho novelas ejemplares), 20, *82-92*, 93, 96, 97, 110
Harlan, Mabel M., 60

Index [163]

Hartzenbusch, Eugenio, 51
Hasell, E. J., 105
Heliodorus, 58, 59
Hermosa Aurora, La. See *Beautiful Aurora*
Hermosilla, Martín de, 127
Hesse, Everett W., 33, 44, 60
Hijo del serafín, San Pedro de Alcántara, El. See *The Son of the Seraphim, St. Peter of Alcántara*
Hijos de la Fortuna, Teágenes y Clariquea, Los. See *The Children of Fortune, Teágenes and Clariquea*
Historia ejemplar de las dos constantes mujeres españolas, La (The Exemplary History of the Two Constant Spanish Women), by Luis Pacheco de Narvaez, 128
Honorable Dishonor (La deshonra honrosa), 57
How Honor is Guarded (Cómo se guarda el honor), 63

Idea de la Comedia de Castilla deducida de las obras cómicas del Doctor Juan Pérez de Montalván (Idea of the "Comedia" of Castile Deduced from the Plays of Dr. Juan Pérez de Montalván), by José Pellicer de Tovar, 67-68
Index librorum prohibitorum (1640), 85
Index of the Eminent Authorities of Madrid (Índice de los ingenios de Madrid), in *For Everybody*, 109, 110-11, 112
Introducción a la semana. See *Introduction to the Week*
Introduction to the Week (Introducción a la semana), 82, 92, 93, 106, 109, 116, 117
Isidro de Madrid, El, by Lope de Vega, 110

Jacquot, Jean, 142n13
Jáuregui, Juan de, 19, 78, 80
Jerusalén conquistada (Jerusalem Regained), by Lope de Vega, 21, 123
Jiménez de Enciso, Diego, 111
Judges, Book of, 58
Juliá Martínez, Eduardo, 75

Kennedy, Ruth Lee, 24, 65
King, Willard F., 93, 117, 118, 137n21, 149n1
Knight of Phoebus, The (El caballero del Febo), 26, 36, 37-38

Lágrimas panegíricas (for Montalván). See *Panegyric Tears*
Laurel de Apolo, El (The Laurel of Apollo), by Lope de Vega, 21
Lealtad, amor y amistad (Loyalty, Love and Friendship), by Sebastián Francisco de Medrano, 70
León Suárez, Miguel de, 127
Leonard, Irving A., 65, 66
Ley, Charles David, 65
Life and Purgatory of St. Patrick, The (La vida y purgatorio de San Patricio), 18, 82, 98-105, 110, 114, 130
Like a Lover and Like an Honorable Woman (Como amante y como honrada), 54-55, 132
Like Father and Like King (Como padre y como rey), 63, 65
Lindona de Galicia, La. See *The Noble Lady of Galicia*
List of Those Who Write Plays in Castile Only (Memoria de los que escriben comedias en Castilla solamente), in *For Everybody*, 109, 111-12
Little Gypsy Girl, The (La Gitanilla), 65, 72-77, 81
Lo que son juicios del cielo. See *What the Judgments of Heaven Are*
Lomba y Pedraja, José R., 64
Longfellow, H. W., 72
Louis XIV (King of France), 65
Love, Loyalty and Friendship (Amor, lealtad y amistad), 53, 70
Lover Cousins, The (Los primos amantes), 82, 89-90, 97
Lovers of Teruel, The (Los amantes de Teruel), 50-51, 131
Lucky Misfortune, The (La desdicha venturosa), 63
Luna, Álvaro de (courtier), 47

MacCurdy, Raymond R., 47, 70
Macarene Gate, The (La puerta macarena), Parts I and II, 64

Maldonado de Guevara, Francisco, 15
Malkiel, María Rosa Lida de, 76
Mancini, Guido, 64
Marcus, Raymond, 74
Marguerite de Navarre, 85
Mariner, Vicente, 23
Mariscal de Virón, El. See *The Marshal of Virón*
Marqués de las Navas, El, by Lope de Vega, 49
Marshal of Virón, The (El mariscal de Virón, 44-45, 47, 48
Martell, Daniel E., 73
Mártir Rizo, Juan Pablo, 45
Más constante mujer, La. See *The Most Devoted Fiancée*
Matos Fragoso, Juan de, 24
Mayberry, Robert E., 76
Mayor confusión, La. See *The Greatest Confusion*
Mayor prodigio, El, o El purgatorio de la vida (The Greatest Prodigy or Purgatory in Life), 104
Mayor virtud de un rey, La (The Greatest Virtue of a King), by Lope de Vega, 121
Medel del Castillo, Francisco, 72
Médicis de Florencia, Los (The Medici of Florence), by Diego Jiménez de Enciso, 111
Medinilla, Baltasar Elisio de, 20
Medrano, Sebastián Francisco de, 19, 53
Mena, Fernando de, 59
Mesón del mundo (Inn of the World), by Rodrigo Fernández de Ribera, 126
Mesonero Romanos, Ramón de, 72, 131
Milagrosa elección de San Pío V, La. See *The Miraculous Election of Pius V*
Mira de Amescua, Antonio, 23, 35, 47, 66, 104, 111, 112, 133
Miraculous Election of Pius V, The (La milagrosa elección de San Pío V), 65
Molière, 30
Monja alférez, La. See *The Nun Ensign*
Monstruo de la Fortuna, la lavandera de Nápoles, Felipa Catanea, El. See *The Prodigy of Fortune, the Laundress of Naples, Felipa Catanea*
Montemayor, Jorge de, 88
Moreto, Agustín, 24, 60, 104, 131
Morir y disimular. See *To Die and to Conceal*
Morley, S. Griswold, 27, 65, 70, 71, 79, 104
Most Devoted Fiancée, The (La más constante mujer), 32-33, 109, 116, 132
Most Happy Braggart, Don Pedro Guiral, The (El valiente más dichoso, Don Pedro Guiral), 61-62
Most Sacred Host of Alcalá, The (Las santísimas formas de Alcalá), 36-37, 38, 41
Muñoz Cortés, M., 35

Niseno, Fray Diego, 24, 67, 80
No hay vida como la honra. See *There Is No Life Like Honor*
Noble Lady of Galicia, The (La lindona de Galicia), 65
Northup, G. T., 65, 76
Nun Ensign, The (La monja alférez), 64

Obregón, Bernardino de, 53, 54
Ocampo, Manuel de, 127
Oficio del Príncipe Cristiano (Office of the Christian Prince), by Roberto Belarmino, trans. Miguel de León Suárez, 127
Olimpa and Vireno (Olimpa y Vireno), 47-48
Olimpa y Vireno. See *Olimpa and Vireno*
One Pleasure Brings a Thousand Pains (Un gusto trae mil disgustos), 63
Orfeo (Orpheus), by Juan de Jáuregui, 78
Orfeo en lengua castellana. See *Orpheus in the Castilian Language*
Orlando furioso (Mad Roland), by Ariosto, 48
Orpheus in the Castilian Language (Orfeo en lengua castellana), 41, 69, 77-79, 81, 110, 115, 130
O'Sullevan, Philip, 98

Pacheco de Narváez, Luis, 80, 128
Paetz, Bernhard, 66

Index [165]

Palacín Iglesias, Gregorio, 73
Palacio encantado, El. See *The Enchanted Palace*
Palmerín de Oliva. See *Palmerín of the Olive Tree*
Palmerín of the Olive Tree (Palmerín de Oliva), 59, 64, 95
Panegyric Tears (Lágrimas panegíricas), 22, 23, 24-25, 67
Papell, Antonio, 21
Para todos. See *For Everybody*
Parker, J. H., 28, 30, 41, 59, 64, 65
Pastoral de Jacinto, La (Jacinto's Pastoral), by Lope de Vega, 120
Peasant Girl of Pinto, The (La villana de Pinto), 82, 88, 97
Pedro el cruel (King), 64
Pellicer y Tovar, José, 67 68, 116, 125, 128
Peregrino, El (The Pilgrim), by Lope de Vega, 71
Perellós, Ramon de, 98, 99
Pérez, Alonso (Father), 15, 16, 18, 19, 20, 22, 25, 28, 39, 49, 52, 122, 123
Pérez, Ángela (Sister), 15, 22
Pérez, Cristóbal (Brother), 15, 22
Pérez, Isabel (Sister), 15, 22
Pérez, Petronila (Sister), 15, 22
Pérez de Montalván Juan: ancestry, 15, 16, 25; birth, 15; character, 24-25; death and burial, 23; education, 16, 17, 20; family of, 15, 16, 22; illness, 22-23; in Alcalá de Henares, 16, 17, 61; Madrid, 15, *et passim*; Seville, 18; literary academies, 19; literary friends, 19-22; literary polemics, 18-19, 114-16; notary of the Inquisition, 17, 18; plays: *autos*, 33-38, 130; classification of, 27; *comedias*, 39-51, 52-62, 63-66, 130, 131-32; *comedias* in collaboration, 35, 40, 66; number of, 18, 26, 110; poetry, 17, 18, 125-29; portraits of, 137n1; priesthood, 16, 17, 18; problems of authorship, 63-66, 69-81; prose, 18, 82-105, 106-18, 119-24; pseudonym ("Montano"), 18, 93, 109; self-entry, in his Index of writers, 110; surname, 135n1
Perinola, La (The Teetotum), by Quevedo, 10, 21, 29, 34 45, 69, 79, 80, 97, 115

Persiles y Sigismunda, by Cervantes, 59, 86
Piadoso bandolero, El. See *The Compassionate Bandit*
Poesías dirigidas al Monte Vesuvio (Poems Addressed to Mount Vesuvius), ed. Juan de Quiñones, 126
Poesías varias de grandes ingenios españoles (Varied Poetry of Great Spanish Writers), ed. José Alfay, 126
Poesse, Walter, 26, 27
Polifemo, El. See *Polyphemus*
Polifemo y Circe. See *Polyphemus and Circe*
Política de Dios, La (The Politics of God), by Quevedo, 110
Polo de Medina, Salvador Jacinto, 24, 127
Polyphemus (El Polifemo), 33-35, 37, 100
Polyphemus and Circe (Polifemo y Circe), 35, 40, 66
Porqueras Mayo, Alberto, 67, 68
Porras, Jerónimo de, 126
Posthumous Fame, The (La fama póstuma), 20, 22, 23, 66, 117, 119-24, 125, 130
Praag, J. A. van, 73
Práctica de boticarios (Practice of Apothecaries), by Pedro Gutiérrez de Arévalo, 126
Primero tomo de las comedias, El. See *The First Volume of Plays*
Primos amantes, Los. See *The Lover Cousins*
Príncipe Escanderbey, El (Prince Skander Beg), by Vélez de Guevara, 35
Privilege of Women, The (El privilegio de las mujeres), 66
Privilegio de las mujeres, El. See *The Privilege of Women*
Prodigiosa, La. See *The Prodigious Story*
Prodigiosa vida de Malhagas el embustero, La. See *The Prodigious Life of Malhagas the Trickster*
Prodigious Life of Malhagas the Trickster, The (La vida prodigiosa de Malhagas el embustero [not written?]), 23, 110
Prodigious Story, The (La prodigiosa), 89, 90-92

Prodigy of Fortune, the Laundress of Naples, Felipa Catanea, The (El monstruo de la Fortuna, la lavandera de Nápoles, Felipa Catanea), 66
Profeti, Maria Grazia, 15, 26, 27, 28, 30, 32, 36, 37, 38, 40, 41, 44, 45, 46, 47, 48, 49, 59, 64, 67, 68, 132, 133
Próspera fortuna de don Álvaro de Luna, La (The Prosperous Fortune of Don Álvaro de Luna), by Mira de Amescua (?), 47
Puerta macarena, La (Parts I and II). See *The Macarene Gate*
Purgatorio de San Patricio, El (The Purgatory of St. Patrick), by Calderón de la Barca, 104

Quevedo y Villegas, Francisco Gómez de, 16, 19, 21, 22, 23, 24, 34, 45, 69, 79, 80, 97, 110, 111, 113, 115, 116, 118
Quintana, Francisco de, 16, 23, 61
Quiñones, Juan de, 126
Quiñones de Benavente, Luis, 112, 113

Ramillete de flores de la Retama (Bouquet of Flowers of the Broom), by Fray Pedro Beltrán, 128
Reinar para morir, El. See *To Reign Only to Die*
Remedio, industria y valor. See *Remedy, Industry and Valor*
Remedy, Industry and Valor (Remedio, industria y valor), 64
Remón, Fray Alonso, 137n18
Rennert, Hugo A., 73, 122
Restori, Antonio, 116
Retrato panegírico de Carlos de Austria (Panegyric Portrait of Charles of Austria), by Gabriel Bocángel y Unzueta, 127
Reynolds, C. Russell, 63
Rigor en la inocencia, El, o Privarse de privar. See *Cruetly in Innocence, or To Deprive Oneself of Favor*
Rimas de Tomé Burguillos (Rhymes of Tomé Burguillos), by Lope de Vega, 21
Rimas humanas, by Lope de Vega, 110
Rimas nuevas, listed for Lope de Vega, 123
Rimas varias (Varied Rhymes), by Jerónimo de Porras, 126

Ríos, Blanca de los, 51
Rojas Zorrilla, Francisco de, 24, 66, 70, 131
Romeo and Juliet, 51
Romera-Navarro, Miguel, 77
Rouanet, Léo, 74
Rubens, Peter Paul, 48
Rufián dichoso, El (The Happy Ruffian), by Cervantes, 104
Ruiz de Alarcón, Juan, 23, 26, 27, 112, 113, 126, 131, 133

St. Dominic in Soriano (Santo Domingo en Soriano), 64
Sainz de Robles, Federico Carlos, 28, 38
Salas Barbadillo, Alonso J., 114
Salomon, Noël, 29, 66
Salvá, Pedro, 73
San Felipe Neri, 17
San Francisco Xavier, 17, 18
San Franco de Sena (St. Franco of Siena), by Moreto, 104
San Ignacio de Loyola, 17
San Isidro, 17, 18
San Pedro de Alcántara, 40, 41
San Pedro Nolasco, 18
Sánchez Escribano, Federico, 67, 68
Sánchez Mariño, Rafael, 19
Sansovino, Francesco, 85
Santa María de la Cabeza, 18
Santa Teresa de Jesús, 17, 41
Santísimas formas de Alcalá, Las. See *The Most Sacred Host of Alcalá.*
Santo Domingo en Soriano. See *St. Dominic in Soriano*
Schack, A. F. von, 72, 128, 131
Schaeffer, Adolf, 73
Schevill, Rudolph, 76
Sebastian (King of Portugal), 41
Second Seneca of Spain, The (El segundo Séneca de España), Part I, 28-29, 50, 56, 106, 109, 132
Second Seneca of Spain, The (El segundo Séneca de España), Part II, 28, 49, 50, 55-56, 132
Second Volume of Plays, The (El segundo tomo de las comedias), 23, 26, 27, 28, 49, 52-62, 63, 69, 70, 95
Segundo Séneca de España, El (Parts I and II). See *The Second Seneca of Spain*

Index [167]

Segundo tomo de las comedias, El. See *The Second Volume of Plays*
Sejanus' Fortunes and Most Unhappy End, or Love, Favor and Punishment (El fin más desgraciado y fortunas de Seyano, o Amor, privanza y castigo, 45, 46-47
Sentinel of Honor, The (La centinela del honor), 63
Señor don Juan de Austria, El. See *Don Juan of Austria*
Ser prudente y ser sufrido. See *To Be Prudent and To Be Devoted*
Silva, Feliciano de, 57
Simón Díaz, José, 18, 125, 126, 127, 128
Skander Beg (Escanderbech), 33, 35-36, 37, 108
Sloman, A. E., 65, 76
Smith, Winifred, 45, 142n10
Solalinde, Antonio G., 98, 99, 104, 105
Solís y Rivadeneyra, Antonio de, 24, 65, 72-77, 111
Son of the Seraphim, St. Peter of Alcántara, The (El hijo del serafín, San Pedro de Alcántara), 40-41
Success in One's Plans (La ganancia por la mano), 17, 27, 60-61
Sucesos y prodigios de amor, en ocho novelas ejemplares, Los. See *The Happenings and Prodigies of Love, in Eight Exemplary Novels*
Sueños, Los (The Visions), by Quevedo, 110
Suffering Rewarded (El sufrimiento premiado), 54, 70-72, 81
Sufrimiento premiado, El. See *Suffering Rewarded*
Sufrir por querer más (To Suffer Through Greater Love), attributed to Villaizán, 116
Sylvia, Esther, 130, 131, 132, 133

Tan largo me lo fiáis (You Are Giving Me So Much Time), 76
Teetotum, The, by Quevedo. See *La perinola*
Templarios, Los. See *The Templars*
Templars, The (Los templarios), 18, 42-43, 45, 47
Tercera orden de San Francisco, La. See *The Third Order of St. Francis*
Terceros de San Francisco, Los. See *The Third Order of St. Francis*
There Is No Life Like Honor (No hay vida como la honra), 29-30, 107, 132
Third Order of St. Francis, The (La tercera orden de San Francisco; Los terceros de San Francisco), 66, 123
Ticknor, George, 72
Tiempos de regocijo y carnestolendas de Madrid (Time of Rejoicing and Carnival in Madrid), by Castillo Solórzano, 98
Tirso de Molina (Gabriel Téllez), 23, 24, 51, 52, 104, 110, 112, 113, 114, 131, 132
To Be Prudent and To Be Devoted (Ser prudente y ser sufrido), 64-65
To Die and to Conceal (Morir y disimular), 17, 27, 64
To Do One's Duty (Cumplir con su obligación), 17, 27, 42, 65
To Reign Only to Die (El reinar para morir), 64
To Scorn What Is Liked (Despreciar lo que se quiere), 59-60
Toquera vizcaína, La. See *The Cap Seller of Biscay*
Trompa, La. See *The Trumpet*
Trumpet, The (La trompa), 22, 69, 79-81, 82
Two Judges of Israel, The (Los dos jueces de Israel), 63
Tyler, Richard W., 71

Un gusto trae mil disgustos. See *One Pleasure Brings a Thousand Pains*
Unfortunate Friendship, The (La desgraciada amistad), 82, 89

Valdivielso, José de, 112, 127
Valiant Nazarene, Sampson, The (El valiente nazareno, Sansón), 57-58
Valiente más dichoso, Don Pedro Guiral, El. See *The Most Happy Braggart, Don Pedro Guiral*
Valiente nazareno, Sansón, El. See *The Valiant Nazarene, Sampson*
Vallejo, Manuel (actor-manager of a theatrical company), 81
Valor Beset and Treason Avenged (El valor perseguido y traición vengada), 65-66

Valor perseguido y traición vengada, El. See *Valor Beset and Treason Avenged*
Vander Hammen, Lorenzo, 28, 49, 56
Vanity in Villaverde (Gravedad en Villaverde), 63
Varias rimas (Several Rhymes), by Miguel Colodrero de Villalobos, 125
Vega, Lope de, 17, 19, 20, 21, 22, 23, 25, 28, 30, 31, 34, 39, 42, 43, 49, 54, 59, 61, 63, 65, 66, 67, 70, 71, 72, 77, 78, 79, 80, 83, 85, 97, 99, 104, 110, 111, 112, 113, 116, 117, 118, 119-24, 125, 127, 131, 132, 133
Velázquez de Silva, Diego, 19
Vélez de Guevara, Luis, 23, 24, 35, 112
Vida de Elio Seyano (Life of Sejanus), 47
Vida del duque de Virón, La (Life of the Duke of Virón), by Juan Pablo Mátir Rizo, 45
Vida es sueño, La (Life is a Dream), by Calderón de la Barca, 39, 40, 76
Vida y purgatorio de San Patricio, La. See *The Life and Purgatory of St. Patrick*
Vidarte, Juan de, 22
Viel-Castel, Louis de, 73

Villaizán, Jerónimo de, 16, 19, 22, 31, 69, 110, 115, 116
Villana de Pinto, La. See *The Peasant Girl of Pinto*
Vincent, E. R., 152nl
Virgen de la Humildad, La (The Virgin of Humility), by Hernando de Camargo y Salgado, 127

Wade, Gerald E., 76
Waiting-Maid, The (La doncella de labor), *43-44*, 46, 55, 131
What the Judgments of Heaven Are (Lo que son juicios del cielo), 48-49
What's Done Can't Be Undone, and the Mountain Prince (A lo hecho no hay remedio y príncipe de los montes), 35, *39-40*, 92
Whitman, Iris L., 73
Wilson, Edward M., 125
Wisdom, 110
Wurzbach, Wolfgang von, 73

Yerros de naturaleza y aciertos de la fortuna (Errors of Nature and Successes of Fortune), 76

Zayas Sotomayor, María de, 24, 97, 111